Lecture Notes
in Business Information Processing　　　9

D1826912

Printing: Mercedes-Druck, Berlin
Binding: Stein + Lehmann, Berlin

Pekka Abrahamsson   Richard Baskerville
Kieran Conboy   Brian Fitzgerald
Lorraine Morgan   Xiaofeng Wang (Eds.)

Agile Processes in Software Engineering and Extreme Programming

9th International Conference, XP 2008
Limerick, Ireland, June 10-14, 2008
Proceedings

 Springer

Volume Editors

Pekka Abrahamsson
VTT Electronics
90571 Oulu, Finland
E-mail: pekka.abrahamsson@vtt.fi

Richard Baskerville
Georgia State University
Dept. of Computer Information Systems
30302 Atlanta, GA, USA
E-mail: baskerville@acm.org

Kieran Conboy
National University of Ireland
Dept. of Accountancy and Finance
Galway, Ireland
E-mail: kieran.conboy@nuigalway.ie

Brian Fitzgerald
Lorraine Morgan
Xiaofeng Wang
University of Limerick
Lero - The Irish Software Engineering Research Centre
Limerick, Ireland
E-mail: {brian.fitzgerald,lorraine.morgan}@ul.ie, xiaofeng.wang@lero.ie

Library of Congress Control Number: 2008927853

ACM Computing Classification (1998): D.2, K.6

ISSN   1865-1348
ISBN-10   3-540-68254-6 Springer Berlin Heidelberg New York
ISBN-13   978-3-540-68254-7 Springer Berlin Heidelberg New York

Springer is a part of Springer Science+Business Media

springer.com

© Springer-Verlag Berlin Heidelberg 2008
Printed in Germany

Typesetting: Camera-ready by author, data conversion by Scientific Publishing Services, Chennai, India
Printed on acid-free paper   SPIN: 12272334   06/3180   5 4 3 2 1 0

Preface

The XP conference series established in 2000 was the first conference dedicated to agile processes in software engineering. The idea of the conference is to offer a unique setting for advancing the state of the art in the research and practice of agile processes. This year's conference was the ninth consecutive edition of this international event. The conference has grown to be the largest conference on agile software development outside North America. The XP conference enjoys being one of those conferences that truly brings practitioners and academics together. About 70% of XP participants come from industry and the number of academics has grown steadily over the years. XP is more of an experience rather than a regular conference. It offers several different ways to interact and strives to create a truly collaborative environment where new ideas and exciting findings can be presented and shared. For example, this year's open space session, which was "a conference within a conference", was larger than ever before.

Agile software development is a unique phenomenon from several perspectives. Few expected it to last for more than a few years due to the focus on team-level software development and a perceived inability to cope with complex development environments. The roots of agile development ideas can be traced back for several decades as experienced practitioners gradually materialized the ideas in the form of several independently developed methods that shared many common characteristics. Later, these characteristics became better known in their expression as the agile manifesto. Anecdotal evidence and the popular press indicate that large software-intensive corporations who operate in complex global development environments are in the process of deploying agile processes and practices as part of their de-facto approach to software development. This process continues even though attempts thus far to standardize or even set up a list of agreed recommended practices for agile software development have fallen short.

Agile software development is unique from a research perspective as well. Anecdotal evidence suggests that, once applied, it may impact the corporate-wide software development ecosystem. It is therefore one of the few research topics that highlights the benefits of bringing together the applied research done in software engineering with theoretically well-developed information systems research, thereby melding constructive pragmatics into holistic views of organizational impacts and beyond. Together, both disciplines can increase our understanding of the concepts, issues and impacts of agile processes in various development contexts. For the first time in the conference's history, both the IS and SE community are equally present in the Organization Committee, in search of the winning balance between abstract perspectives and the experiences of practitioners from the field.

The XP conference has increased its academic standing year by year. The XP committee will seek to build upon this trend in the coming years as well. The XP paper submissions went through a rigorous peer-reviewing process. Each paper was reviewed by at least two Program Committee members. Of 54 papers submitted, only 16 were accepted as full papers. The papers represent a set of high-quality research studies addressing a wide variety of different topics ranging from history and evolution of agile methods to new conceptual models of agility, human factors in agile development and technical aspects of agile processes. The conference program also included a number of interactive workshops, panels and the conference-within-a-conference open space event. This year's XP also presented a number of high-profile keynotes from Dave Snowden, Kati Vilkki and Philippe Kruchten. XP 2008 presented the largest tutorial offering ever seen in the conference history. The participants had the option to participate in 19 half-day tutorials.

We would like to extend our gratitude to all those who contributed to the organization of the XP 2008 event. The authors, the sponsors, the Chairs, the reviewers, and all the volunteers: without their help, this event would have not been possible.

April 2008

Pekka Abrahamsson
Richard Baskerville
Kieran Conboy
Brian Fitzgerald
Lorraine Morgan
Xiaofeng Wang

Organization

Executive Committee

General Chair   Pekka Abrahamsson (Finland)

Program Chairs   Richard Baskerville (USA)
                                     Kieran Conboy (Ireland)

Organizing Chairs   Brian Fitzgerald (Ireland)
                                     Xiaofeng Wang (Ireland)

Local Committee Chair   Lorraine Morgan (Ireland)

Publicity and Industrial Chairs   Julie Eckstein (Germany)
                                     Brian Hanly (Ireland)

Tutorial Chairs   Steven Fraser (USA)
                                     Angela Martin (New Zealand)

                                     David Hussman (USA)
Panel Chairs   Lasse Koskela (Finland)

                                     Par Ågerfalk (Sweden)
Workshop Chair
                                     Charlie Poole (USA)
Open Space Chair
                                     Daniel Karlstrom (Sweden)
Poster Chairs   Minna Pikkarainen (Finland)

Program Committee

Marco Abis, Italy
Tom Acton, Ireland
Par Agerfalk, Sweden
Scott Ambler, Canada
David Avison, France
Chris Barry, Ireland
David Bustard, UK
Sven Carlsson, Sweden
Val Casey, Ireland
Francesco Cirillo, Italy
Ethan Cleary, Ireland
Gerry Coleman, Ireland
Kieran Conboy, Ireland
Daniela Damian, Canada
Ernesto Damiani, Italy
Torgeir Dingsoyr, Norway
Brian Donnellan, Ireland
Yael Dubinsky, Israel
Christian Federspiel, Austria
Elaine Ferneley, UK
Guy Fitzgerald, UK
Stephen Fraser, USA
Gary Gaughan, Ireland
Goran Goldkuhl, Sweden
Jim Highsmith, USA
Seamus Hill, Ireland
Mairead Hogan, Ireland
Helena Holmström, Sweden
David Hussman, USA
Linda Levine, USA
Karlheinz Kautz, Denmark
Frank Keenan, Ireland
Mikko Korkala, Finland
Lasse Koskela, Finland

Michael Lang, Ireland
Gary Lohan, Ireland
Kalle Lyytinen, USA
Lars Mathiassen, USA
Frank Maurer, Canada
John McAvoy, Ireland
Fergal McCaffery, Ireland
Orla McHugh, Ireland
Grigori Melnik, Canada
Kannan Mohan, USA
Eoin O'Conchuir, Ireland
Markku Oivo, Finland
Padraig O'Leary, Ireland
Minna Pikkarainen, Ireland
Charlie Poole, USA
Rafael Prikladnicki, Brazil
Bala Ramesh, USA
Barbara Russo, Italy
Outi Salo, Finland
Murray Scott, Ireland
Keng Siau, USA
Maha Shaikh, Ireland
Ahmed Sidky, USA
Alberto Sillitti, Italy
Sandra Slaughter, USA
Christoph Steindl, Austria
Giancarlo Succi, Italy
Richard Vidgen, UK
Xiaofeng Wang, Ireland
Barbara Weber, Austria
Don Wells, USA
Werner Wild, Austria
Laurie Williams, USA

Sponsors

Table of Contents

History and Evolution of Agile

People Factors in Agile Environments

Conceptual Models of Agility

Experience Reports

Posters

Workshops

Panels (Abstracts)

Essence: Facilitating Agile Innovation

Ivan Aaen

Department of Computer Science, Aalborg University, Denmark
aaen@acm.org

Abstract. This paper suggests ways to facilitate creativity and innovation in agile development. The paper applies four perspectives – *Product, Project, Process,* and *People* - to identify ways to support creative software development based on agile principles. The paper then describes a new facility - *Software Innovation Research Lab* (SIRL) - and drafts a new method concept for software innovation called *Essence*. Finally the paper reports from an early discovery experiment using SIRL and Essence and identifies further research.

Keywords: Software innovation.

1 Introduction

This paper is motivated by two observations: (1) Globalization and technological development opens new challenges for software development in high-cost countries. A viable software industry in our part of the world will likely depend on the ability to create high-value products in close collaboration with customers. (2) Agile development opens new opportunities for software innovation by allowing for changes and adaptations even late in development projects. Software innovation is one main strategy for creating high-value software products.

Software innovation is a complex topic and to make it more manageable, the paper applies four views on innovation - *Product, Project, Process*, and *People* - to allow for separation of concerns.These views are inspired by Pressman [1] as a way to flesh out important aspects of software development while maintaining an overview.

The paper is very much research in progress. First I contrast traditional and agile software development with respect to software innovation. Then I describe a new facility - *Software Innovation Research Lab* (SIRL) - and a new method concept - *Essence* - intended to facilitate software innovation. Lastly I report from an early experiment on the use of physical space in SIRL and the logical views in Essence.

2 A New Outlook for Software Innovation

A brief look at the Software Engineering Body of Knowledge[2] or the Capability Maturity Model Integration [3] shows that the traditional software development paradigm aims for predictable and documented software production. Agile development - according to the values and principles expressed in the manifesto [4] - aims for software

P. Abrahamsson et al. (Eds.): XP 2008, LNBIP 9, pp. 1–10, 2008.

development. The traditional line of thinking sets one scene for software innovation, while agile thinking sets a quite different one.

2.1 Product

One of the four values in the Agile Manifesto [2] - *Working software over comprehensive documentation* - marks major differences between the two paradigms. These differences are about requirements, design, and testing.

Traditional software development focuses on requirements elicitation, on up-front design in order to get the architecture right from the start, and on verification and validation to ensure, that deliverables are consistent and comply with requirements. Agile development focuses on *whole team* [5], *emergent design* [6], *test-infected development* [7] and sees testing as confirming that user and customer needs are met.

Product innovation is about developing new or changed products and services [8]. Both traditional and agile development sets conditions for product innovation. Traditional development tends to subjugate innovative ideas to the requirements specification. In practice this often leads to an early and small window of opportunity for innovative ideas, as *path dependencies* - costs related to rework - effectively impede later changes. Moreover, these ideas will normally come from the customer. Agile development reduces path dependencies significantly and makes dialogue between customers, users, and developers easier.

Both rely on customers as a main source of innovative ideas. Neither stresses the potential in combining application area expertise with the technological expertise held by developers. Moreover, both approaches are generally reticent on innovation.

2.2 Project

The agile manifesto values *responding to change over following a plan* and thereby emphasizes the project-view on software development.

Traditional project management focuses on cost and schedule, and includes requirements management, predictive planning, resource allocation, risk planning, quality planning, and plan management [2]. Collecting comprehensive information up-front is key. Agile development focuses on adaptive planning with built-in feedback loops [9], and is based on incremental development with frequent releases.

Project innovation here refers to changes in the context, where products or services are produced - what Tidd et al. labels as position innovation [8] - or to the way a software project is managed to achieve innovative solutions. Project innovation is both about stimulating creativity and innovation throughout the project, and about identifying options in previous projects that may offer breakthroughs to a new project.

Requirements management, detailed predictive planning, and plan oversight are essential to traditional project management. Such principles tend to curb project innovation by limiting efforts to use results and experiences from past projects to the beginning of a new project for the sake of scheduling and requirements management. Agile development encourages a gradual formation of solutions combined with adjustments based on previous experience. These principles contribute to build an environment for innovative work via cooperation in the whole team.

There seems to be little advice on how to sustain creative and innovative work throughout a software development project. In agile development the window of opportunity for introducing new ideas widens to cover a larger part of the entire project. This wider window necessitates that managerial ways be found to balance progress and achievement on the one side and creativity on the other.

2.3 Process

By valuing *individuals and interactions over processes and tools* the agile manifesto highlights the gap between a traditional emphasis on standardized software processes and an agile emphasis on practice, competence, motivation, and reflection [10]. Building stable software processes stands at the center of the traditional paradigm. The best-known strategy for this is *software process improvement* (SPI) [2]. In agile development, processes are not products - objects - by themselves, but rather practices that evolve dynamically with the team as it adapts to the particular circumstances.

Process innovation is about developing new or improved ways to produce products or provide services [8]. To separate product and process innovation, process innovation here only denotes changes in software development. Traditional SPI no doubt is the best-known example of process innovation in software engineering. SPI efforts develop process changes to be rolled-out in the organization via descriptions, best practices, and templates to support the process. Agile process innovation strategies are very different. Here processes are cultivated in the team while developing software. Examples of central mechanisms for developing and disseminating good agile development practices are *sitting together*, *pair programming*, *shared code*, and *continuous integration*.

Neither traditional nor agile development methods aid innovative work via methods, techniques, or tools. Innovation and creativity are treated as exogenous to software development - as something to be taken care of by external disciplines.

2.4 People

The people view is about the stakeholders in software projects. Examples of stakeholders are senior managers, project managers, developers, customers, super-users, end users, and marketing people. Here I will focus on the whole development team, i.e. developers and customer representatives. Main concerns are personal and collective development, communication, and cooperation.

The agile manifesto values *customer collaboration over contract negotiation*. Specifically this value concerns the relationship between developers and customers. Traditional development views people essentially as functions. Standardization and division of work are ideal for minimizing communications costs, for getting new staff up to speed quickly and for exchanging staff between projects when needed. Agile development puts more emphasis on self-organization, socialization and tacit knowledge. Whereas interpersonal communication in the traditional line-staff organization is considered a cost that should be minimized, agile teams employ communication as the primary way to exchange information and negotiate options.

People innovation is about changing the 'mental models' which frame what an organization does, e.g. changes in the perception of self, of the development team, of the users, or of the market, corresponding to what Tidd et al. calls paradigm innovation [8]. Changes in mental models may help remove blocks or develop new perspectives opening for novel possibilities and solutions.

Little in traditional software development supports people innovation. SPI involves organizational change but rarely paradigmatic change. Likewise requirements elicitation generally develops a quite conventional understanding of a user organization. Agile software development is not elaborate on people innovation either, but the manifesto value mentioned above points to one significant attribute of agile development that could lead to changed perspectives: *The frequent melding of team and customer views* via customer collaboration and formation of whole teams. Likewise self-organizing teams may add to the readiness for change.

Neither traditional nor agile software development offers much to develop new mental models of the development organization or of application areas and markets.

3 SIRL- Software Innovation Research Lab

In this and the following section I will present SIRL and Essence and outline how they support the four views of software innovation identified above. SIRL (Fig. 1) was established in August 2006 at Department of Computer Science at Aalborg University to facilitate research on software creativity and innovation. The lab supports team-based software development using modern development principles.

The lab is used for all phases in a development project and enables working as individuals, as pairs, and as a team. The lab supports:

- Collective idea-generation via interactive boards
- Creative processes via physical movement and localization
- Applying multiple perspectives via spatial separation
- Maintaining holistic overview via logical coherence
- Flexible arrangement of furniture and equipment
- Free communication and eye contact.

To support multiple perspectives the lab contains four interactive boards representing four generic views: *Earth, Water, Fire* and *Air*. The views were named after *Empedocles* of Acragas (ca. 495-435 BCE), who in his *Tetrasomia*, or *Doctrine of the Four Elements*, argued that all matter is comprised of these four elements.

A great many modern systems of perspectives also come in fours. Examples are *SWOT* (Strengths, Weaknesses, Opportunities, Threats), McCarthy's 4P within marketing (Product, Pricing, Placement, Promotion), Gupta's 4P within Six Sigma process management (Prepare, Perform, Perfect, Progress), Liker's 4P within management (Philosophy, Process, People, Problem solving), Tidd, Bessant & Pavitt's 4P within innovation (Product, Position, Process, Paradigm) and finally Pressman's 4P within software engineering (Product, Project, Process, People). The four generic views of SIRL therefore accommodates many and quite different systems of perspectives of relevance to creative and innovative software development.

Fig. 1. SIRL layout fall 2007

SIRL is equipped with four interactive screens (Smart Board 660) with projectors, four desktop computers, and one server. The main software is Visual Studio™ IDE for software development and Smart Ideas™ for idea generation.

4 Essence – Innovation in the Agile Team

Essence is a method concept currently under development in SIRL. The concept is named after *Quintessence*, the cosmic fifth element added by Aristotle to complement Empedocles' four earthly elements. Essence is based on a number of ideas that can only be briefly listed here:

- Melding creative sessions with agile development to employ development speed and flexibility throughout the project.
- Extending existing agile development methods. Essence is not a separate method.
- Entrusting the development team - rather than external specialists - to be creative.
- Kinesthetic thinking - using location and movement in thinking and simulation.
- Using *roles* to promote the application of multiple perspectives and particularly to strengthen synergies between customer challenges and developer ambitions.
- Using *views* for separation of concerns to provide a conceptual division of problem spaces and to balance overview with detail and coherence with transparency.
- Using *modes* to adapt Essence to incremental development in the project.

Essence is intended to be lightweight, easy and fun to use. Lightweight as ceremony and project overheads must be kept at a minimum so as not to have projects drop Essence for lack of time. Easy to use as the time needed before Essence is useful should be short and the activities in Essence should come natural to the participants. Finally Essence should be fun to use to further motivation and outcome.

The strategy for this is to base activities on principles similar to role-playing games and improvisational theater. Both of these are based on defined *characters, settings* and *situations*, whereas the events and actions are largely left to the participants themselves to develop via disciplined improvisations. To ensure a familiar basis for these improvisations, the characters and settings are based on permanent structures (roles and views respectively), whereas situations reflect a current status or challenge.

Team members have roles defining their *characters*. Each role has a set of ideals or values providing a clear *raison d'être* [11] to the role. The *Challenger* is the customer and has all the responsibilities of an on-site customer, yet should pose project requirements in the more open form of challenges. The *Responder* is the developer employing technical competence to deliver ambitious responses. These two roles engage in a dialogue where solutions are developed by contrasting application area needs and desires with technical opportunity. The *Anchor* serves to keep the team absorbed and focused on delivering exciting solutions - what Zultner referred to as *Exciting Requirements* [12]. The last role is the *Child;* this role is temporary as anyone on the team can take this role temporarily at any given time. The Child may raise any idea or issue - even when contrary to decisions made earlier by the team. This role is named after the child in *The Emperor's New Clothes* who said: *But he hasn't got anything on* and thereby revealed the emperor's folly.

The *setting* is part of framing the story world - the shared view that forms the basis for expressing each characters ideals [11]. To define the setting, Essence maps Pressman's 4P from software engineering onto SIRL's four generic views.

The *situation* introduces the dynamic element to complete the story world: The point of departure for the game. The first part of this comes in the form of Essence Games. Essence Games are inspired by Hohmann's Innovation Games [13] and numerous methods described in Huczynski [14]. Essence Games are based on the principle of saying yes - accepting all offers that other characters bring into the situation [11]. Until now two Essence Games have been outlined and tried. The other part is the project state. Projects are in one of three states defining the situation to be addressed - Idea, Plan, or Growth. *Idea* is the mode for suggesting possible courses of action and for developing concepts. Games in this mode are mainly exploratory. *Plan* is where proposals for doing or achieving goals are developed and necessary preparations are identified. This mode leads to decisions about what to do, when, and by whom. Games in this mode focus mainly on inventory building to identify tasks. *Growth* is where ideas find actual form via evolution, experimentation, selection, maturation, expansion, enlargement, and progress. Games in this mode are mainly confirmatory and investigate if the project maintains a focus on innovation.

To ensure continuity from Essence game to project activities and also minimize game preparations, Essence structures should form part of the project infrastructure. Without this, game sessions may not have any real impact on the project. In the following I will outline how such continuity might be pursued.

4.1 Product

Interactions between stakeholders from the application and development areas may serve as means for exchanging perspectives and developing challenging ideas possibly leading to innovative results. Methodologically Essence stimulates dialogue between Challenger and Responder in order to develop ambitious technical responses and answer application area challenges. Visually the Product view lets the responders represent the product being built - the source code - to make the product and propositions for changes to it more tangible in team discussions.

4.2 Project

Project-wise software innovation faces at least two challenges: How to manage innovative projects, and how to get inspiration from past projects when addressing new problems. The challenge grows as the window of opportunity for innovation widens. This requires project status and progress to be balanced against visions.

A comprehensive response to these challenges has yet to be developed for Essence. One main strategy may be to use *metaphors* as instruments for transferring knowledge and inspiration from one area to another. Methodologically Essence will therefore propose a repository of metaphors derived from past projects and products. Visually the Project view supports the Challenger in maintaining project status and planning throughout the project by giving an overview of status & backlog for the sprint and for the project.

4.3 Process

The Process view supports innovative and creative work by offering an assortment of ways to develop and explore concepts and ideas, to elicit tasks and requirements, and to investigate and confirm if the project upholds an appropriate level of innovation. Methodologically Essence will therefore contain a repertoire of creative methods, tools, and techniques such as Innovation Games (Hohmann, 2006) adapted to Essence with respect to roles, views, and modes. Visually the Process view provides the Anchor with an overview over and access to this repertoire throughout the project. The Process view also contains tools for brainstorming, innovation and creativity such as ThoughtOffice™ and Smart Ideas™.

4.4 People

The People view facilitates the development of new mental models of the development organization or of application areas and markets. Methodologically the Child role in Essence empowers at any time any member of the team to irresponsibly question basic assumptions, values or the like in the project for a while. Interventions from external consultants might also find place here. Visually the People view shows applications of the software under development. Throughout the project this view visualizes use scenarios for example via video footage from the user organization, video link to actual users, etc. This view also serves as main access point to off-site stakeholders using video chat, Skype or similar.

5 Early Experiments with Essence and SIRL

Both SIRL and Essence introduce concepts, structures, and ways of working that to my knowledge have not been combined before. They are still early in their development, and experiments will therefore serve to provide insights and knowledge about their utility and produce ideas for how to apply them. At this stage, experiments cannot provide enough information or evidence to support conclusions, yet they might help in formulating hypotheses to be tested at a later stage. For that reason, the early experiments with Essence and SIRL take the form of *discovery experiments* [15,16]. The aim of discovery experiments is to weed out less promising ideas and put the focus on what can best be achieved as well as on conditions for implementation.

We have worked on SIRL for 18 months now. The idea is to develop SIRL and Essence incrementally by using them for software development. In the following, I will report on experiences using physical space in SIRL in combination with the logical views of Essence. These experiences are based on a term project with four students in the fall of 2007. Based on Scrum the project developed an IDE plug-in supporting pair programming between developers in different locations. This discovery experiment addresses among other things two questions:

- Is it useful to physically distribute views in SIRL on four screens?
- Is it useful to logically split up views in Product, Project, Process, and People?

In four months the project completed four Scrum sprints. The students rotated the Essence roles to ensure that everybody served as Challenger, Responder, and Anchor. The Child role was not used. Related to these sprints the students responded to a questionnaire with 16 questions on their experiences using screens, views relative to their particular role in the sprint. These responses were coded using a 48-node coding tree with TAMS Analyzer, version 3.41.

The responses reflect variations with respect to personality, time (sprint #) of the project, and role. In the following, I will address the two questions. For simplicity, I will refer to roles in the first two sprints as *early Challenger, Responder* etc., and to roles in the two last sprints as *late*.

5.1 Experiences with Physical Space

Early Challengers found the physical distribution helpful for planning and oversight by showing the project and sprint backlogs and the running product simultaneously. One early Challenger observed: *I think the screens were great for splitting up thoughts and discuss issues. The screens help keeping ideas alive. The screens help establish overview. Every discussion was persistent in a way, and because of the physical split they were also more focused.* Late Challengers reported briefly on their experiences, as they played a limited role in the project.

Early Responders saw themselves as developers and did not engage much in dialogue with the Challenger, leaving this dialogue to the Anchor. For that reason, early Responders focused mainly on their own *Product* screen. The physical distribution was useful for overviews and for allocating tasks. Late Responders also focused on detailed development. This reflects the limited size of the software making it fairly easy to maintain an overview of the entire product. Larger projects with more people and more refactoring would likely make more screens useful for Responders.

The group used the Anchor role like a Scrum Master with a stronger managerial role than expected in regular uses of Essence. Early Anchors found separate screens useful to split up and discuss issues, focus on ideas, and maintain overview. Late Anchors pointed more to specific episodes where multiple screens helped maintain overview while addressing details. Thus this early discovery experiment suggests that splitting up physically on interactive screens has potential, but also - not surprisingly - that this calls for the Essence roles to be well understood by all team members.

5.2 Experiences with Logical Views

Early Challenger experiences with logical views are on a par with those of physical space. One of them observed: *Having the ability to see the two backlogs and the running product at the same time helped to understand how each requirement had been seen by the team and how it had been implemented.* The other early Challenger observed that the roles help distribute responsibilities. The People and Project views were deemed most important for communication and discussion. Late Challengers also primarily used the People and Project views to show and prioritize backlog items.

Early Responders used the People and Project views to overview tasks and assignments. The Process and Product views were not sufficiently developed to be fully useful. As one of them observed: *There were unused possibilities in Essence - we should have used more views.* Another late Responder observed that the roles help distribute responsibilities: *This way I have specific responsibilities and can concentrate on them [but] the four views were not easy to use directly.*

The first Anchor saw little use of the views specifically for his role. The second Anchor used the People and Project views in meetings to keep track. The third Anchor used all views episodically and two of them (Product and Project) the rest of the time, while the fourth primarily used the Project view for status.

Consistent for all sprints was that the views were not fully used as intended. The primary use of the views was for project overview and coordination - i.e. for project management - whereas the expected main benefit of them - for creative dialogue under development - was not obtained. Further benefits from using these logical views may not be obtained without a stronger methodological foundation.

6 Conclusion

This paper has presented SIRL, a facility for experimenting with software innovation, and Essence, a method concept drafted with use in SIRL in mind. An early discovery experiment suggests conditions for using physical and logical distribution of project views for agile teams. There seems to be benefits in physical and logical distribution for project management, whereas the potential for creative development has yet to be fully demonstrated. A mature understanding of Essence roles and ideas must be in place in order to investigate this potential. This constitutes one future line of research.

Essence will be based on a *static structure* of roles and modes defining characters,and settings and *dynamic situations* with events and actions developed by the participants themselves via disciplined improvisations. How to build such structures and situations constitutes another line of research in the coming years.

Acknowledgements

Thanks go to Peter Axel Nielsen, Jens Henrik Hosbond, and Jeremy Rose from Institute for Computer Science at Aalborg University for inspiring discussion. My students at SIRL, Morten Andersen, Søren Rode Andreasen, Lasse Bæk, and Philip Bredahl Thomsen (2006-07) and Jeppe V. Boelsmand, Rasmus Jensen, Jan Leckscheidt, and Morten Saxov (2007-08) have been indispensable for building SIRL and for the experiments. Also thank to Søren Hansen, founder of the Aalborg University Creativity Lab, for illustrating the potential in Improvisational Theater.

References

1. Pressman, R.S.: Software Engineering: A Practitioner's Approach. McGraw-Hill Higher Education, Boston (2005)
2. Abran, A., Moore, J.W. (eds.): Guide to the Software Engineering Body of Knowledge: 2004 Version - SWEBOK. IEEE Computer Society, Washington (2004)
3. CMMI Product Team CMMI for Software Engineering, Version 1.1, Continuous Representation (CMMI-SW, V1.1, Continuous). Software Engineering Institute, Pittsburgh, PA (2002)
4. Beck, K., et al.: Manifesto for Agile Software Development (2001), http://www.agilemanifesto.org
5. Beck, K., Andres, C.: Extreme Programming Explained: Embrace Change. Addison-Wesley, Boston (2005)
6. Fowler, M.: Design - Who needs an architect? IEEE Software 20, 11–13 (2003)
7. Beck, K., Gamma, E.: Test-infected: programmers love writing tests. In: Deugo, D. (ed.) More Java gems, pp. 357–376. Cambridge University Press, New York (2000)
8. Tidd, J., Bessant, J.R., Pavitt, K.: Managing Innovation: Integrating Technological, Market and Organization Change. Wiley, Hoboken (2005)
9. Cohn, M.: Agile Estimating and Planning. Prentice Hall Professional Technical Reference, Upper Saddle River (2006)
10. Aaen, I.: Software Process Improvement: Blueprints versus Recipes. IEEE Software 20, 86–93 (2003)
11. Swartjes, I.M.T., Vromen, J.A.F.: Emergent Story Generation: Lessons from Improvisational Theater. In: Proceedings of the AAAI Fall Symposium on Intelligent Narrative Technologies, FS-07-05, November 9-11, pp. 146–149 (2007)
12. Zultner, R.E.: TQM for technical teams. Communications of the ACM 36, 79–91 (1993)
13. Hohmann, L.: Innovation Games: Creating Breakthrough Products Through Collaborative Play. Addison-Wesley Professional, Reading (2006)
14. Huczynski, A.: Encyclopedia of Development Methods. Gower, Aldershot (2001)
15. Alberts, D.S., Hayes, R.E.: Code of Best Practice for Experimentation. DoD Command and Control Research Program, Washington, D.C. (2002)
16. Alberts, D.S., Hayes, R.E.: Campaigns of Experimentation: Pathways to Innovation and Transformation. CCRP Publication Series, Washington, D.C. (2005)

Scrum and Team Effectiveness: Theory and Practice

Nils Brede Moe and Torgeir Dingsøyr

SINTEF ICT
NO-7465 Trondheim, Norway
{nils.b.moe,torgeir.dingsoyr}@sintef.no

Abstract. The scrum software development process has recently gained much popularity as an agile method primarily focusing on project management. Scrum has been derived as a set of principles of good management of software projects, from experienced practitioners. In this paper, we discuss the elements of Scrum in relation to a proposed theory of the "big five" components for effectiveness in small teams. We also discuss the theory of scrum in relation to these components, and in relation to a case study of a start-up Scrum team.

Keywords: Agile software development, scrum, software engineering, team effectiveness, empirical software engineering, case study.

1 Introduction

Agile software development methods denotes a set of practices for software development, created by experienced practitioners [23]. Agile processes deal with the challenge of an unpredictable world by relying on "people and their creativity rather than on processes" [12].

Scrum is one of the most popular agile development methods. Rising and Janoff [14] described Scrum as a development process for small teams, which includes a series of short development phases, "sprints", which typically lasts from one to four weeks. The team captures identified tasks in a backlog, which is reprioritized and updated in the beginning of each sprint. This also includes estimating the effort required to complete each task. The customer participates in the sprint meetings, but is not allowed to influence the team in between the meetings. During a sprint, the team holds short daily Scrum meetings to discuss progress, plans and potential problems. Scrum is thoroughly described by Schwaber and Beedle [18].

The cornerstone argument for the suitability of Scrum is that software development is a complex process where many factors influence the final result. It is therefore difficult or even impossible to plan ahead such as described in traditional waterfall-like development processes. Scrum extends incremental software development to what is called "empirical process control"; where feedback loops is the core element. Abrahamsson et al. [1] describe Scrum as an agile process which primarily deal with project management. Scrum is inspired by a range of fields like complexity theory, system dynamics and Nonaka and Takeuchi's theory of knowledge creation [21], adapted to a setting of software development.

P. Abrahamsson et al. (Eds.): XP 2008, LNBIP 9, pp. 11–20, 2008.

There are few studies of Scrum in the research literature [6]. Most of the studies are reports with little scientific backing of claims. We have found three lessons-learned reports from companies taking up Scrum [14, 17, 20], and three case studies examining the combination of XP and Scrum [7], the overtime amongst developers and customer satisfaction in Scrum [10] and experience with scrum in a cross-organizational development project [5].

Software development processes depend significantly on team performance, as does any process that involves human interaction. This focus on teams has been the motivation of this study, where we want to discuss the relation between the general literature on teams and in particular team effectiveness and Scrum. We ask the following research questions:

- How does Scrum support the factors which influence effective teamwork?
- How can challenges when introducing Scrum be explained by the factors influencing effective teamwork?

2 Research Design and Method

Given the focus above, we have designed a study of a project using Scrum, focusing on factors which influence teamwork in a single-case holistic study [22]. We now describe project context, data sources and analysis.

2.1 Study Context

This case study was done in the context of a larger action research program, where several companies have introduced elements from agile development in response to identified problems. Scrum was introduced in one company because they wanted to improve their ability to deliver iteratively and on time, increase the quality, improve the team-feeling and team communication. All 16 employees in the development department were introduced to Scrum at the same time.

The goal of the first Scrum-project was to develop a plan and coordination system for owners of cables (e.g., electricity, fibre) and pipes (water, sewer). The project produced a combination of textual user-interfaces and map-functionality.

The company was used to having people work independently, in small projects, so the case project was one of the largest so far for the organization. Four thousand hours, six developers, one Scrum-master, and a product owner were allocated to the project. The product owner was from the same company as the developers, but was situated in another city. He acted as a representative for the customer who was the local government of a Norwegian city. The project kick-off was in May 2006, first installation was in October and final installation was planned to be November 2007. Prior to the kick-off some initial architectural work was done, and some coding activities had started. The project used .Net.

2.2 Data Sources and Analysis

The two authors conducted ethnographic observations and used interviews. During the observation periods, we visited the team once or twice a week, in total 60 observations lasting from 10 minutes to 8 hours. In each observation session, we participated in daily scrum meetings, planning meetings, retrospective, review meetings, and observations of developers working. We took notes on dialogues, interactions and activities. The dialogues were transcribed and integrated with notes to produce a detailed record of each session. In addition, we interviewed four of the developers after the second sprint, and all developers, scrum master and product owner after the project was completed. The analysis draws on this broad material, and is structured after a framework for team effectiveness, presented in the following.

3   Team Effectiveness; The "Big Five" and Scrum

Much research has been devoted to the topic of teams. In particular, the question of what processes and components comprise teamwork and how teamwork contributes to team effectiveness has received much attention [9, 16]. Stewart [19] conducted a meta-analysis of 93 team studies examining the relationship between team design features and team performance. He found that teams can indeed be designed for high performance, and proper design has in fact proved critical for success.

There is, however, an important difference between team productivity and team effectiveness. There are several models for team effectiveness in the literature. Some emphasize that team effectiveness must be seen more holistic than productivity, taking also into account the interaction of a team. Productivity will in some cases rely on external factors for the team.

A number of frameworks have been proposed to classify teamwork behaviours (e.g. [11], [8], [16]). However, there is a lack of consensus concerning the conceptual structure of teamwork behaviours [15]. Some have criticized that studies of teamwork have been fragmented and not suitable for practical use [16]. A recent review of this body of research by Salas et al. [16] tries to answer this critique and make the studies practically usable, suggesting the "Big Five" components of teamwork.

Salas et al. [16] argue that teams require a complex mixture of factors that include organizational support and individual skills, and also teamwork skills. Therefore, Salas et al. have condensed the knowledge on teamwork into the "Big Five" framework, see Fig. 1. The five components are: team leadership, mutual performance monitoring, backup behaviour, adaptability, and team orientation. Each of the "Big Five" is required for team effectiveness, but each component may be manifested differently across most teams task types because of constraints of team task and varying needs of the team [16]. The "Big Five" require three coordinating mechanisms: shared mental models, closed-looped communication, and mutual trust.

Building on the theoretically and empirically grounded "Big Five" framework, we will now describe each component of the framework, how this component is addressed in Scrum, and how we observed this component in the project which was adopting Scrum.

3.1   Coordinating Mechanisms

Shared Mental Models: are supported in Scrum through the involvement by the product owner, focus on the project vision, and the planning resulting in a backlog, and the retrospective meeting. The daily scrum is important for understanding team members' tasks.

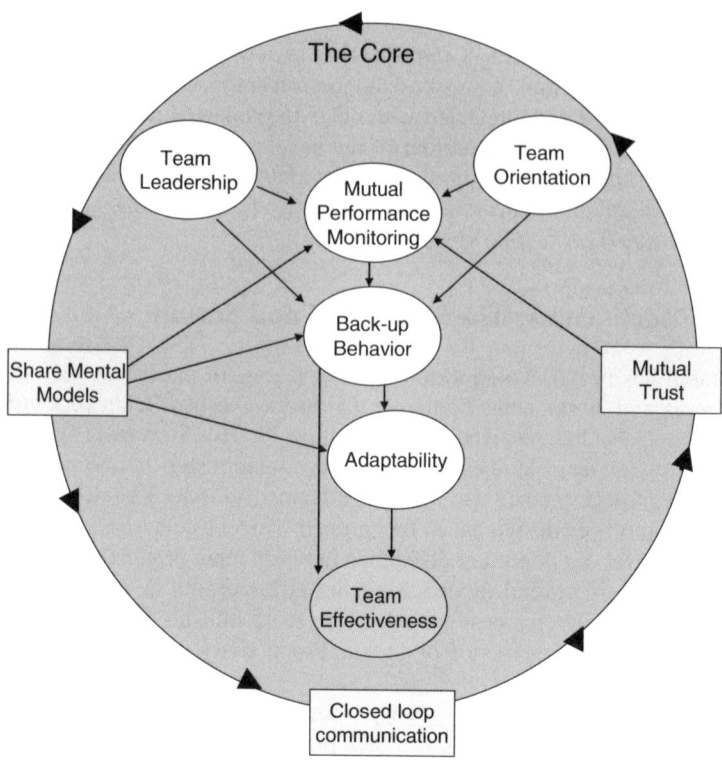

Fig. 1. The proposed model of "Big Five" in teamwork by Salas et al. [16]

In the case, because of highly specialized skills and a corresponding division of work, it was a problem to develop shared mental models both on a project level and on a task level. Without a clear understanding of the system being developed, planning was difficult. The planning meetings turned out to be discussions between the Scrum-master, product owner and the developer that was going to do the work.

Definition [16]: **"**An organizing knowledge structure of the relationships among the task the team is engaged in and how the team members will interact". *Behavioural Makers [16]:* "Anticipating and predicting each other's needs. Identify changes in the team, task, or team-mates and implicitly adjusting strategies as needed".
Scrum: The team is supposed to focus on the high level goal setting in the up front planning. The product owner should provide a vision to help this process. Every stakeholder is involved in this planning which is conducted as a co-located meeting. The sprint and product backlogs describe what is to be developed.
Case-study: The product owner was responsible for communicating the features this system was going to provide. But he lived in another city, was very busy, and became sick in a critical phase. There was a lot of communication between the developers and the product owner but according to the developers it should have been more, to help them better understand how the system was going to be used. A proper vision was also missing.

Closed-Loop Communication: Communication is supported in Scrum with feedback on a daily basis in addition to in the end of each sprint. However, closed-loop communication is only explicitly supported by the review meeting.

In the project, because of highly specialized skills and focus on their own module, the developers did not always listen when others were talking in the daily meeting. Another reason for developers not paying full attention was that the focus of the meetings was often general project problems, not related to development.

Definition [16]: "The exchange of information between a sender and a receiver irrespective of the medium".   *Behavioural Makers [16]:* "Following up with team members to ensure message was received. Acknowledging that a message was received. Clarifying with the sender of the message that the message received is the same as the intended message".
Scrum: The daily Scrum is the most important mechanism, but also the retrospective, planning meeting and review meetings provide feedback loops. There is no mechanism that ensures that sent communication is accurately understood.
Case-study: A database model developed shortly before summer holiday, had to be rewritten during the summer when the person who had made the model was on holiday. The developer thought he had communicated what he did to the others. However, the daily meetings increased the overall communication.

Mutual Trust: Scrum does not have mechanisms to directly develop mutual trust, but assume that there is a culture of mutual trust in the team. Without mutual trust it will be difficult for the team to commit to the backlog, and keep the deadline.

In the project, the three issues mentioned above could have been handled better in order to improve the mutual trust. If team members do not feel that their input is valued or that the information they provide will be used appropriately, they may be less willing to participate in information sharing [2].

Definition [16]: "The shared belief that team members will perform their roles and protect the interests of their team-mates".   *Behavioural Makers [16]:* "Information sharing. Willingness to admit mistakes and accept feedback".
Scrum: The whole team is supposed to commit to what is to be delivered during a sprint. Trust is then needed because team members must be willing to accept a risk to rely on each other to meet deadlines and contribute to the team task.
Case-study: In interviews, most of the people involved in the project stated that they trusted others in the team to do what was expected by the team. However, some events lead to a lack of trust. First, in the beginning of the project, project members thought the scrum master was overreacting to problems stated at the daily meetings. This led them to not reporting problems when the scrum master was present. Second, the fact that developers focused on their own "plan" resulted in a lack of trust from the Scrum-master. Third, the developers discovered towards the end of the project that the deadlines the scrum master presented were not the final deadlines.

3.2   The "Big Five" of Teamwork

Team Leadership: The Scrum-master is presented as a coach, focusing on protecting the team against external noise, removing impediments and facilitating the different processes defined by Scrum. Salas [28] do not directly describe self-organizing teams, however in such teams, leadership should be diffused rather than centralized [22], that is, team leadership should be divided among the Product-owner, Scrum-master, and the self-organizing team. Team leadership should ensure that the tasks are coordinated, and that accurate shared mental models are developed.

In the project, developing shared mental models was difficult, due to the company focus on specialization and corresponding division of work. When the Scrum master acted more like a project manager than a coach, he reduced the ability of the team to self-organize. A developer stated: "There was really little discussion about what we could deliver, more about what we *had to* deliver". Problem solving was often not done in the team, as problems related to a module were often seen as personal, and therefore not reported to the group.

Definition [16]: "Ability to direct and coordinate the activities of other team members, assess team performance, assign tasks, develop team knowledge, skills, and abilities, motivate team members, plan and organize, and establish a positive atmosphere".
Behavioural Makers [16]: "Facilitate team problem solving. Provide performance expectations and acceptable interaction patterns. Synchronize and combine individual team member contributions. Seek and evaluate information that affects team functioning. Clarify team member roles. Engage in preparatory meetings and feedback sessions with the team".
Scrum: The team has authority and responsibility for many aspects of their work, such as planning, scheduling, assigning tasks to members, and making decisions. The Scrum master is often described as a coach or facilitator. The Scrum master works to remove the impediments of the process, runs and makes decisions in the daily meetings and validates them with the management [18].
Case-study: A general problem in the company is to protecting the team against request from other projects, which also in this project resulted in the team in periods losing resources. The scrum master often acted more like a project manager than a coach. According to the product owner, "this was necessary ... everyone are engaged in many projects, so you really need someone to push in order to get things done".

Mutual Performance Monitoring: Scrum enables performance monitoring through feedback loops for each day and iteration.

For the project, participants said they had a better overview than in previous projects, but because of a lack of shared mental models there were individual goals and this reduced the possibility for mutual performance monitoring, since missing shared mental models leads to ineffective feedback [16].

Definition [16]: "The ability to develop common understandings of the team environment and apply appropriate task strategies to accurately monitor team-mate performance".

Behavioural Makers [16]: "Identifying mistakes and lapses in other team members' actions. Providing feedback regarding team member actions to facilitate self-correction".

Scrum: In the daily Scrum each team member answers three questions: What did you do since last Scrum meeting? What are you going to do until next Scrum meeting? What are the obstacles in your way? Daily scrums address impediments, to discover other team-members problems. The sprint burndown gives a daily picture of remaining work and team progress. The project review and retrospective shows what has been done and leads to discussions on performance.

Case-study: The daily scrum was held almost every day, but people did often not listen to what others were talking about. The burndown was not updated regularly.

Backup Behaviour: Scrum only describes the team as multifunctional and self-organizing. However, to fully self-organize backup behaviour is important, because it is a mechanism that affects the team's capability to adapt to changing situations and environments [16].

In the project, the highly specialized skills and corresponding division of work resulted in a lack of redundancy. This lack of redundancy reduced the flexibility and, thus, the possibility for backup behaviour.

Definition [16]: "Ability to anticipate other team members' needs through accurate knowledge about their responsibilities. This includes the ability to shift workload among members to achieve balance during high periods of workload or pressure".

Behavioural Makers [16]: "Recognition by potential backup providers that there is a workload distribution problem in their team. Shifting of work responsibilities to underutilized team members. Completion of the whole task or parts of tasks by other team members".

Scrum: The team is seen as multifunctional. Self-organizing is an important characteristic of a Scrum team, meaning the team is supposed to find out themselves how to solve the tasks they have committed them selves to deliver.

Case-study: Few problems related to development tasks were discussed among the developers as these problems were seen as personal problems. Also, the developers did not want to edit others code, and there were difficulties with doing others work when people were not available to the project (e.g. sick, on vacation, or travelling).

Adaptability: Scrum is designed to adapt to change, by frequent feedback loops and replanning.

In the project, the problem with "highly specialized skills and corresponding division of work" was thoroughly discussed, and the team decided to focus on this challenge. However they did not manage to radically change their working practice during the project. Changing the way of working is difficult, and when it involves a transition from specialized skills to redundancy of functions, it requires a reorientation not only by the developers but also by the management.

Definition [16]: "Ability to adjust strategies based on information gathered from the environment through the use of backup behaviour and reallocation of intrateam resources. Altering a course of action or team repertoire in response to changing conditions (internal or external)".

> *Behavioural Makers [16]:* "Identify cues that a change has occurred, assign meaning to that change, and develop a new plan to deal with the changes. Identify opportunities for improvement and innovation for habitual or routine practices. Remain vigilant to changes in the internal and external environment of the team".
>
> *Scrum:* Continuous planning and feedback from the customer is important in Scrum making it possible to respond to unexpected demands. The retrospective makes it possible to reflect and improve both the project and the process.
>
> *Case-study:* Problems with self-organization lead to problems with developing a new plan, solve problems, and identify improvements. The conditions changed, but they had did not act upon these changes.
>
> The project participants did not give feedback on the problem regarding the structure of the meeting before the last retrospective.

Team Orientation: Scrum foster team orientation through the planning and retrospective meetings, self-organizing and the vision.

The company was lacking a system for support. If a developer became responsible for a solution the developer needed to support it as long as he or she was working in the company. This resulted in the developers not wanting to take responsibility and less willing to contribute their knowledge to problem-solving processes, because when team members feel that the project reflect largely external demands, then they are less likely to identify with the project.

> *Definition [16]:* "Propensity to take other's behaviour into account during group interaction and the belief in the importance of team goal's over individual members' goals".
>
> *Behavioural Makers [16]:* "Taking into account alternative solutions provided by team-mates and appraising that input to determine what is most correct. Increased task involvement, information sharing, strategizing, and participatory goal setting".
>
> *Scrum:* The team does high level goal setting in the up front planning. The Product owner should provide a vision to help this process. Further goal setting are done through sprint planning and somewhat through daily scrums. The team members are empowered to make commitments that fit themselves, while the team as a union is responsible for end results. Scrum is also focused on team consensus rather than dictatorial project managers.
>
> *Case-study:* Specialisation and the lack of cohesion between short-term and long-term planning are signs of reduced team orientation. However, many commented on a good team atmosphere.

4   Conclusion and Further Work

In this paper, we have described the agile process Scrum and a software development project, using the "Big Five" framework for team effectiveness. We have seen that Scrum has several mechanisms in place in order to support the factors in the framework, but we have also seen that many of these mechanisms were not easy to implement in practice in the case organization. As for our first research question, "how does Scrum support the factors which influence effective teamwork?", we found the following:

The aspect of team leadership is not appropriately addressed in Scrum. In a self-organizing team, leadership should be diffused rather than centralized [4]. Scrum puts emphasis on self-organizing teams and coaching, but does not give clear advice on how this should be implemented. Second, back-up behaviour is an issue that is not clearly described in Scrum. In the literature on self-organizing teams, we find that redundancy or back-up behavior has been identified as an important prerequisite for self-organization [4, 13]. Combining Scrum with for example the practice of pair programming in XP [3] would improve this aspect. Third, Scrum is not very specific on how to establish mutual trust in the development team, although this is implicitly a prerequisite for a self-organizing team.

As for our second research question, "how can challenges when introducing Scrum be explained by the factors influencing effective teamwork?", we found:

The main deviations from the recommended practices in the framework were first that the project suffered from lacking long-term planning, handling of problems and establishment of mutual trust. Second, the mutual performance monitoring was hindered by the team not using the burn-down charts throughout the project. Third, the team orientation suffered from specialization in the team, which lead to participants primarily focusing on their own issues. Fourth, mutual trust was not fully developed, which resulted in problems not being reported and a lack of self-organization.

In the future we plan to use the "Big Five" framework in studying more projects, in order to get a better understanding of what the main challenges are when companies are seeking to promote effective teamwork through implementing agile development processes.

References

[1] Abrahamsson, P., Salo, O., Ronkainen, J., Warsta, J.: Agile Software Development Methods: Review and Analysis. VTT Technical report (2002)

[2] Bandow, D.: Time to Create Sound Teamwork. The Journal for quality and participation 24(2), 41 (2001)

[3] Beck, K., Andres, C.: Extreme Programming Explained: Embrace Chage, 2nd edn. Addison-Wesley, Reading (2004)

[4] Morgan, G.: Images of Organizations, p. 504. SAGE publications, Thousands Oaks (2006)

[5] Dingsøyr, T., Hanssen, G.K., Dybå, T., Anker, G., Nygaard, J.O.: Developing Software with Scrum in a Small Cross-Organizational Project. In: Richardson, I., Runeson, P., Messnarz, R. (eds.) EuroSPI 2006. LNCS, vol. 4257, pp. 5–15. Springer, Heidelberg (2006)

[6] Dybå, T., Dingsøyr, T.: Empirical Studies of Agile Software Development: A Systematic Review. Information and Software Technology (2008) doi: 10.1016/j.infsof.2008.01.006

[7] Fitzgerald, B., Hartnett, G., Conboy, K.: Customizing Agile Methods to Software Practices at Intel Shannon. European Journal of Information Systems 15(2), 200–213 (2006)

[8] Hoegl, M., Gemuenden, H.G.: Teamwork Quality and the Success of Innovative Projects: A Theoretical Concept and Empirical Evidence. Organization Science 12(4), 435–449 (2001)

[9] Kay, J., Maisonneuve, N., Yacef, K., Reimann, P.: The Big Five and Visualisations of Team Work Activity. In: Intelligent Tutoring Systems, pp. 197–206 (2006)

[10] Mann, C., Maurer, F.: A Case Study on the Impact of Scrum on Overtime and Customer Satisfaction. In: Proceedings of Agile 2005. IEEE Press, Denver (2005)

[11] Marks, M.A.: A Temporally Based Framework and Taxonomy of Team Processes. The Academy of Management review 26(3), 356 (2001)

[12] Nerur, S., Sikora, R., Mangalaraj, G., Balijepally, V.: Assessing the Relative Influence of Journals in a Citation Network. Communications of the ACM 48(11), 71–73 (2005)

[13] Nonaka, I., Takeuchi, H.: The Knowledge-Creating Company. Oxford University Press, Oxford (1995)

[14] Rising, L., Janoff, N.S.: The Scrum Software Development Process for Small Teams. IEEE Software 17(4), 26 (2000)

[15] Rousseau, V., Aube, C., Savoie, A.: Teamwork Behaviors - a Review and an Integration of Frameworks. Small Group Research 37(5), 540–570 (2006)

[16] Salas, E., Sims, D.E., Burke, C.S.: Is There A "Big Five" In Teamwork? Small group research 36(5), 555–599 (2005)

[17] Schatz, B., Abdelshafi, I.: Primavera Gets Agile: A Successfull Transition to Agile Development. IEEE Software, 36–42 (May/June 2005)

[18] Schwaber, K., Beedle, M.: Agile Software Development with Scrum. Prentice Hall, Upper Saddle River (2001)

[19] Stewart, G.L.: A Meta-Analytic Review of Relationships between Team Design Features and Team Performance. 32, 29–55 (2006)

[20] Sutherland, J.: Agile Development: Lessons Learned from the First Scrum. Cutter Agile Project Management Advisory Service: Executive Update 5(20), 1–4 (2004)

[21] Takeuchi, H., Nonaka, I.: The New Product Development Game. Harvard Business Review, 137–146 (January 1986)

[22] Yin, R.K.: Case Study Research: Design and Methods, 3rd edn. Sage Publications, Thousand Oaks (2003)

[23] Ågerfalk, P., Fitzgerald, B.: Flexible and Distributed Software Processes: Old Petunias in New Bowls? Communications of the ACM 49(10), 27–34 (2006)

Misfit or Misuse? Lessons from Implementation of Scrum in Radical Product Innovation

Jens Henrik Hosbond and Peter Axel Nielsen

Department of Computer Science, Aalborg University, Denmark
{joenne,pan}@cs.aau.dk

Abstract. In this paper we report from a study of the implementation and early experiences of using Scrum for radical product innovation in a traditional, matrix-organized software company. The empirical data was collected in an interview-based case study. The case data show a company undergoing significant change due to a recent corporate take-over which has lead to a re-thinking of the roles and tasks of the organization at all levels. We draw on an already established framework for analyzing the organizational change process. The analysis results in a set of observations that we use subsequently in the discussion of practical lessons for organizations facing similar challenges.

Keywords: Agile, Scrum, Product innovation, Organizational change.

1 Introduction

The case we have studied reveals some significant challenges and lessons to be learned which will be relevant for many software companies. The software company is in the midst of changing from a traditional way of organizing and developing software to a more modern way that is much more agile. As part of their agile process the company has selected Scrum as their main method. At the same time, the company's primary task is to deliver radical product innovation for the mobile phone market and in particular to innovate the software services delivered on a mobile phone. Hence, we are here at the intersection between the challenges with implementing Scrum and implementing innovative product thinking.

We take Scrum to be the process, set of techniques, principles and perspectives that are defined by [1]. In the words of Schwaber and Beedle, Scrum is an approach that "reintroduces flexibility, adaptability, and productivity into systems development" [1]. Scrum implements an empirically based approach to process control which is contrary to the traditional defined process control model. A method is usually seen as a way to control a development process. This is not in the sense of the *one* method, but rather in the sense of a method being bits and pieces which fit together and which might be useful for particular purposes. It thus makes sense to at look at the literature for what to do with implementing such a method. The research on methods for software development sees this process as a learning process [2] and as a process of adaptation [3] where the dined method is just a small element and where the main focus should be on the methods-in-action.

P. Abrahamsson et al. (Eds.): XP 2008, LNBIP 9, pp. 21–31, 2008.

Tidd et al. suggest that four types of innovation exist; product innovation, process innovation, position innovation, and paradigm innovation [4]. We take the process for product innovation to include the four activities of *searching* and *selecting* ideas, implementation, and learning from the innovation process [4]. The existing literature on product innovation has nothing to say on software development and it is therefore relevant for modern software companies to bring these two different lines of thinking, organizing and working together in a single study.

2 Related Work

Scrum is not the only method for agile software development, but it is certainly a significant one amongst Beck's XP [5] and Cockburn's Crystal Methodologies [6].

Like any of the methods ever studied for software development Scrum is never just *applied*. It is implemented in many different forms. It is adapted to the specific needs in the company or in a specific project. The experience with using it will vary depending on who is using it, how it is used and for what purposes. It has been argued in information systems research that the practice of developing does not follow methods, and it is a-methodical [7]. Others follow a similar view on methods and have found through empirical studies that method emerges through practice [8], that methods are never used by-the-book [9], or that it is necessary to have a critical view on the use of methods [9]. Another strand of research on methods has been concerned with tailoring methods to the unique situation where they are to be used, e.g. as combinations of methods [10, 11]. Harmsen et al. [12] and Brinkkemper [13] suggest that methods are engineered on the spot to fit the current situation and needs. Reports from empirical studies show how this has been done in practice at Motorola [14] and at Intel [15].

Product innovation on the other hand is not really a method. It is a task that a company or a project can undertake. There are many ways in which product innovation have been undertaken in organizations. Based on a literature study Slappendel [16] suggests the individualist perspective (innovation is driven by champions), the structuralist perspective (innovation is determined by structural characteristics, e.g., type of organization, environment etc.), and the interactive process perspective (innovation is dependent on the interplay between actors and the organizational structures) as three different theoretical perspectives on innovation in organizations. As one example, the work on innovation in organizations by Nonaka and Takeuchi [17] belong to the interactive process perspective.

Whereas Slappendal [16] takes a process view on innovation, Tidd et al. [4] represents a product view on innovation. That is, they separate innovation according to the type of output resulting of an innovation process. They distinguish between product innovation (output is often a technology or service), process innovation (changes in how products or services are created or delivered), position innovation (changes related to positioning or re-positioning a product), and paradigm innovation (changes in the mental models of the organization itself and of what it does). It is on this background of related work that we have engaged in the following case study.

3 Case Study

In the following section we present the background of the case study, the research approach, and the analysis framework applied.

3.1 Case Background

The history of this software company dates back to the late 1980s. It started out as a Scandinavian company developing mobile phones. Due to a financial crisis in the mid-1990s a larger company acquired the company. During its lifetime it has experienced several take-overs by multi-national corporations. During the years the company has been engaged mainly in development, but also in production of mobile phones. In 2000 the company was acquired by a dominant player in the mobile phones development industry. Being one of 9 development sites worldwide the company changed its organizational structure into a matrix organisation fitting the corporate structure. The matrix organization was divided into functional units each headed by a functional manager, e.g., a functional unit handling connectivity issues. Developers were split into functional departments and from here they were assigned to work on specific development projects. At that time the company counted approximately 300 employees. The type of work was intended to be R&D, but only on rare occasions was it characterised as research-driven. The organization of work was highly managed. Developers were given specific and concrete tasks with fixed deadlines. The development practice followed a very structured adaptation of the specify-and-test model also known as the V-model and was characterised by considerable documentation work.

In 2004 the company was acquired by a relatively new player within the mobile phone industry in Europe. This did not last long as it was sold again in 2005 to the corporation under which it operates today. In late 2007 the organisation has more than 400 employees.

After the last take-over in 2005 the company has been given a new role. The company has been attached to an already established division within the corporation. The division worked on wireless innovative technologies and the company was given the task of developing unique and radically different and innovative mobile phones. This differed from what previously had been the company's primary task. This new task required that the company became more research-driven. Due to the new task and desire to show that the division got value for money, the company's top management decided to try a different approach to product development. The approach had to be more focused on products, on shorter development cycles, and on responsiveness to change. Because of a top manager's prior positive experiences with Scrum at another company, Scrum was chosen as the new development method for software projects. Certification programmes for Scrum masters were initiated in 2005 and the first Scrum projects were started in the late summer of 2005.

3.2 Research Approach

This study may be classified as qualitative research [18] and it uses the case study approach [19] as foundation. The study was carried out in the spring 2006 spanning a period of 4 months. Empirical data was collected through 20 semi-structured interviews, reading of historical data, and through several informal face-to-face conversations at the site. Prior to the interviews an interview template was prepared serving as inspiration and as guidance during the interviews. The questions in the template related to prior and current development practice. Each interview varied from 30 minutes to more than an hour. All interviews were audio recorded. Interviewees came from several development projects as well as managerial levels. These were software project managers, product owners, scrum masters, developers, functional managers, staff in the technical requirements department, and people from the quality assurance function. Upon completion of the interviews the audio recordings were transcribed which were then used for the subsequent data analysis. The data analysis was conducted in an iterative manner allowing for a continual refinement of the categorisation and selection of observations for further interpretation.

3.3 Analysis Framework

This case study is a study of an organization undergoing significant change. For structuring and scoping the search spaces of our analysis we adopt the multivariate framework proposed by Leavitt [20] more commonly referred to as *Leavitt's diamond*, see Figure. 1. The framework consists of the four variables actors, structure, task, and technology. *Actors* are the people part of the change process. *Structure* reflects the system of authority and power. *Task* defines the job to be done by the actors and lastly *Technology* represents the means (i.e., tools, techniques, know-how etc.) by which the tasks are carried out. These four elements are interdependent and change in one will change the state of each of the remaining three variables.

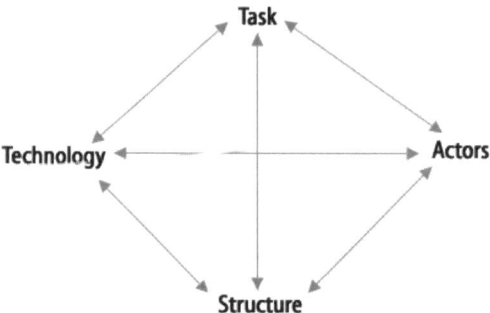

Fig. 1. Leavitt's diamond

The framework by Leavitt is simple yet powerful in that it captures the multifaceted nature of change in an organizational context. The framework is relevant in this study as the implementation of Scrum and the new task of radical product innovation facing the organisation cause a significant change process. Much in line with Lyttinen et al. [21], we found the framework very useful for scoping and structuring our search for central issues in the change process.

4   Analysis

In this section we present the central observations in the empirical data.

4.1 Observations

Observation 1: *There is a misfit between employee competences and the competences required to do radical product innovation and mastering Scrum.*

This observation relates to two relations in Leavitt's diamond, see Figure 1. That is, the relations *task-actors* and the relation *technology-actors*. The *task-actors* relation is bound to the misfit between employee competences and the new task of doing radical product innovation. The *technology-actors* relation refers to misfit between people competences in following Scrum as a new model for software development.

As part of the recent take-over in 2005 the company experienced a significant change in focus. Coming from software development projects predominantly concerned with known and existing technologies the company was now given the new task of developing radical innovative mobile phones. This had several implications. A development project's task was now unknown a priori or was at the most only loosely defined and then often changed on a regular basis. Most likely only a product vision was passed on to the product owner and the Scrum team. This level of uncertainty bound to these projects had never before been experienced. Traditionally the company had been an internal subcontractor on larger and already defined and on-going development projects with clear feature requirements. Now, the development teams had to be proactive, creative yet disciplined, and self-confident in order to live up to the demand of producing tomorrow's mobile phones. In addition, top management had decided to implement Scrum as a new development method. The integration of Scrum did not happen over night, but as about 20 people had been certified either as Scrum Masters, product owners or both, the initiative was rolled-out completely replacing the old V-model. However, the interviews showed that not all developers, Scrum Masters, and product owners at the time of enrollment felt they had the proper training in conducting Scrum in a proper way. This re-focusing of the task and the implementation of Scrum required a complete turn-around in mindset throughout the organization. Not surprisingly, the empirical data indicated a shortage of developers' and managers' competences in dealing with these changes.

Observation 2: *Management relied solely on Scrum as enabler for innovation.*

This observation relates to the relation *technology-task* in Leavitt's diamond. The task is changed to product innovation and it relates directly to the technology (Scrum as a method). Scrum is however an insufficient response to the changed task.

As a response to the new focus on innovation, top management decided to implement a new way of organizing software projects. Scrum was chosen as the new method for development. The decision to drop the traditional development process was especially pushed by one of the managers as he had had positive experiences in using Scrum in similar projects at a different company. The apparent strengths of Scrum such as increased focus on product output, the ability to change course, and fostering developer commitment and ownership all seemed relevant in achieving the task of product innovation. Through self-organizing teams and co-location enabling free communication, the creation of a shared understanding of the problem to solve, and ideas for solving these seems intuitively as very good instruments in an innovation process where idea generation, mutual understanding and communication are necessities. However, Scrum does not say anything specific about innovation. It does not address the question on what is required to do innovation: How are ideas generated, selected, re-fined, and later re-formulated as tasks on a product backlog? These questions are important in an innovation process and the latter especially in bridging the innovation process with Scrum.

Observation 3: *Unclear and shifting power structures between functional managers, scrum masters and product owners as a result of implementing Scrum.*

This observation concerns the relation *technology-structure*. The introduction of Scrum as a method (technology) really requires a changed organization and management practices (structure), but these changed were never fully realized and hence never implemented.

The implementation of Scrum as the new development method has had an impact on the existing system of authority and power within the organization. Prior to the Scrum implementation the organization could be characterized as a traditional matrix organization. A matrix organization divided into functional departments each managed by a functional manager responsible for a group of experts within a pre-defined knowledge domain, e.g., wireless connectivity. In a functional department all the experts are grouped in the same room creating a community of experts. The functional manager decides how many and who is to be allocated on to which software project. In addition, the functional manager is responsible for further educating his developers. Even though developers within a department belong to different projects they are still and have always been physically present in the same room.

With the introduction of the Scrum method the focus has now shifted away from the functional departments to the Scrum projects. This shift is caused by an increased focus from top management on product output. A product output coming only from the Scrum teams. With the integration of the roles in Scrum, namely the product owner and the Scrum master role, the power structure within the organization is changing. In the new structure the power and authority of the functional manager decreases at the expense of the increasing power of products owners and Scrum masters. The previous central role of the functional department is in the eyes of the functional managers in danger of turning into a mere supplier of expertise for Scrum projects. But, what is maybe more interesting is that the functional departments stand the risk of becoming nearly obsolete or they may only exist as virtual groups. That is, if a full-scale co-location as prescribed by Scrum is carried out. Co-location was not implemented during the case study period though it was discussed. Co-location is further elaborated on in observation 4.

Observation 4: *Co-location was not implemented, but wanted by developers and Scrum masters.*

As for observation 3 this observation concerns the relation *technology-structure*.

During implementation of Scrum all principles within Scrum was sought integrated into existing practice. However, one central aspect of Scrum was not implemented. That is, co-location was for several reasons found either not important or impossible to carry through in the company. One reason that some of the interviewees mentioned were inadequate office space. The current office space was characterized by large and open rooms that did not facilitate working in isolated small teams as recommended in Scrum. Another reason was that several Scrum teams working side by side in one room would break a corporate security rule. Upon the take-over in 2005 a new and much tougher security policy had been introduced at the company. This was done to ensure that the work on innovative technologies was not compromised. What this meant was that all paperwork related to a project should be locked off when leaving ones desk. At the end of a work day it should be possible to lock off a room belonging only to that project. Hence, grouping several teams in one large room would make this impossible.

Yet another reason for not implementing co-location is believed to be connected with the apparent power struggle in observation 3. Co-locating Scrum teams would mean having people physically grouped according to their Scrum team relation making the functional departments and functional managers much less necessary or simply serving as virtual departments that group developer' competences and that is responsible for further training and education.

Product owners, Scrum masters, and Scrum teams perceived the lacking co-location as frustrating and a wrong decision made by top management. It was perceived by several interviewees as frustrating as it prohibited them in exploiting the full potential of Scrum.

Observation 5: *There was a misfit between the agile desire for light-weight documentation and the corporate quality assurance system.*

This observation concerns the relation *technology-structure*. The Scrum method (technology) advocates significantly less documentation than what was required by the corporate structures. The implementation of an agile approach through Scrum was decided not only as a response to changes in the company's primary task; it was also introduced in order to lessening the documentation work. Documentation work had previously taken significant resources and time in performing analysis, design and requirements documentation.

With the introduction of Scrum the management took the opportunity to only spend resources on activities deemed value-generating such as coding and hence minimize documentation work. The reduced focus on documentation was throughout the organization received positively. However, the agile principle of "working software over comprehensive documentation" [22] did not coincide with the demands for documentation set by the corporate quality assurance system. The quality assurance system that was maintained by an external quality assurance department had the purpose of tracing and validating the maturity level of a product under development. From project initiation until final market launch the project/product must pass a number of maturity steps in the quality assurance system. For passing a maturity step comprehensive documentation of the current state of the product must be provided. The current quality assurance system measures product maturity from a number of metrics that all are quantitative measures such as lines of code, number of completed function points, test coverage, etc. The level of documentation for passing a maturity gate is substantial and the documentation is not readily or easily extracted from the projects and therefore has to be laboriously created. The project manager of software had to prepare a 70 pages report on a weekly or bi-weekly basis documenting the current progress and maturity of the projects. As noted by the project manager, it would suit their new way of working if products could to a larger extent be measured qualitatively rather than quantitatively. A qualitative evaluation would focus on the look-and-feel of the product more than it would be based on for instance lines of code.

4.2 Summary

The analysis of the empirical data has led to five central observations. These five observations concern the relations in Leavitt's diamond as displayed in Figure 2.

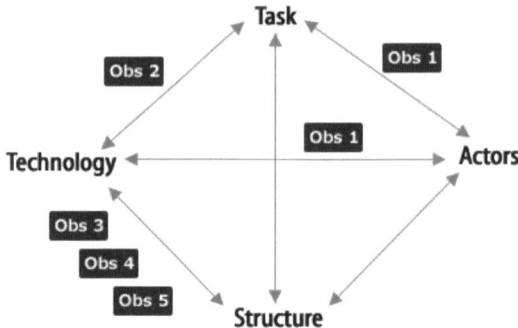

Fig. 2. Mapping of observations onto Leavitt's diamond

5 Discussion

As with any major change process much depends on peoples' competence and this case show a similar pattern. Observation 1 addresses this directly. The developers needed considerable training in Scrum, which they then went through. It is fair to state that they were then sufficiently competence to start using Scrum and that a new balance between the developers and their technology use had been established. This relation will certainly improve when the developers gradually gain more experience. The framework points to the conclusion, that Scrum and the developers' competences will remain different entities and it will thus make little sense to see the developers' practice as the same as Scrum or that Scrum have been 'internalized'. This coincides with previous results of previous studies, e.g., [2] [3, 23]. Observation 1 becomes more interesting when we see it in conjunction with observation 2, that management had their eyes firmly focused on Scrum (the technology dimension) to enable the developers to gain the competence (the actors dimension) necessary to do product innovation (the task dimension). It seems evident that the new technology does not directly address the new task. Further, changes in actors' competences could not alone enable the new task.

It is interesting that the interview data points to three central observations concerning the relation between Scrum and the structure: Scrum and power structures (observation 3), Scrum and co-location (observation 4), and Scrum and documentation rules (observation 5). The interviews were addressing both Scrum and the radical innovation task and the interviewer did probably not cause the considerable focus on Scrum. We find that this bias appeared in the company and that the main reason can be found in observation 2. All management attention has gone into Scrum as the primary enabler for the task of product innovation.

It is clear from observations 1, 3, 4 and 5 that this is not a case of successful application of Scrum for the purpose of radical product innovation. The developers are simply too troubled by how to deal with the new task and how to practice Scrum. In terms of Leavitt's diamond the relations between the four dimensions are out of balance. Without assuming that equilibrium would ever occur we may still use the theory to point at four dimensions and six relations to be very aware of in agile software development. From the viewpoint of managing agile software development it is apparent that too little attention has been paid to other dimensions than technology and how changes in the task must lead management to create changes in both the *structure* dimension and in the *actor* dimension which they have not.

Let us now return to the question posed in the title: Misfit or misuse? That is, is there a misfit between using Scrum for radical product innovation or is it a case of misuse of Scrum? If Scrum is not useful for radical product innovation, it would be misfit. Misfit would in this case have been caused by poor management decisions. If the developers in this particular company did not use Scrum well or properly, it would be misuse. Misuse would in this case have been caused by lack of developers' competence. From the viewpoint of research methodology it is a question that has always bothered researchers. Most of the research on development methods evaluate methods in the context of their use and hence seek to relate features of methods to particular contingencies or at least explain how methods and situations can be matched given a particular situation. This line of research is not particularly helpful in explaining what is troubling the developers in our case. What should they do to turn a growing failure into success?

Based on our case study and our use of Leavitt's framework we should now like to abandon the simple dichotomy of misfit-misuse. It is not valuable to the company to discuss the features of Scrum. The observations and the framework suggest that the singleton focus on technology inhibits the further development of the whole agile process. The structures would also have to be changed. Not only to comply the guidelines in Scrum, but also to cater for the complex task of product innovation. The actors' competence would have to be further developed. Not only to become more skilled in Scrum, but also to address directly the task's complexities. The applied technologies will have to be extended beyond Scrum to address other aspects of the task at hand. Hence, the research scope for an agile method like Scrum must be wider than the method and its features.

6 Limitations and Future Work

In this study we have looked at an organisation undergoing significant change. A change caused by an implementation of Scrum as the enabler for radical product innovation. The study points at interesting lessons to be learned for practices in similar contexts. With that being said, we also know that our study has limitations. The study only covers one case which limits the general applicability of our findings. In addition, the study was carried out over a period of four months. In this particular case it could have been interesting to follow the organisation over a greater time period making it possible to observe in greater detail how the organisational change process came along. However, due to time and resource constraints we did not have that option. With respect to future work, we would like to conduct similar studies in order to look for similar observations earning credibility and validity to our findings, but also to extend our understanding of the issues emerging when applying Scrum or other agile approaches as enablers of product innovation.

7 Conclusion

We have studied a case where a software company have tried to use Scrum to enable radical product innovation. The empirical data came from a series of interviews with key informants in the company. Leavitt's framework has then been applied to structure the findings and that has led to five central observations. The observations are: (1) There is a misfit between employee competences and the competences required to do radical product innovation and mastering Scrum, (2) Management relied solely on Scrum as enabler for innovation, (3) Unclear and shifting power structures between functional managers, Scrum masters and product owners as a result of implementing Scrum, (4) Co-location was not implemented, but was wanted by developers and Scrum masters, and (5) There was a misfit between the agile desire for lightweight documentation and the corporate quality assurance system. In the discussion we relate the observations to a wider concern. First the observations were discussed within Leavitt's framework and then the discussion extended beyond the question of misfit or misuse of Scrum. The conclusion is that the observations are valuable on the way to turn a growing failure into a possible success if attention is put on other dimensions than technology.

References

1. Schwaber, K., Beedle, M.: Agile Software Development with Scrum. In: Martin, R.C. (ed.) Agile Software Development. Prentice Hall, Upper Saddle River (2002)
2. Nielsen, P.A.: Reflections on development methods for information systems: a set of distinctions between methods. Office, Technology and People 5(2), 81–104 (1989)
3. Fitzgerald, B., Russo, N., Stolterman, E.: Information Systems Development: Methods-in-Action. McGraw-Hill, London (2002)
4. Tidd, J., Bessant, J., Pavitt, K.: Managing Innovation, 3rd edn., p. 582. John Wiley & Sons Ltd, West Sussex (2005)
5. Beck, K.: Extreme Programming Explained: Embrace Change. The XP Series. Addison-Wesley, Boston (2000)
6. Cockburn, A.: Agile Software Development. In: Cockburn, A., Highsmith, J. (eds.) The Agile Software Development Series, p. 304. Addison-Wesley Professional, Reading (2001)
7. Truex, D., Baskerville, R., Travis, J.: Amethodical Systems Development: The Deferred Meaning of Systems Development Methods. Accounting, Management, and Information Technologies 10, 53–79 (2000)
8. Madsen, S., Kautz, K., Vidgen, R.: A Framework for Understanding how a Unique and Local IS Development Method Emerges in Practice. European Journal of Information Systems 15(2), 225–238 (2006)
9. Fitzgerald, B.: Formalized systems development methodologies: a critical perspective. Information Systems Journal 6(1), 3–23 (1996)
10. Avison, D., Nandhakumar, J.: Information Systems Development Methodology in Use: An Empirical Study. In: Lessons Learned from the Use of Methodologies. BCS, London (1996)
11. Vidgen, R.: Constructing a web information system development methodology. Information Systems Journal 12(3), 247 (2002)

12. Harmsen, F., Brinkkemper, S., Oei Han, J.L.: Situational method engineering for informational system project approaches. In: Proceedings of the IFIP WG8.1 Working Conference on Methods and Associated Tools for the Information Systems Life Cycle. Elsevier Science Inc., Amsterdam (1994)
13. Brinkkemper, S.: Method engineering: engineering of information systems development methods and tools. Information and Software Technology 34(4), 275–280 (1996)
14. Fitzgerald, B., Russo, N., O'Kane, T.: Software development method tailoring at Motorola. Communications of the ACM 46(4), 64–70 (2003)
15. Fitzgerald, B., Hartnett, G., Conboy, K.: Customising agile methods to software practices at Intel Shannon. European Journal of Information Systems 15(2), 200–213 (2006)
16. Slappendel, C.: Perspectives on innovation in organizations. Organization studies 17(1), 107–129 (1996)
17. Nonaka, I., Takeuchi, H.: The Knowledge-Creating Company: How Japanese Companies Create the Dynamics of Innovation. Oxford University Press, New York (1995)
18. Patton, M.Q.: Qualitative Evaluation and Research Methods, 2nd edn., p. 536. SAGE Publications, Thousand Oaks (1990)
19. Yin, R.K.: Case study research - design and methods. SAGE Publications, Thousand Oaks (1994)
20. Leavitt, H.J.: Applying organizational change in industry: Structural, technological and humanistic approaches. In: March, J.G. (ed.) Handbook of organizations. Rand McNally, Chicago (1965)
21. Lyytinen, K., Mathiassen, L., Ropponen, J.: A Framework For Software Risk Management. Scandinavian Journal of Information Systems 8(1), 53–68 (1996)
22. Beck, K., et al.: Manifesto for Agile Software Development (2001),
    http://agilemanifesto.org/
23. Mathiassen, L., Purao, S.: Educating reflective systems developers. Information Systems Journal 12(2), 81–102 (2002)

Method Configuration:
The eXtreme Programming Case

Fredrik Karlsson[1] and Pär J. Ågerfalk[2]

[1] Dept. of Informatics (ESI), Methodology Exploration Lab
Örebro University, SE-701 82 Örebro, Sweden
fredrik.karlsson@esi.oru.se
[2] Department of Information Science
Uppsala University, SE-751 20 Uppsala, Sweden
Lero – The Irish Software Engineering Research Centre
par.agerfalk@dis.uu.se

Abstract. The Method for Method Configuration (MMC) has been proposed as a method engineering approach to tailoring software development methods. This paper evaluates MMC during three software development projects where it was used to tailor eXtreme Programming (XP). The study has been justified by the need to complement earlier evaluations of MMC and providing more conclusive tests to determine the effectiveness of the meta-method in practice. Also, since MMC originates from the plan-based method community, no tests have so far been made on agile methods. Many method engineering concepts have similar roots and it is of interest to evaluate their applicability also in the agile context. We report on the migration results together with lessons learned.

Keywords: Method Configuration, Method tailoring, Method Engineering, eXtreme Programming, Agile Method.

1 Introduction

An often used dichotomy within the field of software and information systems development is that of plan-driven vs. agile methods [1]. While agile proponents emphasise 'just enough method', plan-driven methods often try to cover every aspect of software and systems development. As a consequence, the latter have been criticized for being too inflexible and hard to comprehend [2].

Agile methods, which can be viewed as a reaction towards plan-driven methods [3], started to evolve in the mid 1990's with methods such as DSDM [4], eXtreme Programming [2] and SCRUM [5], and characteristics inherited from Rapid Application Development [6]. Despite the large number of agile methods, they all share a number of characteristics, such as iterative development models [1], emphasis on interaction with the end users [7] and face-to-face communication [8], and low confidence in intermediate artefacts [9].

However, practical experience shows that all projects are unique and require unique methodological support [10]. Hence, there is no one-size-fits-all method—neither

P. Abrahamsson et al. (Eds.): XP 2008, LNBIP 9, pp. 32–41, 2008.

plan-based nor agile [11, 12]. Method configuration [13] has been proposed as a possible solution to this problem. Here, one method, often termed base method, is taken as the starting point for configuring a situational method suitable to the project at hand. This is particularly useful when an organization wants to establish an organization-wide method to be used across all projects. Incentives for such an effort include more effective communication, reduced training costs due to common modelling languages and the utilization of industry standards, as well as the access to existing computerized tools.

The Method for Method Configuration (MMC) [13, 14] has been proposed as a structured way to carry out method configuration. The approach is anchored in Activity Theory [15] and the concept of method rationale [16, 17] to emphasize the collaborative aspect of methods during method tailoring. Furthermore, MMC has been proposed as a tool to manage method knowledge between projects, since it builds on the idea of reusing method sections based on similarities in project characteristics.

MMC has so far only been evaluated using a limited number of methods [14]. None of which are particularly agile. Therefore, more conclusive tests, to determine the effectiveness of MMC, are needed. Aydin et. al [18] state that only a few studies exist on tailoring of agile methods. In addition, as with most method engineering concepts and tools, MMC has its roots in the plan-based method community. Consequently, it is of interest to see if it can successfully be moved to the agile context. Thus, the aim of this paper is to report on the use of MMC and its conceptual framework during method configuration of the agile method eXtreme Programming (XP).

The paper proceeds as follows. Section 2 presents the adopted research approach. Section 3 introduces a selection of key MMC concepts. Section 4 reports on the empirical experiences from the use of MMC during three agile software development projects. Finally, Section 5 provides a concluding discussion.

2 Research Approach

The study was carried out as a case study in a small software development company in Sweden. Their business is mainly to provide project management expertise and run systems development projects that bring together a network of external partners. The company agreed to evaluate MMC through the use of MC Sandbox[1] [19] in three commercial software development projects. The choice of XP as the base method was the industrial partner's. They do not use it as a true organization-wide method, but only with some specific clients.

The first author of this paper was the project manager during all three projects. However, he was not responsible for the method engineering, except for mentoring one of the software developers when modularizing the base method (XP). Rather method engineering was distributed among the developers and the majority of the method configuration decisions were taken together during method-user-centred method configuration [19] workshops. Since the teams were unfamiliar with MMC and MC Sandbox they received an introduction to both—lasting for approx. three hours. Furthermore, some of the developers participated in more than one of the projects, which facilitated

---

[1] MC Sandbox is the computerized implementation of MMC. For the sake of simplicity we will only refer to MC Sandbox in the presentation when explicitly needed.

knowledge sharing. All of the developers had at least four years experience from systems development and had used XP in earlier projects. The selection of projects was based on the industrial partner's current project portfolio. A summary of the projects' characteristics is shown in Table 1.

Table 1. Characteristics of Projects

Project	Type of Information System	Person-hours	Calendar Months	No of Developers
1	Web-based inventory system	1500	4	5
2	Web-based time report system	800	2	4
3	Web-based quotation system	1100	3	5

Empirical data was collected using MC Sandbox, logbooks, and interviews with the developers. MC Sandbox allows for free text comments to be associated with each method configuration decision, thus containing developers' comments. The log books, written by the first author during the method configuration workshops, are a complement that focuses on the configuration process as such. The interviews were semistructured using the logbooks and data from MC Sandbox as a form of interview guide [20]. The subsequent analysis focused on categorizing emerging issues into (a) conflicting design principles between MMC and XP, (b) inexperience with MMC/MC Sandbox, and (c) the developers' knowledge of XP. In this paper we focus on the results from (a), which are presented in Section 5.2. Within (a), we grouped problems into categories that were associated with one or more design principle in MMC, XP or both. In cases where we only could associate the category with a design principle in either MMC or XP we searched for a conflicting design principle in the other approach. Interview quotes are used to illustrate the developers' opinions about these issues.

3   Method for Method Configuration—Key Concepts

The aim of the MMC is to support method configuration: the planned and systematic adaptation of a specific method through the use of reusable assets. The meta-method embraces the need for both structure and flexibility in software development practice and is anchored in the following design principles [14]:

(1) The principle of modularization: (1a) self-contained modules, (1b) internally consistent and coherent modules, (1c) support for information hiding; (2) The principle of method rationale for selecting method parts: (2a) support analysis of potential to achieve rationality resonance (2b) support method-in-action decisions; and (3) The principle of a multi-layered reuse model.

These design principles are implemented as three core concepts providing the possibility to work with reusable method assets: method components [15], configuration packages [14], and configuration templates [14]. The presentation below focuses on these three key concepts. A more extensive treatment of all concepts can be found in [14] and [15].

3.1 The Method Component Concept

A modularization concept is needed to enable systematic ways of working with method configuration. Through such a concept, specific parts can be suppressed, added or exchanged within the confines of a coherent method. A *method component* is a self-contained part of a method expressing the transformation of one or several artefacts into a defined target artefact, and the rationale for such a transformation. A method component has two parts: its *content* and its *interface*.

Method Component Content. The content of a method component is an aggregate of method elements: A *method element* is a part of a method that manifests a method component's target state or facilitates the transformation from one defined state to another. Method elements are constituted by prescribed actions (e.g. draw class diagram), concepts (e.g. class), notations (e.g. UML class), artefacts (e.g. class diagram), and actor roles (e.g. analyst). A development activity is essentially a set of prescribed actions with associated sequence restrictions that guide project members actions in specific situations. In performing these actions, developers' attention is directed towards specific phenomena in the problem domain. These are concepts that express an understanding of the problem domain, and also of the method itself. Results of actions are documented by artefacts using a prescribed notation, giving the concepts a concrete representation. Artefacts are thus both deliverables from and input to (subsequent stages of) the process. In MMC, methods are viewed as heuristic procedures and hence specified inputs are only recommended inputs. Finally, actor roles describe the functions that actors play in the method component. The selection of actor roles is determined by the prescribed actions that are needed for the transformation process.

The rationale part of the method component has two concepts: goals and values. Each method element is included in the method component for reasons, which are made explicit by associating method elements to goals. Moreover, these goals are anchored in values of the method creator. Together these goals and values reflect the underlying perspective of the method from which the method component originates. When working with MMC, method rationale is more important than the deliverable as such. Through the method rationale it is possible to address the goals that are essential in order to fulfil the overall goal of a specific project. Prescribed actions and artefacts are viewed as means to achieve those goals. Hence, method rationale can help developers not to loose sight of the ultimate result, and also help them find alternative ways forward.

The Method Component Interface. The purpose of the interface is to hide unnecessary details during method configuration. It draws on the general use of the component construct in software engineering and that the primary interest during method configuration is the results offered and the required inputs needed, not how a task is executed. This reduction of complexity is achieved through the *method component interface*: A reference to a selection of method elements and rationale that is relevant for the task at hand. The interface becomes an external view of method components. The interface's content depends on the task at hand [15]. During method configuration, the method component's overall goals and the artefacts are the primary selection. The artefacts are designated as input and/or deliverable (output), as discussed above. This is necessary in order to deal with the three fundamental actions that can be performed on an artefact: create, update and delete. An artefact is classified as a deliverable when it is only created by the method component. If the artefact can be updated by the same method component it is classified as input as well. In addition, we stipulate that a component can take one or several input artefacts, but has only one deliverable. Finally, the interface expresses the method component's overall goals, representing the method rationale. These goals are used to discuss the rationality resonance possible to achieve during a project with certain characteristics.

3.2 The Configuration Package

Method configuration is mainly about deciding whether or not method components in a base method are to be performed, and to what extent. In MMC this is facilitated by the use of method rationale, which is expressed in the method components' interfaces. The result of this selection, with respect to particular project characteristics, is represented in a configuration package. This selection of method components can, if required, include components from complementing methods. A characteristic is viewed as a question about one isolated aspect of the development situation. Such a question typically has several possible answers that constitute the characteristic's dimension; one possible answer is called a *configuration package*. A configuration package is thus a configuration of the base method suitable for a characteristic's value. Each characteristic addresses one or several method components and their purpose. A configuration package is thus a classification of method components with regard to how relevant their overall goals are for a specific answer in a characteristic's dimension. The characteristic sets the scope of a configuration package—the method components that are of interest for classification. The *scope* is used in order to reduce the number of classification operations that have to be performed when creating a configuration package. The classification of method components is based on a two-dimensional classification schema, as shown in Table 2.

The vertical dimension focuses on how much attention the developers should devote to a particular method component: 'None,' 'Insignificant,' 'Normal' or 'Significant'. If at this stage a method component is found to be unimportant, it can be classified as 'Omit' outright. The three aspects of the horizontal dimension— 'Satisfactory,' 'Unsatisfactory' and 'Missing'—cut across the vertical dimension. This dimension is referred to as the potential for achieving rationality resonance between the base method's content and the software developers' intensions. Together this scheme provides different variants of the fundamental method configuration scenarios that need to be supported: selection, exchange and addition.

Table 2. Classification Schema for Method Components

| | | Potential to achieve rationality resonance | | |
		Satisfactory	Unsatisfactory	Missing
Attention given to method component	None	Omit	-	-
	Insignificant	Perform informal	Exchanges informal	Added informal
	Normal	Perform as is	Exchanges as is	Added as is
	Significant	Emphasize as is	Exchanges emphasized	Added emphasized

3.3 The Configuration Template

While configuration packages and characteristics are used to simplify analyses of the base method, we also need to be able to handle more complicated situations where characteristics exist in combinations. This is the purpose of the *configuration template*. A configuration template is a combined method configuration, based on one or more configuration packages, for a set of recurrent project characteristics. The concept allows the reuse of combined configuration packages that target development situation types common within the organization. In MMC the selection is based on the set of available characteristics and configuration packages. One configuration package can be chosen per characteristic and if a characteristic is irrelevant, it can be left out when selecting configuration packages.

MC Sandbox semi-automatically builds a configuration template based on the selections made. If conflicts arise between overlapping configuration packages, these are listed together with the reasons. Relevant configuration templates can be retrieved with a search engine based on a selection of characteristics and configuration packages. It is thereby possible to tailor the base method more efficiently.

The situational method is based on a selected configuration template and is the method delivered to the project team for use. When the situational method is enacted in a project, experiences should be fed back to the configuration process in order to improve configuration templates and/or configuration packages and to facilitate knowledge sharing between projects. Such experience is typically fed back continuously throughout the project.

4 Empirical Examples

The empirical work in this research included method configurations in three different projects. One important aspect of MMC is the idea of reuse. The three projects shared a number of aspects, such as involving development of web applications. Table 3

Table 3. Overview of Configurations

Characteristic	Configuration Package	Project 1	2	3
Knowledge about business process?	High	•		
	Low		•	•
On-site customer?	Yes	•		
	No		•	•
Co-located project team?	Yes		•	•
	No	•		
Project risk?	Normal (normal planning)	•	•	•
	High (extended planning)			
Degree of management commitment?	High	•	•	•
	Low			
Modeling of web aspects	Yes	•	•	•
	No			
Type of testing	Automated		•	•
	Manual	•		

contains the characteristics and configuration packages resulting from the method configuration work. The three rightmost columns in the table show the combination of configuration packages for each project; i.e. they illustrate the configuration templates used. From this table we find that the second and third project shared one configuration template. The first project differed in several respects, but shared the three configuration packages concerning project risk, degree of management commitment and modelling of "web aspects", with the other two projects.

Table 4. Configuration Package: On-site customer = No

Method component	Method component's rationale	Classification
Vision card	To capture the purpose of the system	Perform as is
Metaphor	To describe the system's likeness	Perform informal
User story	To describe a path through the system	Omit
Use case	To understand the system's behavior	Exchanges as is

We choose to exemplify the reuse aspect with the shared configuration package 'On-site customer = No'. This configuration package focuses how the project teams plan to handle the fact that no costumer will be on-site. The developers demarcated the configuration package to requirements aspects of XP (the base method).

Table 4 shows the method components and their classifications. The first component is the Vision card. The systems developers expressed that it was important for the customer to be able to "depict the future system" and that the feasibility of this method component "does not change with this kind of relationship to the customer." Hence, the method component was to be performed as described in the base method. The second method component, the Metaphor, was to be used on an informal basis. As one of the systems developer expressed during a method configuration workshop: "we use them frequently but usually we do not document them." According to the MMC classification scheme, such a use is classified 'Perform informal.' The last two method components in Table 4 illustrate the replacement of User stories with Use cases. The rationale for this exchange is captured in the statements: "we need to compensate [the increased distance] with more details", "one needs tools that are not that interaction intense", and "I view it [the use case] as a more suitable way." Consequently, the user story component was suppressed for the benefit of use case component.

5   Lessons Learned

Three major lessons can be drawn, centring on MMC's design principles and its origin in the plan-based method tradition. They are summarized in Table 5.

Table 5. Major lessons learned

No	Lesson
1	Different preferences for the use of up-front designs.
2	Different preferences for the use of intermediate artefacts.
3	Different preferences for method size.

The first lesson concerns MMC's plan-based preference for up-front design. Here the systems developers had mixed views. The following represents the voices of three developers: "it is impossible to anticipate everything", "unproductive, we were such a small team ... we could have dealt with these issues during the project", and "these adaptations are still plans." However, other developers value in a shared understanding of the ways of working before the projects and sharing experiences between projects: "[MMC] increased my understanding of how to mitigate [project] risks through systematic addition of methods", "[MMC] is a vehicle for sharing knowledge, strengthened with experience", "I guess you must view it [the configuration] as a sketch of your project ... a sketch on how to collaborate", and "we created an understanding of what we think is needed."

The second lesson concerns the agile methods' lack of confidence in intermediate artefacts and MMC's reliance on the method component concept, which centres on the artefact. This difference in philosophy is obvious in the content administration process of MMC. The content administration process is the process where MC Sandbox is populated with method components and the base method (XP in this case). Due to space limitations, this process is not covered in detail in this paper but is fully elaborated in [14]. Basically, the modularization process has its starting point in the intermediate artefacts (models, etc) to which the remaining parts of the method component's content are traced. However, all central prescribed actions of XP cannot be traced to intermediate artefacts. One of the developers expressed the following confusion about the content administration process: "I interpreted the main result as the artefact ... even if it is not an artefact in its true sense."

The third lesson concerns the size of the base method. A central aspect of MMC and method configuration when working with plan-based methods is deciding what to exclude from the base method. The base method itself is the starting point for these discussions with developers. The content serves as an encyclopaedia of possible paths to take. However, XP is a lightweight method providing less guidance when it comes to suggesting possible paths. Consequently, method configuration came to focus on extension rather than exclusion.

6   Concluding Discussion

In this paper we have reported on software developers' experience from using the Method for Method Configuration (MMC). The method was used during three systems development projects to tailor the agile method eXtreme Programming (XP). This study has been justified by (a) the need to complement earlier evaluations of MMC providing more conclusive tests to determine the effectiveness of the meta-method, and (b) MMC's origin is in the plan-based method tradition. Many method engineering concepts have their roots in this tradition and it is of interest to evaluate the possibility to transfer such constructs to an agile method context.

Through content examples of method configurations we have shown that it is possible to use MMC and its conceptual framework on XP. Furthermore, we have identified reuse of both configuration templates and configuration packages between the three projects we have studied. This corroborates earlier evaluations of MMC. Moreover, three lessons have been learned about applying MMC to XP with respect to MMC's origin in the plan-based method tradition.

The first lesson concerns MMC's preference for up-front designs. We can report on mixed views concerning this aspect of MMC. Three systems developers viewed method configuration according to MMC as up-front designs of the project, expressing a fear of adapting the project and the people to the method. Others expressed value in creating a shared understanding of the way of working before the projects started and sharing experiences between projects. The second lesson concerned different preferences regarding the use of intermediate artefacts. While XP reflects a low confidence in intermediate artefacts, the method component concept of MMC centres on the artefact concept. Hence, the MMC design was to some extent difficult to apply and in some cases more attention was paid to the type of development results than the actual artefacts. The third lesson concerned the support the base method (XP) provided during the method configuration activities. MMC uses the base method as a source of possible paths to follow. XP, however, does not provide that extensive coverage of different project paths. Hence, it was more demanding in terms of requiring the developers to contribute ideas for how to solve different development tasks.

Finally, it should be acknowledged that the interpretive nature of this research might have induced researcher bias. Also, since we have evaluated MMC using only one agile method, XP, further research is clearly needed in order to be able to generalize the results.

References

1. Nerur, S., Balijepally, V.: Theoretical reflections on agile development methodologies. Communication of the ACM 50(3), 79–83 (2007)
2. Beck, K.: Extreme Programming explained: embrace change, p. 190. Addison-Wesley, Reading (1999)
3. Sharp, H., Robinson, H.: An Ethnographic Study of XP Practice. Empirical Software Engineering 9, 353–375 (2004)
4. Stapleton, J.: DSDM: dynamic systems development method: the method in practice, vol. xviii, p. 163. Addison-Wesley, Harlow (1997)
5. Schwaber, K., Beedle, M.: Agile Software Development with Scrum. Prentice Hall, Upper Saddle River (2001)
6. Martin, J.: Rapid application development, p. 788. Macmillan, New York (1991)
7. Hansson, C., Dittrich, Y., Gustafsson, B., Zarnak, S.: How agile are industrial software development practice? The Journal of Systems and Software 79, 1295–1311 (2005)
8. Radding, A.: Extremely agile programming. Computerworld 36(6), 42–44 (2002)
9. Meso, P., Jain, R.: Agile Software Development: Adaptive Systems Principles And Best Practices. Information Systems Management 23(3), 19–30 (2006)
10. van Slooten, K., Hodes, B.: Characterizing IS development projects. In: Brinkkemper, S., Lyytinen, K., Welke, R. (eds.) Method Engineering: Principles of method construction and tool support, pp. 29–44. Chapman & Hall, Boca Raton (1996)
11. Henderson-Sellers, B., Serour, M.K.: Creating a Dual-Agility Method: The Value of Method Engineering. Journal of Database Management 16(4), 1–23 (2005)
12. Fitzgerald, B., Hartnett, G., Conboy, K.: Customising agile methods to software practices at Intel Shannon. European Journal of Information Systems 15(2), 200–213 (2006)
13. Karlsson, F., Ågerfalk, P.J.: Method Configuration: Adapting to Situational Characteristics while Creating Reusable Assets. Information and Software Technology 46(9), 619–633 (2004)

14. Karlsson, F.: Method Configuration - Method and Computerized Tool Support. Linköping University, Linköping (2005)
15. Karlsson, F., Wistrand, K.: Combining method engineering with activity theory: theoretical grounding of the method component concept. European Journal of Information Systems 15, 82–90 (2006)
16. Rossi, M., Ramesh, B., Lyytinen, K., Tolvanen, J.-P.: Managing Evolutionary Method Engineering by Method Rationale. Journal of Association of Information Systems 5(9), 356–391 (2004)
17. Ågerfalk, P.J., Fitzgerald, B.: Exploring the Concept of Method Rationale: A Conceptual Tool for Method Tailoring. In: Siau, K. (ed.) Advanced Topics in Database Research, pp. 63–78. Idea Group, Hershey, PA (2006)
18. Aydin, M.N., Harmsen, F., van Slooten, K., Stegwee, R.A.: On the Adaptation of an Agile Information Systems Development Method. Journal of Database Management 16(4), 24–40 (2005)
19. Karlsson, F., Ågerfalk, P.J.: Method-User-Centred Method Configuration. In: Situational Requirements Engineering Processes - Methods, Techniques and Tools to Support Situation-Specific Requirements Engineering Processes (SREP 2005), University of Limerick, Paris, France (2005)
20. Patton, M.Q.: Qualitative evaluation and research methods, 2nd edn., p. 532. SAGE, Newbury Park, CA (1990)
21. Kruchten, P.: The rational unified process: an introduction. Addison-Wesley object technology series, vol. xiv, p. 255. Addison-Wesley, Reading, MA (2004)

Adopting Agile in a Large Organisation

José Abdelnour-Nocera[1] and Helen Sharp[2]

[1] Thames Valley University, St Mary's Road, Ealing, London, W5 5RF
jose.abdelnour-nocera@tvu.ac.uk
[2] The Open University, Walton Hall, Milton Keynes MK7 6AA, UK
h.c.sharp@open.ac.uk

Abstract. Much has been written about adopting agile software development within a large organisation. A key aspect of this significant organisational change is to ensure that a common understanding of the new technology emerges within all stakeholder groups. We propose that an analysis framework based on the concept of Technological Frames (TFs) can identify where understanding is in conflict across different stakeholder groups. We used TFs to analyse data collected in one organisation in the process of adopting an agile development approach. In doing so, we identified several dimensions (called 'elements' in TFs) which characterise a group's understanding of agility. In this paper, we present these elements and describe the TFs for four distinct groups. We suggest that these elements may be used by other organisations adopting agile methods to help understand the views of different stakeholder groups.

Keywords: Technological frame, human aspects, empirical, qualitative.

1 Introduction

Many aspects have been identified as important in the process of adopting agile development, especially in a large organisation. For example, which practices to adopt [1], how to accommodate restrictive regulations [2] and how to balance repeatable processes with uncertainty [3]. A key issue underlying these concerns is the need for a common understanding of the new technology within all stakeholder groups. But where will conflicts arise in this process? How can different groups be helped to converge on a common understanding?

The aim of this paper is twofold: to suggest that Technological Frames (TF) [4] provide a useful analysis framework for studies wishing to answer these questions; and to present the results from such an analysis of one organisation. TF analysis helps to identify the elements that shape the process of translation by the key stakeholders [5], and hence offers a way to characterize where differences may arise. Using this framework provides a snapshot of the assumptions, knowledge and expectations of stakeholders during the adoption of agile methods in an organisation, and the practices constraining, framing and emerging in this process. To illustrate how TFs may be used, the specific framework of elements derived from a qualitative case study of one organisation adopting agile methods is presented; this specific framework may be a useful starting point for others attempting to understand conflicts between stakeholder groups.

P. Abrahamsson et al. (Eds.): XP 2008, LNBIP 9, pp. 42–52, 2008.
© Springer-Verlag Berlin Heidelberg 2008

Section 2 introduces key literature on adopting agile development in a large organisation. Section 3 introduces technological frames. In section 4 we present the qualitative case study from one organisation. The analysis and interpretation of how "agile" is defined and implemented by the different stakeholders is presented in Section 5. Section 6 discusses our results; section 7 provides some conclusions.

2 Adopting Agile in Large Organisations

Software process changes represent complex organisational change and cannot be accomplished merely by replacing tools and techniques [6]. Adopting agile development is no different from other organisational change events in this sense, and several authors have identified key challenges from their experience.

Lindvall et al. [7] identify the greatest challenge to adopting agile practices as being the need to integrate with the existing environment, while Cohn and Ford [8] say that failing to persuade any stakeholder group to use the new process can impact negatively on the project's outcome. Both of these emphasise the need to understand the wider organisational culture as well as the processes and structures that support it.

Boehm and Turner [9] report the results of workshops aimed at identifying barriers to agile acceptance in large organisations. They describe three groups of issues that act as barriers to agile adoption: development process conflicts, business process conflicts, and people conflicts. People conflicts are identified as the most crucial to the success of agile adoption.

At a more fundamental level, Weyrauch [10] points out that a common language needs to be developed between stakeholder groups. However this is not simply a matter of using the same vocabulary since this common language also needs to represent the same concepts.

3 Technological Frames

A TF is made up of two parts: elements of interpretation and elements of practice [4] Elements of interpretation include assumptions, knowledge and expectations about technology which shape a group's understanding of the new technology, while elements of practice describe the constraints from their existing practices on adopting the new technology. The study of practices includes the existing network of artefacts, such as manuals, policies, etc. and the practices they represent. Underlying the TF view is that a community can be divided into different social groups. All members of one group share the same TF to various extents, but different groups may have different TFs. Understanding a group's TF with respect to a particular technology uncovers how that technology is being viewed by that group, and hence may identify conflicts between groups.

The TF concept was originally developed to understand the sociocultural processes that guided the interactions of groups of scientists and technologists in the invention and development of a number of technological artefacts - the bicycle, bakelite and the fluorescent lamp [4]. Subsequently, TFs have been used to investigate other kinds of technological change. Some studies, e.g. [11], use the concept of TF to successfully explain in what ways groups differ in their interpretation of systems and how this leads to changes in the way they are designed and adopted. Others have used TFs to understand conflicts among stakeholders: between producers and users of ERP software [12]; in the adoption of intranets in large organisations [13]; and in participatory design [14]. In this study, we use TFs to understand the conflicting perceptions of stakeholder groups adopting agile methods in one organisation.

A key characteristic of sociotechnical change is that groups in favour of the new technology tend to view existing practices as problematic, whereas groups not in favour of the technology say that the problem lies in the new tools. This key element of TF construction is referred to as 'problem locus construction' [12].

4   The Empirical Study: Data Gathering and Analysis

4.1   The Case Study Organisation

The organisation provides voice and data services around the world, building a 'new wave' business based upon networked IT services, broadband and mobility and is divided into several businesses, one of which focuses on software development. The organisation employs approx 100,000 staff, about 7500 of whom are software developers. Their headquarters is located in the UK, although a large portion of development work is carried out off-shore. At the time of study, the agile adoption process had been running for approximately 2 years. The main thrust for agile adoption came from the software development business where the CEO mandated it, and it is here that most adoption work had been accomplished.

4.2   Data Gathering

Data was gathered through a variety of techniques including individual interviews, observations, face-to-face and telephone meetings, documents, and a wiki. We attached ourselves to one project (Project Z) and also gathered data from representatives of stakeholder groups not part of this project.

Project Z was chosen because the individuals involved in the project had shown willingness and interest in adopting the agile approach, and hence had tried to understand the technology. Also, the contractor working with the team developed code using some agile practices, which we thought might influence Project Z's adoption of agile. Four people involved in Project Z were interviewed: the delivery manager, the user experience manager, the technical architect, and an outside contractor. One user stories meeting which included customer representatives, developers and agile advocates, two user interface design meetings (by telephone with an off-shore contractor), and two delivery meetings (by telephone with an off-shore contractor) were observed.

Three agile coaches, and members of a four-person agile development team not connected to Project Z were also interviewed. The team was observed for two days.

Data consisted of interview summaries and transcriptions, meeting notes, observation notes, artefacts and images, wiki pages and documents. In the interviews we were keen to investigate what the individual understood by the term 'agile', what their experience of agile was, and what it meant to them in their day-to-day work to apply agile principles. A semi-structured interview style was therefore adopted, allowing individuals to discuss other agile-related issues if they seemed important to them.

During observation we looked for examples of the use of agile terminology, evidence that an agile approach had been adopted to any degree, and whether the push to adopt agile methods had impacted on normal work patterns.

A key document was a manual of agile development which captured the particular flavour of agile that the organisation was adopting. The online tracking system and repository of information (a wiki) for the four-person agile development team was also an important artefact. A particular emphasis in all the data gathering was to identify examples of conflict or breakdown [15]. TFs seek to understand how adopters interpret the new technology, and so studying breakdowns helps to explicate TFs.

4.3 Data Analysis

Following Critical Discourse Analysis (CDA) [16], the data was regarded as text reflecting stakeholders' interpretive frames and actions, which, in turn, were taken as an indication of the social context and ideologies surrounding agile adoption. People's interpretive frames are considered to have discursive properties, in accordance with the ideas of [17]. Following the TF framework, the data was analysed to identify elements of interpretation and elements of practice. Therefore the TF framework provided a top-down view of the data, and CDA provided a perspective for analysis from the bottom-up.

Analysis focused on the situations of instability and fluctuation in which the value and usefulness of agile methods was defined. This process enabled the comparison of stakeholder groups in terms of their different TFs.

5   Results: Making Sense of Agile

Accounts about agile and its uses were present in interviews, observational data, policy documents, and on the wiki. Data analysis identified four elements of interpretation and five elements of practice that shaped how agile methods were defined and adopted within the organisation. These elements divided our participants into four groups each with a different TF. These elements and groups are shown in Table 1. In the discussion below, we summarise the key observations for each group.

5.1   Agile Advocates and Coaches

A group of Agile Advocates and Coaches is driving the agile 'push'. Their mission is to disseminate knowledge of agile methods and facilitate their successful adoption across the organisation. From a TF perspective, this means that advocates must persuade other staff to adopt the same elements of interpretation and practice to frame agile adoption as their own. One of the biggest challenges they were facing was to move Agile from the development teams into the rest of the business.

Elements of interpretation. Agile was seen by the advocates and coaches as a flexible development method that represents a natural way of doing things – as "*a subset of common sense*". They see agile as delivering "*what the customer wants not what they asked for*", and this reflects their understanding of agile as enabling an increased collaboration between developers and other stakeholders.

According to the advocates, increased collaboration does not mean letting customers and users fully steer the process of design and development, however. Instead, usability professionals and other user researchers from within the organisation should help customers and users to make decisions. We only saw one instance of this happening where a user proxy attended a user story workshop.

This group believed that the collaboration brought by agile should benefit all areas of the business not just the development effort, including groups such as marketing and retail. They saw the applicability of agile as being across the entire business.

Overall, the value seen by this group for agile adoption is increased customer satisfaction. As one lead advocate reported, the motivation to bring agile into the organisation was "*to be responsive to the changing needs of the business*".

Elements of practice. One reported practice directly aimed at introducing agile methods was 'embedded coaching', where a coach joined a team of developers and transferred knowledge to them. However there were too many teams for the number of coaches, so new coaches were being trained. Translating agile principles to the rest of the business was attempted through special workshops and presentations. This was complemented by events of public recognition such as internal 'Agile Awards'. A key tool was a manual of agile adoption generated by this group, but it was not designed to carry agile methods beyond software engineering, i.e. to the business environment. In terms of problem locus construction, advocates highlighted the inflexibility of current production processes as being a problem, while middle managers questioned the ability of agile to be integrated with current practice. The main mind shift required according to them was the need to think of projects as having flexible as opposed to fixed scope. One of the advocates said in this respect: "*it is a big cultural change. We develop what we need and we keep things flexible.*" To overcome this, the advocates developed workarounds and ways of knowing how agile a team has become. The agile manual lists five principles of agility: customer involvement, user stories, iterative development, automated testing and continuous integration. Advocates have translated what each of these means to non-development staff but not all stakeholders find this translation logical or relevant to what they do. One instance of this translation is creation of 'business scenarios', which attempt to capture not only the IT activities but other activities related to the product, including technical and market research. As one of the lead advocates said, "*there is no point in delivering an IT solution if the business has not done its job*".

Table 1. Technological Frames relating to Agile for the four groups identified

	Advocates and Coaches	Agile Team	Project Z Team	The Business
Elements of Interpretation				
The value of Agile for me is	Customer Satisfaction, Responding to changing needs of business and market. Re-use.	Customer Satisfaction, Business Value, Continuous Delivery	Faster delivery, Structure to what we do. Re-usability.	Redundant
Applicability of Agile	Entire business process	Software Engineering	Entire product process	N/A
Project Scope should be	Flexible	Flexible	Fixed (but understand rationale for flexibility)	Fixed
Increased collaboration for a better product	Agree	Agree	Agree	Agree
Elements of Practice				
How to be agile	In negotiation: coaching, workshops, training.	Highly defined	Ad Hoc (willing to bring Agile for structure)	Highly Defined User Research
Tools and Artefacts	Agile manual, change process documents, wikis, online resource. story cards, MRDs.	The wall, user story cards, charts, wikis, audio 'culture'.	Ad Hoc: excel sheets, wireframes, flowcharts, audio 'culture', MRDs.	Audio 'culture', MRDs.
User Input	Workshops and meetings before and during the production process.	Continuous, they should be part of the team.	Only before production process. Then deadlines more important - but want to change	Only before production process. Then deadlines more important.
Problem Locus Construction: Agile vs. Existing Production Process	Agile will improve production. Senior Management Confirms this.	Agile will improve production. Senior Management Confirms this.	Agile will improve production processes, but do not know how.	Agile is not adequate for our product research processes. On the contrary, it is redundant.
Workarounds on adoption	Translating Agile to entire business: - User stories from MRDs. - Business Scenarios	Retrospective writing of detailed documents to fit the organisation official processes.	Extracting User Stories from MRDs	N/A

Summary. The TF of this group constructs agile as delivering a product of increased quality that responds to the changing needs of the market. Most of the knowledge publicly accessible refers to software development and not to product design and research.

5.2   The Agile Software Development Team

Of the four groups described here, this one followed most of the agile manifesto principles. They mainly delivered internal systems and their interpretation of agile was more focused and consistent than that presented by the advocates and coaches.

Elements of interpretation. The team was proud of being agile and valued the approach: "*It is not just doing one or two things to tick a box. It is the whole methodology that counts. We can deliver if we want every two days. The fact that we can do that shows that we are agile. The customer is very happy!*" They used agile to identify themselves as different from the rest by claiming that several areas within the organisation did not understand what agile is.

A central element in their interpretation of agile was collaboration with the customer: they were able to discuss the product with customers on the same level, delivering a solution closer to their needs. The team leader developed this point by saying "*it is 'I need to speak to my customer and see what he says' rather than thinking 'this is my requirement I will go and do it'. The key change is to consider the customer as a part of the team and help them to get the most business value from the system.*" Customer collaboration was viewed as being able to deliver business value to the development process and its product. Indeed, they saw agile as a set of software engineering practices that help to deliver business value and they all believed that agile requires a mental shift where the scope of the product remains flexible.

Saving wasted effort was another defining idea: "*Being agile is about continuously getting feedback. You deliver small things quickly and then you build on them so you save a lot of wasted effort. Historically we used to deliver things that were not used.*"

Elements of practice. This team followed most of XP's principles and techniques. They claimed to have been practicing agile working before the organisational adoption and had used a number of workarounds in order to comply with incompatible but established processes in the wider organisation. For example, it was reported that long and detailed design documents were written in retrospect to fit the system rather than because they had any value.

A key practice is continuous customer feedback, mostly through a wiki and fortnightly telephone meetings. The co-located team used a 'wall' where user story cards and charts were presented, and a wiki recorded their progress, including current user stories and related acceptance tests. This was especially useful for other project members who were working remotely, e.g. the testers who were based offshore.

From the interviews and observations conducted, it was not evident that this team has been directly influenced by any of the workshops or documents prepared by the advocates. For instance, they confirmed being aware of the agile manual and sharing most of what it prescribes, but they had not fully read it or used it as a guide. This team was awarded an agile prize within the organisation, but they have not applied agile techniques beyond their role as programmers and software engineers.

Summary. Most elements of this group's TF led to a definition and practice of their development methods very close to the agile manifesto. They have used this to differentiate themselves from the rest of the organisation and have in the past used workarounds in order to comply with an incompatible sociotechnical network.

5.3 Project Z

Project Z team is a bigger and more complex team than the agile team presented above. Project Z is made up of different stakeholders located in different areas of the organisation. In addition, most of the development work has been done by an outsourcing partner. In consequence, this project has many external dependencies.

The introduction of agile was received positively by Project Z in the early stages. At the user stories workshop the team were enthusiastic and could see various opportunities in using agile, although we also observed some conflicts between marketing and other groups. Six months later, we could not identify a consistent agile approach or influence in what they had produced. However, they still stood by their initial perceptions of what agile methods could offer them.

Elements of interpretation. Their recurrent element of interpretation in describing the main benefit of agile was that it would allow them to deliver solutions much faster than they normally do. This idea was shared by developers, delivery and usability managers, product managers and technical architects. Another element used especially by usability and user interface designers, was the opportunity to bring end users closer to the design and production process as well as giving the user experience group a more coherent role in the production cycle. The usability manager for Project Z expressed this by saying: *"The key is getting user experience people involved earlier, it's not about getting requirements and handing them over the wall"*.

Despite these positive perceptions, we identified frustration because the team had not been able to adopt agile fully. One indication of this was the absence of user stories in the discourse, or in any physical or electronic representation. The staff did not feel 'touched' by the organisation's agile revolution, and there was a general feeling that *"decisions were made at the top but it is not coming down"* according to one delivery manager. He said: *"big executives say you do this but people on the ground do not understand what it is all about"*.

Another element of interpretation was the need for greater collaboration and communication across all stakeholders and the problems associated with it, especially between marketing managers and IT delivery managers. The IT delivery manager characterized the differences by saying: *"I (marketing says) want that box and I want that now, whereas we (IT delivery) unpack the box"*. The technical architect agreed that all communities need to engage earlier in the process so that decisions make sense from a customer, business and technical point of view.

Elements of practice. Some of the practices shaping agile adoption reflect the interpretative elements discussed above, the most obvious being the need for increased collaboration and communication across all stakeholders, including customers. However the organisation structure was hierarchical and the process of user input was constrained once the product requirements were identified.

There was some evidence of behaviours such as stand up meetings and user story workshops, and we identified several workarounds to integrate agile into the current way of working. One was the 'hothouse' a kind of workshop that brings together all the key stakeholders to build and refine prototypes and to agree on the next 90-day delivery. Extracting user stories from existing, very detailed 'marketing requirements documents' (MRDs) was another workaround. These MRDs were a prominent artifact found across the organisation. Leaders of Project Z claimed that it was very difficult to work with such detailed documents in a project whose scope could change rapidly; one agile developer described MRDs as "*not based in reality at all*".

"*Engrained processes*" arising from existing practices were mentioned by most members of the project team. According to the delivery manager, these address contracts and integration with larger systems which are issues when adopting agile. To maintain appropriate communication with geographically distributed team members, wikis and a culture of phone meetings were encouraged.

A practice identified by technical architects, delivery managers and usability managers was that staff were trying to deliver in 90-day cycles, which meant that they had only 'shrunk' the Waterfall process without any qualitative change.

Summary. A less refined understanding of agile, and a number of engrained processes that hinder adopting agile are evident in Project Z's TF. However, we also found a positive perception of agile and efforts to integrate agile into what they do that respond to this basic understanding.

5.4 The 'Business' (or Customer Proxy)

We did not have the opportunity to interview and visit the premises of the 'business' companies within the organisation. However, they played a major role in the first user stories workshop, our interviewees made reference to them, and we had the opportunity to meet representatives of this group informally, which helped us to confirm the validity of other accounts that we gathered. Although we have less data from this group, we consider them here as they represent an important reference point in trying to describe and understand agile adoption.

Elements of interpretation. The main interpretation of agile in this group is that they did not see any value in creating user stories. From their perspective, the MRD already reflected their work on user research and did not need to be repeated. However, there was no discussion or comment on the value of continuous user or customer feedback during the production process from this group.

Elements of practice. Marketing have historically been physically separated and distant from the IT division. This affects the amount and quality of collaboration between the two groups.

Summary. Overall, marketing's perception of agile is very basic. A higher interaction with other groups in the organisation, especially advocates and mature agile teams may have an impact on the elements of interpretation of their TF about product development processes.

6 Discussion

Table 1 shows that the TFs of the four groups we have studied are quite different, but there are also similarities. Advocates and the agile team have a clear agile frame as part of their described production methods whereas Project Z shows an initial transition from their *ad hoc* methods towards agile. In the case of the business's TF, we could not find any strong indication of agile integration.

Three of the groups saw agile as having value for them, while 'the business' apparently do not see the value of agile at all. One of the challenges faced by this organisation is how to extend an agile way of thinking beyond the developers, and both the Agile Advocates and Project Z believed that agile should cover the entire process, while the development team were content with focusing on implementation only. This shows a tension in the process of sociotechnical change: trying to translate principles created for the development of software into broader knowledge and processes to an audience with different roles, understandings and expectations, sharing a contrasting TF. One thing (the only thing) which all groups agreed upon was that increased collaboration would result in a better product. There is more variability evident in the elements of practice for each group, which is a consequence of each working to adapt to their own circumstances. As might be expected, the problem locus constructions for the first two groups identify problems in existing practices, while Project Z is unsure how to proceed and 'the business' blame agile itself. Agile advocates, the agile team and Project Z, agreed that the biggest cause of resistance to adopting the new methods lay in the need for cultural change in middle management.

According to Bijker, TFs show power dynamics in the constitution of technology. Powerful members of a social group try to frame other members with their own meanings and prescribed uses for a technology. For example, Advocates are trying to bring staff into their TF by rewarding mechanisms and faster delivery targets.

7 Conclusions

The Technological Frames developed here provide a snapshot of how agile was being interpreted and adopted in one organisation at the time of the research. They have identified some clear issues faced by the organisation and have highlighted areas of confusion and uncertainty. The analysis reinforces others' findings regarding the adoption of agile processes within a large organisation. In particular, the importance of ensuring that all stakeholder groups are consulted and engaged in the adoption process, and that existing practices need to be understood and taken into account in devising new procedures. A key issue faced by individuals and groups appears to be coming to terms with what adopting agile means to everyday processes: What do I do when I get up in the morning? But also, what does it mean for the whole business to adopt Agile?

The TF framework has provided a novel way to analyse the issues of integrating agile into an organisation. The TF elements presented here emerged from the data and hence are specific for one organisation, but they provide initial indications of where others may find areas of conflict.

Acknowledgements

We would like to thank all our collaborators for their time and patience.

References

[1] Lawrence, R., Yslas, B.: Three-way cultural change: Introducing agile within two non-agile companies and a non-agile methodology. In: Proceedings of Agile 2006, pp. 255–259. IEEE Computer Society, Los Alamitos (2006)

[2] Wils, A., van Baelen, S., Holvoet, T., de Vlaminck, K.: Agility in the Avionics Software World. In: Abrahamsson, P., Marchesi, M., Succi, G. (eds.) XP 2006. LNCS, vol. 4044, pp. 123–132. Springer, Heidelberg (2006)

[3] Lycett, M., Macredie, R.D., Patel, C., Paul, R.J.: Migrating agile methods to standardized development practice. IEEE Computer 36(6), 79–85 (2003)

[4] Bijker, W.E.: Of bicycles, bakelites, and bulbs: toward a theory of sociotechnical change. MIT Press, Cambridge (1995)

[5] Latour, B.: The Powers of Association. In: Law, J. (ed.) Power, action, and belief: a new sociology of knowledge, p. viii, 280. Routledge & Kegan Paul, London (1986)

[6] Nerur, S., Mahapatra, R., Mangalaraj, G.: Challenges of migrating to agile methodologies. Communications of the ACM 48(5), 73–78 (2005)

[7] Lindvall, M., Muthig, D., Dagnino, A., Wallin, C., Stupperich, M., Kiefer, D., May, J., Kähkönen, T.: Agile software development in large organisations. IEEE Computer 37(12), 26–34 (2004)

[8] Cohn, M., Ford, D.: Introducing an agile process to an organisation. IEEE Computer 36(6), 74–78 (2003)

[9] Boehm, B., Turner, R.: Management Challenges to Implementing Agile Processes in Traditional Development Organisations. IEEE Software 22(5), 30–38 (2005)

[10] Weyrauch, K.: What are we arguing about? A framework for defining agile in our organisation. In: Proceedings of Agile 2006, pp. 213–220. IEEE CS, Los Alamitos (2006)

[11] Orlikowski, W., Gash, D.C.: Technological Frames: Making Sense of Information Technology in Organisations. ACM Transactions on Information Systems 12, 174–207 (1994)

[12] Abdelnour-Nocera, J., Dunckley, L., Sharp, H.: An approach to the evaluation of usefulness as a social construct using technological frames. International Journal of Human-Computer Interaction 22, 157–177 (2007)

[13] Pellegrino, G.: Thickening the Frame: Cross-Theoretical Accounts of Contexts Inside and Around Technology. Bulletin of Science Technology Society 25, 63–72 (2005)

[14] Sarkkinen, J.: Examining a Planning Discourse: How a Manager Represents Issues within a Planning Frame and How the Other Could Do the Same. In: Participatory Design Conference, Toronto, Canada (2004)

[15] Winograd, T., Flores, F.: Understanding Computers and Cognition: A New Foundation for Design. Ablex Pub. Corp., Norwood (1986)

[16] Fairclough, N.: Language and Power, 2nd edn., Harlow, England, Longman (2001)

[17] Harré, R., Gillett, G.: The Discursive Mind. Sage, Thousand Oaks, Calif. (1994)

An Observational Study of a Distributed Card Based Planning Environment

Robert Morgan[1], Frank Maurer[2], and Mike Chiasson[3]

[1,2] Department of Computer Science, University of Calgary,
2500 University Drive NW Calgary, AB, Canada, T2N 1N4
robertemorgan@gmail.com, frank.maurer@ucalgary.ca
[3] Department of Management Studies, Lancaster University,
Lancaster, UK LA1 4YW
m.chiasson@lancaster.ac.uk

Abstract. Providing support for distributed agile teams as they conduct planning meetings is tricky. In distributed settings, the use of paper index cards for planning isn't convenient, as some of the team members do not have access to the physical cards. We present the results of an observational study where a distributed card based planning tool was evaluated against planning with physical cards. The feedback we received from the participants was encouraging. Results indicated that teams were excited to use the tool in part because telepointers made knowledge of the other participants actions easier. We also found that communication was improved as the tool kept teams interested in the meeting and conversations on topic.

Keywords: Distributed Planning, Groupware, Agile Planning, Story Cards.

1 Introduction

Many software development teams today are involved in projects where the ability to have all team members sit together and plan the next iteration is difficult. Dispersed & distributed teams and off-shoring development is commonplace in the software industry. The reality is that distributed software projects are here to stay and with them so are distributed planning meetings. Planning in an agile environment is something that does not fit well with distributed projects. Being able to see story cards as they are created and negotiating whether they are in or out of an iteration is something that is much easier to do when all team members can see and manipulate the story cards.

Planning processes in the agile community varies from team to team. However, most teams follow the idea of using index cards (or similar sized sheets of paper) to record stories and subsequently organize then into iterations [1, 3]. Pen and paper allow easy and quick creating of stories during a meeting and makes organizing them either on a table or board effortless. This cannot be said when planning with distributed team members. As team members are not at the same location, sharing the current state of the iteration plan becomes substantially more difficult. Picking up a pen and writing on an index card and placing it on the table is not helpful in creating a shared understanding of

P. Abrahamsson et al. (Eds.): XP 2008, LNBIP 9, pp. 53–62, 2008.
© Springer-Verlag Berlin Heidelberg 2008

the current state of the plan. Cards need to be created and manipulated on multiple sites. This replication can – and often does – lead to inconsistencies between sites resulting in misunderstandings and an overall slowdown of the planning process.

Tools that support distributed planning must allow for easy and intuitive creation and modification of stories and iterations during the planning meetings and not after the meeting. This implies that digital representations of story cards and iterations must be as easy to create, modify and destroy as their physical counterparts. DAP [9, 10] is an open-source distributed project planning tool that supports card based planning in a fashion that resembles pen and paper based planning. For reasons discussed below, we picked this tool for evaluating if tools improve the effectiveness of distributed iteration planning meetings. In this paper, we present the results of a qualitative evaluation where DAP and distributed paper based planning were compared.

The paper is structured as follows: Section 2 takes a look at existing works relating to agile project planning and groupware applications. Section 3 highlights DAP distributed planning features. Section 4 looks at the qualitative evaluation process, participants, and context. Section 5 presents the results of our evaluation. We summarize our results in Section 6.

2   Related Works

Software systems that provide support for both collocated and distributed agile project planning have been around for quite some time. Existing options such as: Scrum Works [4], XPSWiki [11], Rally [12], Version One [16], and XPlanner [17] provide basic functionality for creating and organizing stories in one way or another. Most of these systems use traditional web technologies and as a result present planning information in the form of tables supporting create, read, update and delete operations.

The collaborative aspect of these systems, though effective, leaves a lot of room for improvement. Awareness information that allows others to know who is online and working or editing information is often limited or not available at all. Research into supporting collaboration with computers has been around since the early 1960's. Many researchers focusing on Human Computer Interaction have made significant strides in improving our understanding of how to build more collaborative tools. This collaboration aware [15] or groupware research has tended to focus on generalized group activities in order to better understand the entire groupware spectrum. A large part of the literature in this area looks at tasks such as drawing and or editing text [5, 15]. The focus on general group tasks has provided significant amounts of insight for tool developers to draw upon. Recommendations, however, tend to be generalized to all groupware applications and their relevance to agile planning tasks is varied.

Early work by Tang [15] produced a number of recommendations on how to approach the design of groupware applications. Of significant importance when building groupware applications is the consideration of: hand gestures during communication, the importance of the workspace tools for mediating collaboration, and the role of spatial orientation in structuring the collaborative activity.

Specifically for planning tasks, workspace awareness is important to understand in more detail. Gutwin et al. [8] breaks down workspace awareness into three parts: knowing what others are able to see, knowing where their mouse is located and when it is moving (telepointers), and finally seeing the movements and modifications of artifacts in the workspace as they happen (What You See Is What I See, or WYSI-WIS). Research into workspace awareness puts a strong emphasis on sharing the workspace with everyone connected. With a shared workspace, one important aspect is knowing where and what others are doing. To provide this information to everyone all three aspects need to be supported.

To ensure that everyone sees the same information, an interface that supports the WYSIWIS paradigm is essential [13, 14]. This ensures that when one artifact is moved or changed that those changes are shared with everyone immediately (in real time), thus duplicating the environment on every client.

An important aspect for workspace awareness involves supporting telepointers [6, 7, 15]: the ability to point to locations in the shared workspace on *all* connected clients. Support for telepointers in the workspace provides support for gestures in the workspace as it shares all the interactions of one mouse with the other clients. Tele-pointers alone do not completely address gesturing in the workspace, however, they drastically increase team members abilities to refer to an artifact in the workspace.

Recently, two agile planning tools were developed that incorporate ideas from the groupware community. We used one of them, DAP, for our study and describe it in detail below. The 2nd tool, CardMeeting [2], is a web-based agile planning application that moves away from existing implementations by representing planning information as colored cards in a shared environment. The system provides users the ability to create blank index cards that look identical to their physical counterparts. The cards can be moved around the workspace with ease. When compared to existing agile planning tools, however, there are no accounting features or indicators of which card belongs to any given iteration. It simply creates digital cards in a workspace that can be managed and modified by every distributed individual.

The use of a shared environment that simulates face-to-face planning presents the requirement that updates to that environment are near real-time. When comparing DAP and CardMeeting against collocated agile planning performance levels were noticeably different. Both tools were tested with two clients located next to each other. CardMeeting experienced substantial delays, with interactions taking in excess of two seconds, interactions in DAP were substantially shorter. (See section 5.3 for more on DAP's performance).

3 Distributed AgilePlanner (DAP)

DAP provides a shared planning environment (Figure 1) that helps distributed teams to conduct a planning meeting synchronously in real time [9,10]. DAP uses visual objects to represent the various different planning artifacts. These visual artifacts allow team members to plan in a way that mimics paper based planning with the added benefit that team members do not have to be in the same room to share a planning space. Besides providing standard effort accounting functionality, DAP is able to reconstruct previous planning sessions effortlessly. This allows teams to quickly remember the context of the last meeting and track the progress of the project.

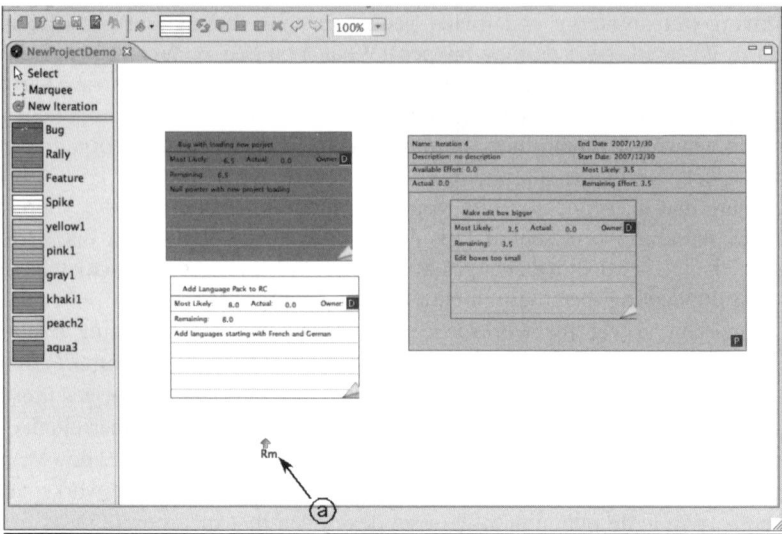

Fig. 1. DAP environment

3.1 Interacting with Planning Artifacts

Story card and iteration creation is straightforward and mimics paper based planning. Clicking or selecting the story card or iteration button and then clicking or dropping the artifacts at the desired location creates the artifact. Once the artifact is dropped at the desired location it is immediately shared with all other connected clients. DAP's flexibility allows for story cards and iterations to be created anywhere in the workspace.

Editing of story or iteration information again mimics team members using paper cards. Card fields are quickly edited by clicking on the desired field and changing its contents. Editing of the text is done directly on the card so that all team members, distributed and collocated, can see the changes happening in real-time.

DAP takes great care in making card organization intuitive while leaving teams free to organize cards in a way that best suits them. A large component of card organization is moving a card from a given location to another. In DAP this is accomplished via a simple drag-and-drop action. Moving multiple cards involves selecting multiple cards and dragging the group. Iteration objects containing cards are also moved by the same means. Iterations act as containers for story cards and when moved they keep the internal organization of the stories.

3.2 Distributed Planning

Our primary reason for choosing DAP for our study is its distributed team support. Traditionally, as we saw earlier, tools to support distributed agile teams do not provide much synchronous and immediate feedback to the others participating in the meeting at a different location. DAP attempts to provide team members with as much as possible non-verbal information as team members would get if they were all sitting in the same location. In order to provide this kind of awareness, artifacts are shown in all the shared workspaces as soon as they are created.

In order to support pointing to artifacts for distributed teams, DAP makes use of telepointers [8] (Figure 1:a). DAP's telepointers provide connected clients the ability to point out, highlight artifacts or gesture to others in real time. This feature provides team members with a natural and non-verbal means communicating, in addition to verbal communication.

4 Study Design

To understand the impact of a distributed planning tool that uses two dimensional representations of story cards as well as groupware features, a preliminary but structured qualitative study was conducted. The study looked at how teams interacted with story cards in both a paper-based environment and then using the DAP tool. The purpose of the study was to determine if tool support for distributed planning improves upon existing paper based planning approaches. In addition, the study hopes to highlight the strengths and shortcomings of such a tool.

4.1 Participants and Context

The evaluation of DAP took place over the course of six months in early 2007. During this time five teams were observed (amounting to twenty six participants) as they conducted various planning meetings. All five teams were predominantly composed of graduate students from the areas of software engineering and management studies. The teams can be categorized into two groups Case Study Teams (two teams) and User Study Teams (three teams). The case study teams were involved in existing software development projects for clients. The user study teams were participating in mock project planning meetings organized by the researchers, but no development was carried out afterwards. User study teams were used to provide a larger user base for observation, as no other development teams were available.

The Case Study teams had existing projects for delivery to a customer. User Study teams, on the other hand were given a high level project description, a vague description of a point of sale application. Teams were given a short and limited (30 second) introduction to the DAP planning tool, comprising of a short tour of the tool.

The five teams were observed in a variety of situations. The three user Study teams participated in two distributed planning meetings, one with paper index cards and one with the DAP tool. Of the two Case Study teams the first participated in three distributed planning all using the DAP tool as they were already using the tool for their development, while the second team participated in one collocated planning meeting with paper index cards, one distributed planning meeting using paper index cards and another distributed planning meeting using the DAP tool. Collocated planning was not possible for most of the teams due to the geographical limitations.

Participants were located in Canada, the United States and the United Kingdom. Developers for all the teams were located in one Canadian city with customers located in another Canadian city, a city in the United States and a city in the United Kingdom. Participants experience with story card planning varied from team to team, with more then half of the participants having little to no experience with the planning approach.

4.2 Data Collection and Evaluation Criteria

Data was collected from the meetings through observations of the planning meetings, and interviews. Observations were conducted by means of video and the researchers taking notes during the planning meetings. Researcher observations were conducted by one researcher in the United Kingdom and one in Canada. No researchers were able to be on site with the US team.

After the planning meetings, participants were asked a variety of questions relating to their experience in the study. Questions focused on: the perceived learning curve of the tool, the perceived ease of use and interaction with the tool, the impact the tool's use had on productivity compared to previous meetings and experiences.

5 Study Results

Feedback from the participants in addition to the observations from the planning meetings was affirmative. Participants were generally positive towards their experience with DAP. We did not observe any difference between participant responses based on location nor user type. Participants seemed excited and expressed a desire to use and interact with DAP. However, this does not mean that there weren't issues that manifested. Issues surrounding communication as well as tool related issues did occur.

5.1 Observations

Observations from the teams highlighted a number of positive and negative effects that DAP brings to distributed environments. The case study teams demonstrated that a tool like DAP has an impact on synchronizing the entire team while at the same time keeping everyone involved and engaged in the planning when compared against distributed paper based planning. Based on our own experiences as educators, we decided to use eye contact and fidgeting as a way to subjectively determine team member engagement.

Team members engagement was most noticeably affected with the introduction of DAP. The levels of perceived engagement in the meeting as expressed by eye contact and the amount of fidgeting from each team member increased while using the tool. When comparing the three meetings of the second Case Study team (collocated, distributed and DAP) the meetings with the most eye contact and the least amount of fidgeting were the collocated and the DAP meetings. The distributed planning meeting where no tool was used saw almost everyone on the team looking around the room, closing their eyes for long periods of time and continuous fidgeting in their chairs. The collocated and DAP planning meetings saw all team members focusing on the customer, either physically in the room (collocated) or on their interactions on a large shared display (DAP). Only rarely did a team member shift their focus away from the planning tasks. In addition team member's body language differed: during the collocated and DAP meetings team members positioned themselves to face the customer /display and a tendency to lean towards the customer/display. This type of body positioning was not seen during the paper-only distributed planning meeting.

Tool usage across all five teams was relatively similar. Team interaction with DAP was dominated by the developers with the customers interacting on occasion. The exception to this was the third user study team. The interactions with the tool changed mid meeting when one of the customers asked if they could use the tool as well. Once they started using the tool, they dominated its control, creating new story cards adding descriptions and even adding the estimate values after discussing them with the developers. All throughout the meeting both the customers and the developers expressed excitement about using the tool. Comments like: "this is neat" or "oh cool".

A point of significant interaction and discussion for all teams were the telepointers. Team members liked the idea of being able to point to an object in the workspace and having their colleagues at the other location see their actions. The customer for one of the case studies commented during one of the planning meetings: "this is exciting. This is great!" after using the telepointers to point to a story card being discussed. Following that same meeting a project manager commented "It's the first time that I really saw that [telepointers] was useful, because when [he] said look here!" Similar sentiments regarding telepointers were expressed during the other planning meetings with everyone making positive comments regarding them.

Although participants were excited about using DAP, teams did experience some trouble interacting with the tool. Every team had trouble with editing story card content. Editing of story cards was implemented as a single click on the field once the card was selected. However, everyone used a double click to try and edit the fields. Double clicking resulted in the card collapsing instead of entering edit mode, as the participants expected. This resulted in frustrations amongst the teams and resulted in the teams asking the observer for help.

The second point of frustration came from creating story cards. One of the user study teams was trying to create a story card on top of another story card. It appeared that the team wanted to keep the story cards in the same visible workspace and not have to scroll around. This was a much smaller point of frustration and resulted in the team making a few attempts before resizing the other cards and then creating the card on top of an iteration.[1]

5.2 Feedback

Of the twenty-six participants, in the five teams, twenty provided feedback on their experiences in the study. The feedback was encouraging with similar comments being made by many of the participants. We did not see any differences between feedback from developers and customers. Generally, participants found that DAP was "... very very easy to use", with the exception of editing cards. In addition, participants commented on the visual representations of the cards indicating that "...it gave [them] an exact picture of the planning project".

During conversations with the participants telepointers again came up as an important part of DAP. Participants indicated that they liked how "...[they] could monitor whatever was happening on the screen of the other party" and "...that simple pointing [was] possible". In addition to the telepointers, participants liked the fact that the story cards had explicit areas for the story name and a description. In particular the description area was an important feature as it encouraged them to add more information to the story. One user study participant, acting as a developer, compared the virtual cards to paper cards and commented that when using the paper cards "...there was nothing

---

[1] Most of the usability issues identified by our study have now been fixed by the DAP developers.

that forced me to enter a description but the tool had the description [area] so I felt like, you know, I should fill this in".

Comments from participants continuously highlighted the impact that DAP had on communication during the meetings. The majority of those interviewed felt that the tool helped with keeping the discussions on track. They felt that during the distributed planning meetings where no tool was used that team members would easily and often go off topic or get caught up in an idea and they would then have a hard time getting back on track or interjecting to pose a question.

Participants perceived productivity[2] was slightly increased with the introduction of DAP. Participants felt that with the conversations being more directed and on topic in addition to being able to see, read and interact with the planning artifacts in near real-time helped increase the productivity of the meetings. Participants also believed that they had a better understanding of the stories for the current iteration and spent less time discussing individual stories. They also found that creating cards was just as simple and quick as creating paper cards.

5.3 Real-Time Performance

Response times for various actions in DAP are near-real-time. Actions in DAP were tested both in a controlled laboratory setting with limited network activity and in a cross-continent setting (Canada - United Kingdom). For both time trials the DAP server was located in Canada. Table 1 summarizes the times for the various different actions in DAP. Times were calculated by hand with a stopwatch, researchers communicated verbally (via VIOP system in the cross-continent case). Action starts were verbalized by one individual and when the other individual had seen the change they would verbally indicate to stop the clock.

Table 1. DAP Performance

	Create Story Card	Create Iteration	Move Story Card	Move Iteration (Empty)	Move Iteration (12 Story Cards)	Move Mouse	Edit Text (<12 Chars)	Edit Text (>12 Chars)	Delete Story Card
Canada - UK	0.75s	1.5s	1.2s	1.5s	2.0s	1.5s	1.5s	1.5s	1.5s
Laboratory	0.5s	0.5s	0.5s	0.25s	1.75s	0.25s	0.25s	0.25s	1.0s

As we can see, the majority of actions in DAP takes two seconds or less regardless of the network settings. Results from the laboratory setting were considerably faster resulting in near instantaneous changes to the workspace. We can see that there is a delay introduced when collaborating over greater distances, however, the delay is still relatively short and did not have an impact on the user study teams ability to collaborate.

5.4 Limitations

The research into the effectiveness of DAP has provided insight into supporting distributed agile planning. The results of our initial study – although encouraging – suffer from

---

[2] When interviewing study participants, we did not define "planning productivity" but let them use their own understanding of the term.

a number of limitations. Specifically, the participants for the user study are graduate students and it is unclear how well they represent agile teams working in an industrial setting. The participants are also volunteers – creating a potential positive bias in the results.

Secondly, biases are introduced due to the fact that half of the volunteers that participated in the user studies were colleagues of the primary researcher. The bias introduced by the volunteers knowing the researcher, are partially kept in check by having the remaining half of the participants in the user study teams being from other universities where there was no prior contact with the researcher or knowledge of the tool.

Finally, industrial evaluation is extremely minimal (one individual on one case study team) and DAP was only compared against paper based planning. No comparative evaluation was conducted between DAP and other distributed agile planning tools and no comparison where the order in which the planning methods were examined were conducted. The lack of comparison against other industrial tools and the limited involvement of industrial participants introduce a bias into the results presented here and demand further investigation. The reason for focusing on DAP instead of alternative tools was our desire to primarily compare paper-based distributed planning with tool-based distributed planning. We picked what we consider the best-of-breed tool as the basis for our study. After our study indicates the benefits of tool support, a next step would now be to compare different agile planning tools and evaluate if there are any differences in planning effectiveness.

6 Conclusions

Tools to support distributed agile planning have made significant strides in bringing the benefits of collocated planning to distributed teams. Research from the groupware community like a shared workspace and telepointers provide teams with additional non-verbal information that is missing from paper based distributed planning meetings.

The results from our observational study are encouraging in that teams found the additional awareness information beneficial. Participants were very receptive of the tool and felt that communication and productivity were positively affected when compared to the paper based distributed planning they experienced. In addition, participants' feedback regarding the use of telepointers is important and suggests that future agile planning tools consider their inclusion.

Further investigation into the effects of distributed planning tools that use physical representations of planning artifacts is warranted. In addition, a comparative evaluation that examines the impacts of the various different agile planning tools is needed.

Distributed AgilePlanner provides card-based planning to agile teams – but it uses a shared vertical surface to display iterations and story cards. Our ongoing work looks into using digital tables for distributed planning and promises to be even closer to collocated agile planning meetings.

References

[1] Beck, K.: Extreme Programming Explained: Embracing Change. Addison-Wesley, Reading (2000)
[2] CardMeeting, http://www.cardmeeting.com

[3] Chon, M.: Agile Estimating and Planning. Pearson Education Inc., London (2006)

[4] Danube Technologies Inc - ScrumWorks, `http://danube.com/scrumworks`

[5] Ellis, C.A., Gibbs, S.J., Rein, G.: Groupware: some issues and experiences. Communications of the ACM 34, 19 (1991)

[6] Greenberg, S.: Sharing views and interactions with single-user applications. ACM SIGOIS Bulletin 11(2-3), 10 (1990)

[7] Gutwin, C., Greenberg, S.: Workspace awareness for groupware. In: Conference companion on Human factors in computing systems (CHI 1996). ACM Press, Vancouver, British, Columbia, Canada (1996)

[8] Gutwin, C., Greenberg, S.: Effects of awareness support on groupware usability. In: Conference on Human Factors in Computer Systems (SIGCHI). ACM Press/ Addison-Wesley Publishing Co., Los Angeles, California, United States (1998)

[9] Morgan, R., Maurer, F.: MasePlanner: A Card-Based Distributed Planning Tool For Agile Teams. In: Porceedings, International Conference on Global Software Engineering (ICGSE 2006). IEEE Computer, Los Alamitos (2006)

[10] Morgan, R., Walyn, J., Kolenda, H., Ginez, E., Maurer, F.: Using Horizontal Displays for Distributed & Collocated Agile Planning. In: Concas, G., Damiani, E., Scotto, M., Succi, G. (eds.) XP 2007. LNCS, vol. 4536, pp. 38–45. Springer, Heidelberg (2007)

[11] Pine, S., Mauri, S., Lorrai, P., Marchesi, M., Serra, N.: XPSwiki: An Agile Tool Supporting the Planning game. In: Marchesi, M., Succi, G. (eds.) XP 2003. LNCS, vol. 2675, pp. 104–113. Springer, Heidelberg (2003)

[12] Rally Software Development Corp, http://www.rallydev.com/products.jsp

[13] Reinhard, W., Schweitzer, J., Volksen, G., Weber, M.: CSCW Tools: Concepts and Architectures. Computer 27(5), 8 (1994)

[14] Stefik, M., Bobrow, D., Foster, G., Lanning, S., Tatar, D.: WYSIWIS revised: Early experiences with multiuser interfaces. ACM Transactions on Information Systems (TOIS) 5(2), 20 (1987)

[15] Tang, J.C.: Findings from observational studies of collaborative work. Interantional Journal of Man-Machine Studies 34(2), 17 (1991)

[16] VersionOne LLC, http://www.versionone.net/products.asp

[17] XPlanner, http://xplanner.org

The TDD-Guide Training and Guidance Tool for Test-Driven Development

Oren Mishali[1], Yael Dubinsky[2], and Shmuel Katz[1]

[1] Computer Science Department
The Technion, Haifa, Israel
{omishali,katz}@cs.technion.ac.il
[2] IBM Haifa Research Lab
31905 Haifa, Israel
dubinsky@il.ibm.com

Abstract. A tool is presented for guiding Test-Driven Development (TDD), called TDD-Guide. The tool is integrated into an existing development environment and guides the developer *during* the development by providing notifications that encourage use of TDD. The TDD practice is defined through rules that can easily be changed and are used to generate code incorporated to a development environment using an aspect-based framework, so that the development of the tool has agile characteristics. Feedback from user experiments both validates the rules and suggests refinements to improve TDD-Guide, as is shown in descriptions of two user experiments.

Keywords: Rule-based framework, test driven development (TDD), software process support, user evaluation.

1 Introduction

Test-Driven Development (TDD) is widely considered both one of the central contributions of Extreme Programming to general agile techniques [1], and one of the most difficult practices to internalize [2, 3]. In this paper the TDD-Guide tool is shown both to effectively encourage use of test-driven development, and to allow incremental and flexible integration into an existing general development environment. The tool can detect conformance or deviation from test-driven practice as coding or testing steps are being developed, and provide valuable notifications to the developer. Some of the notifications provide the developer with positive feedback when the practice is followed, while others identify deviations from TDD. When deviations are detected, the tool can guide the developer to correct the deviation or even strictly enforce TDD by not allowing the developer to perform an operation deviating from the practice.

TDD-Guide is an application of the Aspect-Oriented Process Support (AOPS) framework. This framework, whose concepts were first introduced in [4], facilitates the definition and deployment of support for a variety of software processes in the form of rules and here the framework is used to define rules to support TDD. As its name suggests, the framework is based on aspect-oriented technology [5]. Using the

P. Abrahamsson et al. (Eds.): XP 2008, LNBIP 9, pp. 63–72, 2008.

support definition, code containing aspects and classes is automatically generated, ready to be integrated into the target development environment. Such integration guarantees the customization of the environment according to the defined rules. This aspect-based integration approach is used here on the Eclipse platform and thus the generated types are in AspectJ[1] and Java. The rules for TDD, code generated from this set of rules, a repository of key TDD events and their connection to the environment, together with a user-interface common to all framework products, all integrated into Eclipse, comprise the TDD-Guide tool.

The rules defined using the framework are simple to express, and it is relatively easy to add, remove or modify rules. The framework is especially appropriate for defining development practices that are flexible, may need frequent adjustment, and can be seamlessly integrated with an existing, familiar, development environment. This differs from previous Process Centered Engineering Environments (PCE's), such as [6, 7], that generally replace existing environments and are oriented to a fully detailed process model.

The current version of TDD-Guide is the result of ongoing research whose goal is to define practical and effective TDD rules. Given that goal and the flexible nature of the framework, we chose to define the rules in an agile fashion, starting from a basic and simple set of rules that is iteratively refined. In each iteration, the existing set of rules is tested on real developers and the gathered user feedback is used to refine the set toward the next iteration. In this paper, two such iterations are described, focusing on the experiments within them. In each experiment, student developers with novice TDD skills were given a Java development task, and were asked to develop the task using TDD. TDD-Guide was integrated in advance into the users' development environment (Eclipse), and significant development steps were logged. Based on the logs and questionnaires, we searched for and developed possible rule refinements. We were also interested in examining the reaction of the developers to this kind of on-line guidance.

We present results showing that TDD-Guide is in general perceived by the users to be helpful and that the tool indeed is effective in guiding TDD. More importantly, we show how the experiments provide important user feedback that helps both to improve the rules themselves and to refine the user-interface. In the next Section we present the user-interface and rules of TDD-Guide while explaining how rules are defined using the framework. The experiments' goals, description, and results are presented in Section 3, and conclusions and future directions are provided in Section 4.

2   TDD-Guide and the AOPS Framework

We metaphorically view a software development process as a trail defined by the process methods and practices; the developers are considered as hikers who are supposed to follow the trail but, for various reasons, once in a while deviate from it. Accordingly, an AOPS rule can be of kind *deviation* or *on-track*; a rule of kind on-track when triggered denotes that the developer is following the trail, and encourages the developer by providing positive feedback. Similarly, a rule of kind deviation is activated when the developer deviates from the desired trail; here, the rule may force the developer to return to the trail, or alternatively provide the developer with the choice to deviate while presenting negative feedback with different severity levels.

---

[1] The AspectJ Project, http://www.eclipse.org/aspectj/

2.1 TDD-Guide User-Interface

Upon activation of an AOPS rule, its message is presented to the developer in the AOPS view (Figure 1), where an appropriate icon denotes the type of the message. In addition, the AOPS bar (Figure 2) updates its color according the kind of the activated rule and also supplies a tooltip to quickly observe the rule's message.

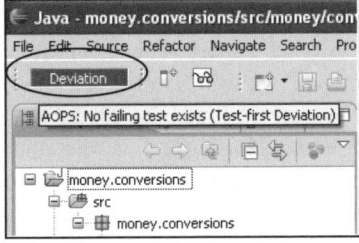

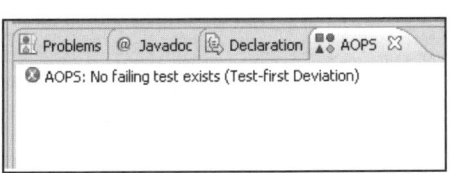

Fig. 1. The AOPS view   **Fig. 2.** The AOPS bar

Rule messages may also be presented to the developer within Eclipse dialogs and wizards. In Figure 3, for instance, we see the same "No failing test exists" message, but presented within the Java class creation wizard. This tight integration with Eclipse allows natural enforcement of the rule by simply disabling the 'Finish' button. However, in editing mode the same rule is not mandatory and can be overridden.

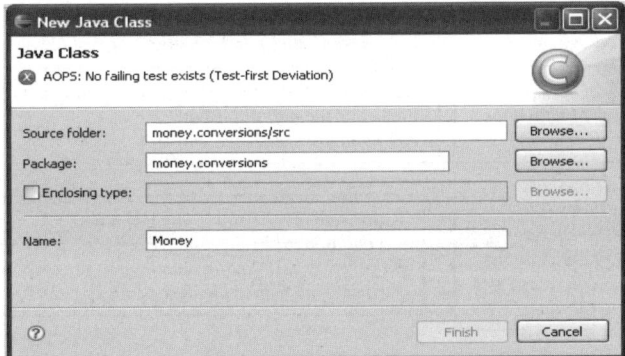

Fig. 3. Java class creation wizard augmented with an AOPS message

2.2 Rule Definition

To define AOPS rules, the manager/governor (the one who defines the rules) should first define an abstraction of the underlying development process, namely a set of entities that represent important elements in the process. Then, rules are defined that operate on the entities.

In Figure 4 we see some of the entities and the rules that constitute TDD-Guide. Two entities are defined, *CodingSpace* and *TestingSpace*, representing the space where the functional code is developed and where the unit tests are developed, respectively. Each entity can have *key-events* and *attributes*; key-events represent abstract events that occur during the development related to the modeled process element, and attributes are meant to hold related important values. Both entities have two key-events representing creation and modification of types in the space, and in addition, *TestingSpace* has two attributes *numOfFailingTests* and *numOfBrokenTests*; both attributes are of type Integer and hold the current number of failing tests and broken tests (that do not compile), respectively. An AOPS rule is activated when one of the key-events defined in its *condition* part is activated and its predicate, also defined there, holds. The rule *NeverWriteCodeWithoutFailingTest* is therefore activated when the developer creates a new type/class or modifies an existing one and neither a failing test nor a broken test exists. Activation of this rule is the most severe deviation from TDD and therefore a *strategy* of type error is defined (a strategy describes the general course of action taken upon rule activation). The second rule *ChallengeExistingCode* is of kind *on-track* and is activated when the developer is modifying a test and no failing test exists. The rule encourages the developer by clarifying the task ahead: writing a test that is not passed by existing code.

Four more rules are defined. Two of them enforce coding standards that distinguish between coding and testing elements, and another one *HaveOneActiveTest* recognizes deviations from the TDD recommended guideline of not trying to fix several things at a time[2]. The last rule *MakeExistingCodePass* encourages the developer to fix the code when in the coding space and having one failing test.

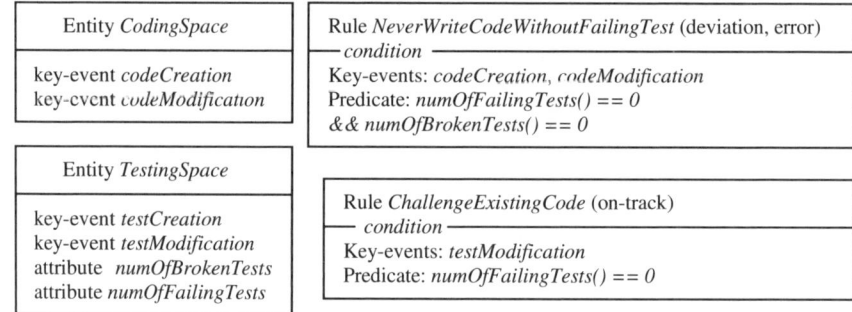

Fig. 4. Sample TDD entities and rules

The defined entities are just declarations and thus should be connected to the underlying development environment. This process of connecting the entities to the environment is called entity-mapping and uses a repository of concrete Eclipse method calls not elaborated here. After the mapping, during development of an application the entities are continuously updated to reflect the state and behavior of the underlying process elements that they represent. The entities, their mapping, and the rules, are all defined using the framework's graphical interface. A public release of

---

[2] http://c2.com/cgi/wiki?OneUnitTestAtaTime

the AOPS framework is expected within several months. An Eclipse plug-in of TDD-Guide is available upon request from the authors.

3   Evaluating TDD-Guide

A support tool to guide TDD can be best validated through user experiments. The validation should involve user experience that is rigorously planned and executed aiming at refining the tool to be more effective [8, 9]. The users in our case are developers in software development teams who work to produce code according to some predefined functionality and need to produce unit tests to support the code.

In this section we describe the two user experiments of the first two development iterations of TDD-Guide. The first experiment was a spike whose major purpose was to examine the initial set of the rules of the first iteration in a real development setup. Based on this spike, several changes were introduced to the tool. The second version of the tool was experimented with in a larger setting, more focused on rule refinement, namely examining the effectiveness of the rules in supporting TDD, and searching for unanticipated development states.

3.1   First Experiment

Six experienced programmers familiar with Java and Eclipse, and less familiar with TDD, were given a simple development task and asked to develop the task while using TDD. The initial feedback was encouraging: all of the participants showed positive reactions to the idea of accompanying the development with messages and alerts, and four participants reported that the messages helped them to develop test-first. No change was noticed in Eclipse performance due to the addition of aspects into it.

The experiment led to changes in the user-interface, in the rules, and in the logging. Four participants reported that paying attention to the AOPS view did not disrupt their concentration in developing the task. The other two felt that it sometimes was a burden. Accordingly, we decided to add the AOPS bar (Figure 2), hoping that colored feedback would be more intuitive than a purely textual one. The rule *NeverWriteCodeWithoutFailingTest* in its first version attempted to treat a special case: when the developer had a broken test, the rule allowed moving to the code without requiring to execute the test (assuming that the developer is interested in creating, e.g., a missing declaration and then returning to the test). However, we observed that two participants did not act according to our assumption. They indeed created a missing declaration, but instead of then returning to the test they continued to develop the code without first running JUnit. We changed the rule so that test execution is required before each move to the code, to make the TDD cycle simpler and more uniform. Since execution of broken tests is also reported by JUnit with red indication, we also added a warning to the rule to remind the developer that the JUnit bar is red due to a compilation error and not because of a failing test. We also added time-stamps to the logs to facilitate better reasoning.

3.2   Second Experiment

The participants in the second experiment were 34 CS-major fourth-year students in an advanced Software Engineering project course. The experiment had three phases:

1. Pre-experiment phase in which participants filled in a questionnaire about the level of their familiarity and experience with programming concepts and tools in general and with TDD in particular. Then, they heard a one-hour lecture about unit testing and specifically about TDD.
2. Experiment experience phase in which participants moved to the computer lab where they were guided in groups of 2-4 to perform a specific programming task. After completing the task they filled in a personal reflection.
3. Post-experiment phase in which participants were asked one week after the experiment to indicate two features of TDD-Guide that they perceive as most significant and two possible improvements or extensions. This feedback was obtained using a web-based feedback mechanism familiar to the students.

Twenty seven of the participants filled in the questionnaire of the pre-experiment phase. The results show that participants felt knowledgeable with Java programming and object-oriented design, less knowledgeable with Eclipse IDE and unit testing, and beginners in JUnit and TDD. Regarding the development process, participants were less experienced with measuring the development process and product, but felt knowledgeable and even expert with working in pairs.

Given a project named money.conversions that contains classes and conversion utilities[3], participants were asked to define a class Money that represents a certain amount of money in a specific currency. In addition, the class should have the method Money add(Money m, String currency) where the returned Money represents the addition of the called Money object and the given Money argument, in the given currency argument. Participants were asked to develop according to the TDD technique (within 35 minutes) and to take notice of AOPS messages. As in the first experiment, aspects were also added to Eclipse to log actual behavior and timing information.

3.2.1   Experiment Outcomes

We illustrate the experiment findings for the *NeverWriteCodeWithoutFailingTest* rule of TDD-Guide that detects a deviation as aforementioned. We considered recurrences of series of events in the logs that show a specific behavior of the developers either before or after the deviation. The logs of twelve groups that completed their task were considered and the following four findings were formulated:

- The first finding deals with the intuitive tendency of developers to start programming with coding rather than with testing. An expected behavior in the beginning of the log is *Test - TestFailed - Code* where *Test* means writing test lines, *TestFailed* means that running JUnit causes a failure, and *Code* means writing code lines. Four logs out of twelve include *Code - DeviationMessage - Test* at the beginning of the log (meaning that they start directly with code as they used to, noticed the AOPS deviation

---

[3] The given task is a simplified version of a well-known TDD example by Kent Beck and Erich Gamma (http://junit.sourceforge.net/doc/testinfected/testing.htm).

message that appears and responded by starting to test). This tendency to start with coding was also found in the middle of the task when instead of the expected *Code - TestSucceeded - Test* we found *Code - TestSucceeded - Code - DeviationMessage - Test.* These cases show that novice developers can benefit from TDD-Guide messages and by following them they overcome their tendency to start coding without testing, and thus adhere to the TDD practice. Since this rule can be overruled in *edit* mode, we found two cases of *Code - DeviationMessage - Code* meaning the deviation message was ignored by the developers who continued to work on the code although there was no failed test. This can be also explained as a refactoring activity and was marked by us for further investigation.

- The second finding concerns getting used to actually run the tests before moving to code. We found eight cases in six logs where developers did *Test - Code - DeviationMessage - TestFailed - Code* meaning they worked on the test and switched to code without receiving the feedback of running JUnit. Following the deviation message they ran the test, causing a test failure, and went back to code.

- The third finding relates to the learning curve that can be observed especially when adding the time measure of the different activities. The following series of events was found starting at the beginning of a specific log:
  - o *Code - DeviationMessage* for 1 minute; no work for 2 minutes;
  - o *Test* for 15 seconds;
  - o *Code - DeviationMessage* for 4 seconds; no work for 7 seconds;
  - o *Test* for 8 minutes;
  - o *Code - DeviationMessage* for 1 second;
  - o *TestFailed - Code*

The deviation message was used three times to correct the development in this trace. We observed here and elsewhere that the time to respond to the deviation messages decreased while the time invested in testing increased.

- The fourth finding reveals strong emotions against testing and can be seen as anecdotal: one group used "i dont want to test" as part of their test file name.

3.2.2 Participants' Reflection on the Experiment

After completing the task, participants filled in their level of agreement with statements related to the experiment. Table 1 summarizes their answers; a clear majority is marked in grey. As can be observed most participants felt that the Eclipse IDE works as usual (statement 1) and that TDD-Guide helped them in working according to the TDD technique (e.g., statement 6). However, statements for which no clear majority exists reveal issues that may suggest rule refinement. For instance, statements 2 and 4 reveal usability issues, and statements 8 and 13 disagreement with the TDD guiding rules (we refer to these issues in Section 4). Statements 7 and 16 uncover resistance to the TDD concept. We believe this only emphasizes the necessity of the guidance, in particular for novices who are not yet familiar with the advantages of TDD.

To assess the longer-term impact of this experience, we asked for feedback one week after the experiment. As noted, participants were asked to indicate two features of TDD-Guide that they perceived as most significant and two possible improvements or extensions to the tool. Thirty two participants responded to this phase.

Table 1. Reflecting on the experiment activity

#	Statement	Agree	Tend to agree	Tend to disagree	Dis-agree	No answer
1	During development, I felt that the Eclipse interface responded as usual	9	15	8	2	
2	Paying attention to the AOPS messages was a burden	3	14	14	3	
3	I have hardly had any AOPS Deviation (Error) messages	1	12	11	8	2
4	Some of the AOPS messages were not comprehensible	5	12	11	5	1
5	Sometimes I didn't agree with what an AOPS message was saying	2	4	15	12	1
6	The AOPS messages helped me to develop test-first	11	13	8	1	1
7	I find test-first an annoying technique	5	14	13	2	
8	Sometimes, I just ignored an AOPS message	9	9	8	8	
9	Sometimes, I felt that an AOPS message was needed but it didn't show up	3	5	18	8	
10	I think that accompanying the development with messages and alerts is not a good idea and just interferes with the fluent work	1	8	17	8	
11	Several times, AOPS messages led to a change in my behavior	4	16	10	4	
12	I looked several times at the reference page to figure out how to develop test-first	3	6	10	15	
13	When a failing test does not exist, the AOPS system should always <u>disallow</u> any coding	5	13	13	3	
14	I got several "false alarms" (incorrect AOPS messages)	2	3	14	14	1
15	The AOPS view was more useful than the AOPS bar	2	18	11	3	
16	I will definitely develop test-first in the future	2	15	10	6	1
17	Most of the AOPS Warning messages were justified	6	24	5	-	

Most of them indicate the main tool features, though some mixed the TDD technique itself with the features of the guiding tool. Following are some of their suggestions for improvements: "A feature can be added to mark code that is already covered by tests thus help with the testing management"; "Better indication of the current stage in the development process, sometimes it was difficult to understand what the environment expects us to do"; "Introduce development tasks into the environment in order to enable the planning of the product roadmap according to the list of tests that should be written"; "An error should not always be created in order to go forward, there can be an option to skip the obvious errors in the beginning or at least to mark them for example as 'preliminary development remarks'"; "In my opinion no significant improvements/extensions are needed"; "I suggest to emphasize the status marker"; "Possible extension is an automatic correction offer when a problem is diagnosed"; "Add voice alert when there is a warning".

4   Conclusion and Future Work

We conclude this paper by describing the implications of the outcomes presented on the TDD-Guide rules, the user-interface, and the log used to gather information.

As previously mentioned (Section 3.1), after the first experiment we added a warning to the rule *NeverWriteCodeWithoutFailingTest* that is activated when the developers write code while having only broken tests. Its purpose was to remind them that the JUnit bar is red due to a compilation error and not because of a failing test. The logs show that although the warning was presented, usually the developers did not execute the test again after the missing declarations were created but continued to code in that state, without knowing for sure that the test fails. One possible remedy could be to activate the warning again after some time. We should also examine whether the warning message is clear enough.

The addition of time-stamps to the logs discovered that a significant aspect of a correct TDD trail is related to time. For instance, we found several cases where tests were developed (for the first time) for more than ten minutes before moving to the code, and cases where the first successful test execution took place only after fifteen minutes, both indicating that the initial TDD steps are too complex. A new story defined for the third development iteration of TDD-Guide is to provide timing alerts, e.g., if the developer stays too long in the testing space.

Although Section 3.2.1 discussed the *NeverWriteCodeWithoutFailingTest* rule, of course the other rules were examined and guidelines for their refinements exist. The rule *HaveOneActiveTest* was defined to be activated when the developer is in the coding space and has more than one failing test. However, one log revealed that coding while having several failing tests is not always a deviation; that may happen when coding indeed starts with one failing test however changes made in the code cause the failure of others. Although it may indicate tests that are not reasonably independent, it should not be classified as a deviation. Thus, the first improvement is to distinguish between that case and the case where the deviation is certain, that is, where coding *starts* with several failing tests. The logs report on three occurrences of the latter and show that the rule's notification was ignored, i.e., the developers continued to code. The reason may be that the guidance was applied in retrospect, i.e., when the developers already had the tests written. The lesson learned here is that a deviation should be reported as early as possible, when its correction is practical.

As noted in Section 3.2.1, the pattern *Code - DeviationMessage – Code* could also be a sign for a refactoring activity and in that case the TDD rules should not report a deviation. Therefore, another new story for the third iteration is to define refactoring as a new state where modified TDD rules apply.

There is a need to emphasize the user interface indications (see statement 2 in Table 1 and the last feedback in Section 3.2.2). In the next iteration we plan to add vocal indications. Another point to consider is the use of interactive communication with the developer, e.g., pop-ups asking for real-time developer feedback or a button whose pressing indicates moving to a refactoring state.

The performance logs were the primary aid for reasoning on the development and the effectiveness of TDD-Guide. During their analysis, we noted that different views of the logged data are needed, e.g., to identify recurrent patterns and to analyze all activations of an individual rule. These views were created manually and we plan to add their automatic creation. We are also considering the use of a relational database that will store the data and allow queries and reports.

As confirmed by the experiments, after two iterations TDD-Guide is already an effective tool for guiding test-driven development. Its flexibility and light-weight integration into the Eclipse IDE, provided by the AOPS framework, increases the potential of widespread adoption for this tool and its extensions to additional agile software processes.

References

1. Beck, K.: Test-Driven Development By Example. Addison-Wesley, Reading (2003)
2. Dubinsky, Y., Hazzan, O.: Measured Test-Driven Development: Using Measures to Monitor and Control the Unit Development. Journal of Computer Science, Science Publication 3, 335–344 (2007)
3. George, B., Williams, L.A.: A structured experiment of test-driven development. Information & Software Technology 46, 337–342 (2004)
4. Mishali, O., Katz, S.: Using aspects to support the software process: XP over Eclipse. In: International Conference on Aspect-Oriented Software Development, pp. 169–179. ACM, Bonn, Germany (2006)
5. Kiczales, G., Lamping, J., Menhdhekar, A., Maeda, C., Lopes, C., Loingtier, J.-M., Irwin, J.: Aspect-Oriented Programming. In: Aksit, M., Matsuoka, S. (eds.) ECOOP 1997. LNCS, vol. 1241, pp. 220–242. Springer, Heidelberg (1997)
6. Bandinelli, S., Braga, M., Fuggetta, A., Lavazza, L.: The Architecture of SPADE-1-Process-Centered SEE. In: Warboys, B.C. (ed.) EWSPT 1994. LNCS, vol. 772, pp. 15–30. Springer, Heidelberg (1994)
7. Junkermann, G., Peuschel, B., Schafer, W., Wolf, S.: MERLIN: Supporting Cooperation in Software Development Through a Knowledge Based Environment. In: Software Process Modelling and Technology, pp. 103–129. John Wiley and Sons, Chichester (1994)
8. Dix, A., Finlay, J., Abowd, G.D., Beale, R.: Human-Computer-Interaction, 3rd edn. Prentice Hall, Englewood Cliffs (2003)
9. Sharp, H., Rogers, Y., Preece, J.: Interaction Design: Beyond Human-Computer Interaction, 2nd edn. John Wiley & Sons, Chichester (2007)

JExample: Exploiting Dependencies between Tests to Improve Defect Localization

Adrian Kuhn[1], Bart Van Rompaey[2], Lea Haensenberger[1], Oscar Nierstrasz[1],
Serge Demeyer[2], Markus Gaelli[1], and Koenraad Van Leemput[2]

[1] Software Composition Group, University of Bern,
Neubrückstrasse 10, 3012 Bern, Switzerland
{akuhn,gaelli,oscar}@iam.unibe.ch,
lhaensenberger@students.unibe.ch
[2] University of Antwerp, Middelheimlaan 1, 2020 Antwerpen, Belgium
{bart.vanrompaey2,serge.demeyer,koen.vanleemput}@ua.ac.be

Abstract. To quickly localize defects, we want our attention to be focussed on
relevant failing tests. We propose to improve defect localization by *exploiting
dependencies between tests*, using a JUNIT extension called JEXAMPLE. In a
case study, a monolithic white-box test suite for a complex algorithm is refactored into two traditional JUNIT style tests and to JEXAMPLE. Of the three refac-
torings, JEXAMPLE reports five times fewer defect locations and slightly better
performance (-8-12%), while having similar maintenance characteristics. Compared to the original implementation, JEXAMPLE greatly improves maintainability due the improved factorization following the accepted test quality guidelines.
As such, JEXAMPLE combines the benefits of test chains with test quality aspects
of JUNIT style testing.

1   Introduction

A well-designed test suite should exhibit high coverage to improve our chances of identifying any defects. When tests fail, we want to quickly localize defects, so we want our
attention to be focussed on the relevant failing tests to identify the root cause of the defect. However, when some part of the base-code gets changed, a small defect can cause
a domino effect of multiple failing unit tests. This is a problem, because the person
changing the code has no other option than to browse all failing unit tests to try and
deduce a single root cause. This task can prove to be quite difficult when that person is
unfamiliar with the test code that fails.

Dependencies between unit tests, the cause of this domino effect, have generated
considerable controversy [6,12,4]. Common wisdom states that defect localization is
improved by avoiding dependencies between tests, yet empirical evidence shows that
latent dependencies exist anyway even in well-designed test suites [9]. This suggests
that, despite the guidelines, dependencies between tests are inevitable.

In this paper we propose to improve defect localization by making dependencies
between tests explicit. For example, a developer can declare that a testRemove test
depends on the successful outcome of a testAdd test. Based on these depedencies,
a testing framework can automatically determine a suitable order to run the tests, and

P. Abrahamsson et al. (Eds.): XP 2008, LNBIP 9, pp. 73–82, 2008.
© Springer-Verlag Berlin Heidelberg 2008

to skip tests that depend on other failed tests. This setup prevents the domino effect of failing tests. We test this hypothesis by means of a case study in which we compare four implementations of the same test suite: a JEXAMPLE-based implementation and three alternative JUNIT-based implementations.

The contributions of this paper can be summarized as:

- We propose explicit test dependencies as solution for the domino effect in defect localization (e.g. in Chained tests),
- We introduce JEXAMPLE, an extension of JUNIT that uses annotations to declare explicit dependencies between test methods,
- We present empirical evidence that JEXAMPLE provides five times better defect localization than traditional JUNIT, without considerable degradation in performance, code size or duplication.

The remainder of the paper is structured as follows: after related work in Section 2, Section 3 introduces JEXAMPLE, illustrating the difference between chained test methods and conventional JUNIT test methods. Section 4 covers the case study, with Section 5 discussing the results and stating some concluding remarks.

2 Related Work

Many authors have been studying techniques to prioritize test cases, selectively execute regression tests or reduce test suites.

Kung *et al.* discuss a cost-effective selective regression testing approach after changes in an object-oriented program, by (i) determining the set of affected classes and (ii) prioritizing the testing of classes to minimize test stub construction [10]. A similar approach is followed by Wong *et al.*, first applying a modification-based selection technique followed by test set minimization (minimal selection preserving a coverage criterion) and prioritization (increasing cost per additional coverage) [19].

Rothermel *et al.* propose several techniques for prioritizing test cases with the goal of improving the rate of fault detection. Coverage and fault-detection ability, in various forms, are used to determine the test cases execution order [14]. Results show that all techniques improve the rate of fault detection compared to the standard, randomly ordered suite.

Stoerzer et al. automatically classify changes depending on the likelihood that they contribute to a test's failure [16], by monitoring test execution and addressing the local change history in Eclipse.

Gaelli *et al.* infer a partial order of unit tests corresponding to the coverage hierarchy of their sets of covered method signatures [8]. Their work shows that most tests either cover a superset of another test method's coverage or cover themselves a subset of another test, concluding that most tests implicitly depend on other tests. In case of test case failures, the developer is guided to tests which were found to be smallest in a previously stored hierarchy of a successful test run. In our *a priori* approach, letting developers explicitly link tests, we do not need a green running suite in the first place.

There exists a consensus about the following quality aspects of test code. When supporting fast and frequent code-test cycles, not only should a test run take minimal time [15,5], but detected defects should be communicated to the developer in an informative manner [6]. This implies that the link between the test error and the responsible unit under test is made explicit. In an evolving system, test code needs to be understood, reviewed and extended by team members. Moreover, knowing that (refactoring) operations to the production system potentially invalidate the corresponding tests, a test suite's code should be easy to understand and change [17]. As test code is typically not verified beyond reviewing (at 150 to 200 lines of code per hour [2]), tests are advised to be short and simple. *Test smells* are described as maintenance prone constructs that are specific for software test code [4,12], in addition to regular deficiencies such as code duplication. As such, they are to be avoided.

Dependencies between unit tests have generated considerable controversy [4,6,12]. As a motivating example to illustrate a test dependency, consider the test code in Listing 1: the unit under test is a simple Stack class, for which two test methods are given, testPush and testPop, both implemented to run independently of each other. However, as each of the two test methods *must* cover Stack's push method (there is no pop without push), an implicit dependency between testPop and testPush is introduced: whenever testPush fails, testPop is likely to fail as well.

Listing 1. Implicit dependency between test methods

```
public class StackTest {
    private Stack stack;

    @Before
    public void setup() {
        stack = new Stack();
    }

    @Test
    public void testPush() {
        stack.push("Foo");
        assertEquals(false, stack.isEmpty());
        assertEquals("Foo", stack.top());
    }

    @Test
    public void testPop() {
        stack.push("Foo");
        Object top = stack.pop();
        assertEquals(true, stack.isEmpty());
        assertEquals("Foo", top);
    }
}
```

On one side of the controversy, detractors consider dependencies to be a form of "bad smell" in testing code. Van Deursen *et al.* use the term *Eager Test* to refer to a test method checking several methods of the object to be tested [4]. They say that dependencies between the enclosed tests make such tests harder to understand and maintain. Van Rompaey *et al.* provide empirical evidence to support this claim [18]. Fewster and Graham state that the efficiency benefit of long tests (where setup and tear-down is only performed once) is far outweighed by the inefficiency of identifying the single point of failure [6]. The xUnit family of testing frameworks, as exemplified by JUNIT, advises its users to avoid dependencies between tests. Test methods are supposed to be independent artifacts, sharing at most a (re-initialized) fixture constituting the unit under test. Meszaros uses the term *ChainedTests* to point to this test design [12], motivating that it may be a valid strategy for overly long, incremental tests. On the down side, the implicit fixture initialized by previous tests may impede the understandability of a single test. On the supporting side of test dependencies, we find testing frameworks such as TESTNG that provide support to define explicit dependencies between test methods and or test cases [3].

3   JExample in a Nutshell

In order to facilitate chained tests, JEXAMPLE extends JUNIT as follows: (i) test methods may return values; (ii) test methods may take arguments; and (iii) test methods may declare dependencies.

When using JEXAMPLE there is no need for fixtures or setup methods. Any test method M_0 may be used as a setup method, using its return value x as the fixture for its dependents. That is, JEXAMPLE takes the return value x of M_0 and passes it on as an argument to all methods that depend on M_0. Chained tests are related to the idea of example-driven testing, which states that fixture instances are valuable objects, and hence, to be reused and treated first-order first order by a testing framework [7].

When executing a standard JUnit test case (*e.g.,* Listing 1), the JUNIT framework executes setup before each test method, using a field to pass the fixture instance from setup to test methods. Considering this, we may say that setup creates an example instance, and that all other tests depend on this instance. Hence, we promote setup to become a test method with return value:

Listing 2. Promote fixture to test with return value

```
@Test
public Stack testEmpty() {
    Stack empty = new Stack();
    assertTrue(empty.isEmpty());
    assertEquals(null, empty.top()));
    return empty;
}
```

Note the assertions in the method body. As setup is now a proper test method we may even test the fixture before passing it on. Next, we rewrite testPush to depend on the result of setup using a @Depends annotation as follows:

Listing 3. Take another test's result as input value

```
@Test
@Depends("testEmpty")
public Stack testPush(Stack stack) {
    stack.push("Foo");
    assertFalse(empty.isEmpty());
    assert("Foo", empty.top());
    return stack;
}
```

When executing the test in Listing 3, the JEXAMPLE framework will first call `setup` in order to fetch its return value and then pass the return value as an argument to `testPush`. As this method might possible modify its argument, we must either clone the example instance before passing it on or call `setup` twice. The current implementation of JEXAMPLE does the former (of course only if `setup` succeeds, otherwise all dependents of `setup` are skipped anyway).

Next, we readdress Listing 1 to find deeper levels of dependencies, turning the test case into a graph of chained test methods. And indeed, there is a test method that implicitly depends upon `testPush`'s outcome: `testPop` cannot be exercised without pushing some element first. Hence we implement `testPop` as follows, avoiding the duplicate call to `push` by depending on `testPush`'s return value:

Listing 4. Avoid code duplication using dependencies

```
@Test
@Depends("testPush")
public Stack testPop(Stack stack) {
    Object top = stack.pop();
    assertEquals(true, empty.isEmpty());
    assertEquals("Foo", top);
    return stack;
}
```

Given a defect in `Stack`'s `push` method, the `pop` test is ignored by JEXAMPLE, thereby pointing precisely to the defect location.

4 Case Study

In this section we report on a case study that compares four different implementations of the same unit test suite. The goal is to check how Chained tests improve defect localization, and how JEXAMPLE promotes quality criteria related to performance, size and code duplication.

The (pre-existing) JUnit test suite under study exercises an implementation of the *Ullmann subgraph isomorphism* algorithm — *i.e.,* an algorithm to compare the structure of graphs. This set of rigorous, white box tests was written to verify the core of a research tool as well as the interaction with a third party graph library.

Ullman Original is the original implementation of the case-study. Figure 1 illustrates how the test suite is implemented as a single test case consisting of six very long test methods. The test methods concentrate on a *growing unit under test* and are hence implemented as an alternating series of initialization and assertion code, entangling fixture and test code.

We refactored this original test suite implementation to three alternatives (i) best practice JUNIT tests; (ii) JUNIT using test case inheritance; and (iii) Chained tests using JEXAMPLE. The goal of this refactoring was to obtain equivalent implementations of the same test suite using different test design styles.

The *Ullmann JUnit-style (UJ)* implementation follows the original JUnit test guidelines as described by Beck and Gamma [1]. Tests on the same unit under test are grouped together, by sharing fixture objects and a setup method. To apply this style

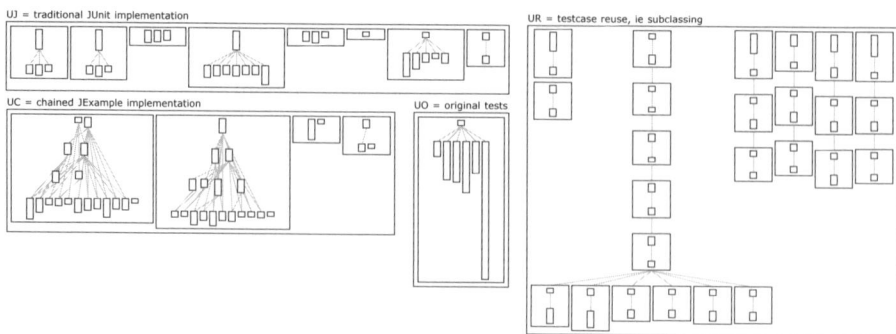

Fig. 1. Polymetric view of the four alternative test suite implementations: The innermost boxes represent test methods (including setup methods); the height of the boxes shows the method's LOC (lines of code) metric; edges show test dependencies. The enclosing boxes represent test cases; edges show test case inheritance.

to the Ullmann case-study, the original test suite is split into eight test cases that each focuses on a different snapshot of the growing unit under test.

The *Ullman test case Reuse (UR)* implementation relies on test case subclassing to build a set of chained yet isolated test cases. This implementation uses a specific subclassing pattern, turning each iterative initialization step of the original test into a subclass that calls `super.setUp()` in its `setup` method to reuse previous initialization code. As such, test dependencies are specified by the test case inheritance hierarchy.

Ullmann Chained JExample-Style (UC), finally, introduces explicit dependencies using JEXAMPLE. Mirroring the iterative initialization code of the original test methods, and using the dependency mechanism presented in Section 3, a root test method creates an example instance of an empty graph object, and passes the instance on to dependent methods. The dependent methods extend the example instance a bit, check some assertions, and eventually pass the instance on to another level of dependent instances, and so on. Dependencies between methods are declared by the developer using `@Depend` annotations, whereas passing on a method's return values to its dependents is done by the framework while running the test suite.

Figure 1 presents the test design of the four implementations using polymetric views [11]. The innermost boxes represent test methods (including setup methods). The height of these boxes show the method's SLOC (source lines of code) metric, while edges show test dependencies. The enclosing boxes represent test cases; edges show test case inheritance.

4.1   Evaluation Procedure

To evaluate *defect localization*, we measure the number of reported test case failures after randomly introducing defects in the system's code with a mutation testing tool (Jester [13]). Using the explicit dependencies between tests, JEXAMPLE ignores tests that depend on a failed test. As such, we expect the UC implementation to report fewer failures than the other three implementations.

Besides defect localization, we select *test suite run-time performance*, *test size* and *code duplication* from the set of common test quality criteria. To quantify the adherence to these criteria, we use the following set of metrics:

- *Performance*. We measure the execution time of each implementation. To measure execution of test suites with failures, we use the created mutations.
- *Size*. We calculate the overall size (source lines of code) of the test suite as well as the number and size of test methods. While the former tells us something about the code base as a whole that needs to be maintained, the latter identifies how well the test suite is factorized.
- *Duplication*. We measure the amount of duplication[1] in each implementation as a result of the presence or absence of reuse possibilities.

For comparison reasons, we control a couple of test suite equality factors. First, we ensured that all four implementations exhibit the same coverage, being 96.9% (Java) instruction coverage (measured using Emma[2]). Secondly, we aimed to keep the same number of assertions. Ultimately, slight differences appeared (between 81 and 85 asserts) due to varying reuse opportunities.

4.2 Results

Defect localization. In order to quantify the traceability quality of the four implementations, we created eight scenarios, named MUT1-MUT8, where a single mutation in the Ullmann code causes the tests to fail. Jester changes constants in the code and adds clauses in boolean conditions to test the defect detection strength of a test suite. For each mutation scenario, we then measure the number of failures JUnit reports. Knowing that only one mutation has been introduced at a single location, ideally only a single failure should be reported.

Table 1. Number of failures: absolute number/ignored tests (relative number)

	UO	UJ	UR	UC
MUT1	4 (66%)	12 (46%)	14 (52%)	2/12 (6%)
MUT2	2 (33%)	2 (8%)	2 (7%)	2/0 (4%)
MUT3	1 (17%)	10 (38%)	9 (37%)	1/12 (3%)
MUT4	1 (17%)	1 (4%)	1 (4%)	1/0 (3%)
MUT5	1 (17%)	10 (38%)	9 (37%)	1/12 (3%)
MUT6	1 (17%)	1 (4%)	1 (4%)	1/1 (3%)
MUT7	1 (17%)	10 (38%)	9 (37%)	1/12 (3%)
MUT8	4 (66%)	11 (42%)	9 (37%)	2/14 (4%)

Table 2. Average execution time (in seconds) of 30 test runs

	UO	UJ	UR	UC
SUCC	0.512	0.600	0.747	0.554
MUT1	0.506	0.603	0.753	0.539
MUT2	0.516	0.609	0.753	0.554
MUT3	0.500	0.597	0.748	0.534
MUT4	0.516	0.600	0.751	0.556
MUT5	0.499	0.594	0.752	0.533
MUT6	0.513	0.610	0.747	0.547
MUT7	0.502	0.600	0.755	0.537
MUT8	0.515	0.613	0.754	0.546

Table 1 presents the failures reported during test runs on the mutated Ullmann code in absolute numbers as well as a percentage of the number of tests. For UC, we add the number of tests ignored by JEXAMPLE. The results show that for a single mutation,

---

[1] Using CCFinderX — http://www.ccfinder.net
[2] http://emma.sourceforge.net

typically multiple tests fail. In the case of the original implementation, the number of failures varies between 1 and 4 (out of 6 test methods). For UJ and UR however, up to 14 tests fail as a result of the factorization of test methods. Due to the ordered test execution of the UC implementation, at most 2 tests fail during a test run, while up to 14 are skipped. Overall, test runs on the UJ and UR implementations report five times more defect locations than the JEXAMPLE tests. The original implementation, however, only reports about 36% more defect locations.

Performance. Table 2 lists the average execution time for the four test suite implementations, and for 5 scenarios. In the first scenario called SUCC(ESS), we execute the tests on the original Ullmann implementation. In the four cases we reuse the mutations of Ullmann created earlier. The results are collected as the average execution time of 30 test runs, measured with the UNIX *time* command on an Intel Pentium 4, 3 Ghz, 1 Gb Ram, Sun JDK 1.6.0, JUnit 4.3.1.

For the successful test run on the original implementation of the Ullmann algorithm, we observe that the original test suite implementation has the fastest average, followed by UC, UJ and UR. We apply Student's t-test to verify whether there exists a significant difference between the test execution time sample sets. As a result, we can indeed conclude — with a confidence of 95% — that UC is 7-8% slower than UO, yet 8-12% faster than UJ and 35-41% faster than the UR approach. The results do only indicate significant performance increases – compared to the SUCCESS scenario – for mutations where 12 to 14 tests are skipped in the UC implementation.

Size. The original Ullmann test implementation, lacking any form of encapsulation for individual tests or set-up, is the most concise one. As a consequence, the UJ and UC implementations are 77% and 87% larger. UR is even 2.4 times as large.

Due to explicit set-ups and fixtures for the multiple test cases the original Ullmann test case (NOTC — number of test cases) has been refactored into, and the method header code for many test commands, the alternative implementations are better factored, as Table 3 shows. The average test method length has dropped from close to 40 to around 10, while the number of assertions per test method decreased from 14 to below 4.

Duplication. To evaluate the level of code duplication, we used CCFinderX to calculate and report code clones. Table 4 summarizes the results. The original implementation contains the least duplication, with 266 tokens (out of 3446) involved in any code clone. The alternative implementations contain between 4200 and 4500 tokens, 13 to 22% of

Table 3. Size of the four implementations expressed in Source Lines Of Code (SLOC), Number Of Test Cases (NOTC), Number Of Test Setups (NOTS) and Number Of Test Methods (NOTM)

	UO	UJ	UR	UC
SLOC	311	551	735	582
NOTC	1	8	26	4
NOTS	1	8	25	0
NOTM	6	52	54	34

Table 4. Code clone results, configured with a minimum clone token size of 50, soft shaper and p-match in CCFinderX

	#tokens	% tokens
UO	266	7.7%
UJ	597	13%
UR	938	22%
UC	780	18%

which is listed in code clones. UC contains about 5% more code covered by clones than UJ.

5   Discussion and Conclusion

In this paper we introduced the idea of making dependencies between tests explicit to improve defect localization. We proposed JEXAMPLE, an extension of JUNIT that allows the tester to annotate test methods with its dependencies. In a case study, JEXAMPLE is compared to more traditional JUNIT-style tests.

The case study showed that compared to alternative test suite implementations, JEXAMPLE tests indeed exhibit an improved defect localization. Moreover, such test suites execute faster and contain less code than traditional JUNIT tests. Compared to a test design style consisting of monolithic test methods entailing long chains of tests, JEXAMPLE tests run somewhat slower and contain some more source code, but rely upon good unit testing practices of encapsulated, concise test methods to ensure maintainability. JEXAMPLE thus combines the best of both worlds: it exhibits the benefits of test chains with the test quality aspects of JUNIT style testing.

There exist a couple of open challenges to consider regarding maintenance of chained tests. First, the dependencies between tests have to be indicated by the developers. Forgetting to do so, or introducing wrong dependencies leads to potentially more failures for a single defect. In the future, automated support to track such dependencies might alleviate this effort. Secondly, with JEXAMPLE, the concepts of a fixture and a set-up become implicit, rendering their identification harder.

Being an extension of JUNIT, JEXAMPLE tests can co-exist with regular tests. Moreover, the migration process merely consists in adding dependency and parameter-passing annotations, as well as cloning the passed-on objects. Our evaluation showed that JEXAMPLE-style tests are especially useful for expressing long test chains as well as for unit tests with obvious dependencies in test suites.

Reproducible Results Statement: A prototype of JEXAMPLE, as well as all four scenarios of the case-study are available for download at: `http://scg.unibe.ch/Resources/JExample`

Acknowledgments. We gratefully acknowledge the financial support of the Swiss National Science Foundation for the project "Analyzing, Capturing and Taming Software Change" (SNF Project No. 200020-113342, Oct. 2006 - Sept. 2008), and IWT Flanders, in the context of the ITEA project if04032 entitled "SERIOUS: Software Evolution, Refactoring, Improvement of Operational & Usable Systems" (Eureka Σ 2023 Programme).

References

1. Beck, K., Gamma, E.: Test infected: Programmers love writing tests. Java Report 3(7), 51–56 (1998)
2. Belli, F., Crisan, R.: Empirical performance analysis of computer-supported code-reviews. In: Proceedings of the 8th International Symposium on Software Reliability Engineering, pp. 245–255. IEEE Computer Society, Los Alamitos (1997)

3. Beust, C., Suleiman, H.: Next Generation Java Testing: TestNG and Advanced Concepts. Addison-Wesley, Reading (2007)
4. Deursen, A., Moonen, L., Bergh, A., Kok, G.: Refactoring test code. In: Marchesi, M. (ed.) Proceedings of the 2nd International Conference on Extreme Programming and Flexible Processes (XP 2001), University of Cagliari, pp. 92–95 (2001)
5. Feathers, M.C.: Working Effectively with Legacy Code. Prentice-Hall, Englewood Cliffs (2005)
6. Fewster, M., Graham, D.: Building maintainable tests. In: Software Test Automation. ch. 7. ACM Press, New York (1999)
7. Gaelli, M.: Modeling Examples to Test and Understand Software. PhD thesis, University of Berne (November 2006)
8. Gaelli, M., Lanza, M., Nierstrasz, O., Wuyts, R.: Ordering broken unit tests for focused debugging. In: 20th International Conference on Software Maintenance (ICSM 2004), pp. 114–123 (2004)
9. Gaelli, M., Nierstrasz, O., Ducasse, S.: One-method commands: Linking methods and their tests. In: OOPSLA Workshop on Revival of Dynamic Languages (October 2004)
10. Kung, D., Gao, J., Hsia, P., Toyoshima, Y., Chen, C., Kim, Y.-S., Song, Y.-K.: Developing and oject-oriented software testing and maintenance environment. Communications of the ACM 38(10), 75–86 (1995)
11. Lanza, M., Ducasse, S.: Polymetric views—a lightweight visual approach to reverse engineering. Transactions on Software Engineering (TSE) 29(9), 782–795 (2003)
12. Meszaros, G.: XUnit Test Patterns - Refactoring Test Code. Addison-Wesley, Reading (2007)
13. Moore, I.: Jester — a JUnit test tester. In: Marchesi, M. (ed.) Proceedings of the 2nd International Conference on Extreme Programming and Flexible Processes (XP 2001), University of Cagliari (2001)
14. Rothermel, G., Untch, R., Chu, C., Harrold, M.J.: Prioritizing test cases for regression testing. Transactions on Software Engineering 27(10), 929–948 (2001)
15. Smith, S., Meszaros, G.: Increasing the effectiveness of automated testing. In: Proceedings of the Third XP and Second Agile Universe Conference, pp. 88–91 (2001)
16. Stoerzer, M., Ryder, B.G., Ren, X., Tip, F.: Finding failure-inducing changes in java programs using change classification. In: Proceedings of the 14th SIGSOFT Conference on the Foundations of Software Engineering (FSE 2006) (November 2006)
17. Deursen, A.V., Moonen, L., Zaidman, A.: On the Interplay Between Software Testing and Evolution and its Effect on Program Comprehension. In: Software Evolution. ch. 8. Springer, Heidelberg (2008)
18. Van Rompaey, B., Du Bois, B., Demeyer, S., Rieger, M.: On the detection of test smells: A metrics-based approach for general fixture and eager test. Transactions on Software Engineering 33(12), 800–817 (2007)
19. Wong, W.E., Horgan, J.R., London, S., Agrawal, H.: A study of effective regression testing in practice. In: Proceedings of the Eighth International Symposium on Software Reliability Engineering, November 1997, pp. 230–238 (1997)

An Agile Development Process and Its Assessment Using Quantitative Object-Oriented Metrics

Giulio Concas[1,2], Marco Di Francesco[3], Michele Marchesi[1,2],
Roberta Quaresima[1], and Sandro Pinna[1]

[1] DIEE, Università di Cagliari, Piazza d'Armi,
09123 Cagliari, Italy
{concas,michele,roberta.quaresima,pinnasandro}@diee.unica.it
[2] FlossLab s.r.l., viale Elmas, 142
09122 Cagliari, Italy
[3] Lab for Open Source Software, ICT District, Sardegna Ricerche, Piazza d'Armi,
09123 Cagliari, Italy
difrancesco80@gmail.com

Abstract. The development of a Web application using agile practices is presented, characterized by empirical software measurements that have been performed throughout the duration of the project. The project is the specialization of jAPS, an open source Java Web portal generation framework, for building a Research Register management system. The agile principles and practices used in the project are described and discussed. During the various phases of the project some key agile practices, such as pair programming, test-based development and refactoring, were used at different levels of adoption. The evolution of some object-oriented metrics of the system, and their behavior related to the agile practices adoption level is presented and discussed, showing that software quality, as measured using standard OO metrics, looks directly related to agile practices adoption.

Keywords: Software metrics, agile methodologies, object-oriented languages.

1 Introduction

Agile methodologies are becoming mainstream in software engineering. More and more projects worldwide are being managed in this way. However, most of them are performed within private firms, and the availability of software data enabling empirical software engineering studies about them is still scarce.

Moreover, classical software engineering evolved studying the typical software projects of the seventies and eighties, where users interact with a centralized system through specific user interfaces running on a terminal or on a client. The first applications of agile methodologies, like the Chrysler C3 project [1] where Extreme Programming was born, were of this kind too. Nowadays, most software development is performed either maintaining existing systems, or developing Web applications. We define Web application development as building software that interacts with the user

P. Abrahamsson et al. (Eds.): XP 2008, LNBIP 9, pp. 83–93, 2008.

through a Web browser, and where many, or most of its functionalities are obtained by assembling together software components already available. A Web application is commonly structured in a front-end using some dynamic Web content technology, a business layer performing suitable computations, and a data repository hosted on one or more servers. For the reasons quoted above, the availability of qualitative and quantitative data about Web application projects using agile methodologies is still quite scarce.

In this work we present in detail a Web software project developed in Java language and carried on using an agile process. Throughout the project we collected metrics about the software being developed. Since Java is an object-oriented (OO) language, we used the Chidamber and Kemerer (CK) OO metrics suite [2]. The adoption level of some key agile practices had been recorded as well during the project.

The goals of this paper are two: (i) to present the principles and practices of the specific agile process we devised for the project, assembling agile practices taken from XP [3], Scrum [4] and FDD [5]; (ii) to present some quantitative measurements performed on the system under development, and relate them with the adoption of some key agile practices, which have been used discontinuously during the development. We found that some key software quality metrics show significantly different mean values and trends during different phases of the project, and that these changes can be positively related with the adoption of some agile practices, namely pair programming, test-based development and refactoring.

The paper is organized as follows: in section 2 we present the agile process we used; in section 3 we present in some detail the software project and the phases of its development; in section 4 we present the OO metrics used and their evolution throughout the phases of the project; in section 5 we discuss the results, relating software quality as resulting from the metrics measurements with the adoption of some agile practices; section 6 concludes the paper.

2 The Agile Practices Used

Before starting FlossAr project, we examined the state of the art of agile software development, and devised a specific agile process using a set of practices that we deemed most suited to our Web application development.

Agile Methodologies (AMs) are a recent approach to software development, introduced at the end of the nineties and now widely accepted worldwide as "mainstream" software engineering [6]. AMs offer a viable solution when the software to be developed has fuzzy or changing requirements, being able to cope with changing requirements throughout the life cycle of a project. Several AMs have been formalized, the most popular being Extreme Programming (XP) [3], Scrum [4], Feature Driven Development [5], DSDM [7] and others. All AMs follow the principles presented in the Agile Manifesto [8].

Very often, software teams intending to pursue and agile approach do not follow "by the book" a specific AM, but discuss and decide a set of agile practices to be used, and from time to time review the project and make adjustments to these practices. This is explicitly referred to in one of the principles of the Agile Manifesto: "*At regular intervals, the team reflects on how to become more effective, then tunes and adjusts its behavior accordingly*" [8].

Web application development is relatively new, and it still lacks the many consolidated programming practices applied with traditional software. One of the main peculiarities of this kind of development is a heterogeneous team, composed by graphic designers, programmers, Web developers, testers. Moreover, the application has typically to be run on different platforms, and to interact with other systems. So, the choice of the development practices to use is of paramount importance for the success of the project. The team first defined some key principles to be followed:

- Modularity and code reuse: the functional blocks of the underlying framework must be kept, and new modules must be added on each of them with no intervention on the framework itself. Moreover, the specialized software produced must be reusable.
- Evolvability and maintainability: it is very important that errors and failures must be fixed quickly, and the software can be easily modified and adapted. In fact, there is no such thing as a general purpose register of research, but each university or research institution wishes to customize such a system to cope with its specific features and requirements.
- Portability: this was a specific requirement of FlossAr, to be able to be sold in the hardware and software contexts of different research institutions. For other specialization projects, it might not be as important.

Following the above principles, the team chose and defined an agile process including some agile practices, most of them derived from XP process [3]. They were:

- Pair Programming: all the development tasks were assigned to pairs and not to single programmers. Given a task, each pair decided which part of it to develop together, and which part to develop separately. The integration was in any case made working together. Sometimes, the developers paired with external programmers belonging to jAPS development community, and this helped to grasp quickly the needed knowledge of the framework.
- On Site Customer: a customer's representative was always available to the team. This customer-driven software development led to a deep redefinition of the structure and features of the system, particularly in the first months of the project.
- Continuous integration: the written code was integrated several times a day.
- Small Releases: the development was divided in a sequence of small iterations, each implementing new features separately testable by the customer, guaranteeing feedback. There were three major releases, at a distance of two months each other.
- Test-Driven Development (TDD): all code must have automated unit tests and acceptance tests, and must pass all tests before it can be released. The choice whether to write tests before or after the code was left to programmers.
- Refactoring: a continuous refactoring was practiced throughout the project, to eliminate code duplications and improve hierarchies and abstractions.
- Coding Standards: the same coding standards of the original jAPS project were kept to increase code readability.
- Collective Code Ownership: the code repository was freely accessible to all programmers, and each pair had the ability to make changes wherever needed.

- Sustainable Pace: this practice was enforced throughout the project, with the exception of the week before the main releases, when the team had to work more than forty hours to complete all the needed features in time.
- Stand-up Meeting: every day, before starting the work, an informal short meeting was held by the team, to highlight issues and to organize the daily activities.
- Feature List and Build by Feature: a list of the features to implement, ordered by their relevance, was kept in a Wiki, and the system development was driven implementing them. These features are user-oriented, meaning that most of them describe how the system reacts to user inputs, and have a priority agreed with the on site customer.

The resulting agile software process proceeds by short iterations and takes advantage of many "classical" agile practices, mainly taken from XP. Its main peculiarity is the control process, which is less structured than Scrum Sprint and XP Planning Game, with less meetings and standard artifacts.

The goal of some of the agile practices quoted above is to enable the team to successfully react to changes in the requirements, to maximize feedback with the customer and among the team, and to enable everybody working better. On Site Customer, Small Releases, Stand-up Meeting, Feature List, Build by Feature and Sustainable Pace are all practices of this kind. These practices were adopted during the whole development process, and moreover do not directly prescribe how code is written. Therefore, it is impossible to assess their impact on the quality of the code, expressed using the quality metrics described in the followings.

The other practices concern how the code is written and upgraded, and have a more direct impact on the quality of the code. Coding Standards and Continuous Integration have been applied throughout the development, so it is not possible to analyze their impact on code quality in the presented project. On the other hand, Pair Programming, TDD and Refactoring had different adoption levels during the phases of the project, so it is possible to study their impact on the quality of the produced software, measured in term of object-oriented software metrics.

3   The Project and Its Phases

The presented project consisted in the implementation of FlossAr, a Register of Research software for universities and research institutes, developed with a complete OO approach, and released with an Open Source license. FlossAr manages a repository of data about research groups and research results – papers, reports, patents, prototypes – aimed to help research evaluation and matching between firms looking for technologies and knowledge, and researchers supplying them. Its architecture is that of a standard Web application, and both researchers who input their profiles and products, and people looking for information access the system through a standard Web browser.

FlossAr has been implemented through a specialization of an open source software project. We intend for specialization the process of creating a software application customized for a specific business, starting from an existing, more general software application or framework. The general framework we customized is jAPS (Java Agile

Portal System) [9], a Java framework for Web portal creation released with GNU GPL 2 open source license. jAPS comes equipped with basic infrastructural services and a simple and customizable content management system (CMS). It is able to integrate different applications, offering a common access point. FlossAr has been developed by a co-located team of four junior programmers, coordinated by a team leader, with limited previous experience of agile development. During the development, FlossAr team adopted the agile process that has been defined in the previous section.

The project evolved through five main phases, each one characterized by an adoption level of the key agile practices of pair programming, TDD and refactoring. These phases are summarized below:

- Phase 1: an exploratory phase where the team studied both the functionalities of, and the way to extend the underlying system (jAPS). It started on February 15th, 2007 and lasted three weeks. We will not consider this phase in the measurements and in the subsequent discussion.
- Phase 2: a phase characterized by the full adoption of all practices, including testing, refactoring and pair programming. It lasted nine weeks, leading to the implementation of a set of the required features.
- Phase 3: this is a critical phase, characterized by skipping the adoption of pair programming, testing and refactoring, because a public presentation was approaching, and the system still lacked many of the features of competitor products. So, the team rushed to implement them, compromising the quality. This phase lasted seven weeks, and included the first release of the system after three weeks.
- Phase 4: an important refactoring phase, characterized by the full adoption of testing and refactoring practices and by the adoption of a rigorous pair programming rotation strategy. This phase was needed to fix the bugs and the bad design that resulted from the previous phase. It lasted four weeks and produced the second release of the system.
- Phase 5: Like phase 2, this is a development phase characterized by the full adoption of the entire set of practices, until the final release on October 1st, 2007, after the last nine weeks. Note that the system development was stopped for three weeks during Summer holidays, so in practice this phase lasted six weeks.

4 Software Metrics

Throughout the project, we computed and analyzed the evolution of a set of source code metrics, including the Chidamber and Kemerer suite of quality metrics (CK) [2], the total number of classes, and the lines of code (LOCs) of classes and methods. The quality of a project is usually measured in terms of lack of defects, or of ease of maintenance. It has been found that these quality attributes are often correlated with specific metrics. The CK metrics that proved to be the most relevant in our test case are RFC and LCOM metrics. Other CK metrics, like CBO and WMC were highly correlated with RFC and LCOM, respectively, as reported also in many other studies [10], and we do not report them here; CK inheritance metrics NOC and DIT are of no interest, also due to the relatively small size of the system. The considered metrics are:

- Response For a Class (RFC): a count of the methods that are potentially invoked in response to a message received by an object of a particular class. It is computed as the sum of the number of methods of a class and the number of external methods called by them.
- Lack of Cohesion in Methods (LCOM): a count of the number of method pairs with zero similarity, minus the count of method pairs with non-zero similarity. Two methods are similar if they use at least one shared field (for example they use the same instance variable).

CK metrics have been largely validated in the literature. In a study of two commercial systems, Li and Henry studied the link between CK metrics and the maintenance effort [11]. Basili et al. found, in another study, that many of the CK metrics were associated with fault-proneness of classes [12]. In another study, Chidamber et al. reported that higher values of CK coupling and the cohesion metrics were associated with reduced productivity and increased rework/design effort [13].

We also consider the LOCs of methods metric, computed for each method of the system. It is good OO programming practice to keep short the method LOCs, because every method should concentrate on just one task, and should delegate a substantial part of its behavior to other methods.

In this paper, we consider just the average values of RFC, LCOM and method LOCs metrics, averaged on all the classes or methods of the system. The average is just a rough measure of the metrics, because it is well known that the distributions of CK and method LOCs metrics follow a power-law [14]. However, also given that the number of classes of the system is of the order of some hundreds, the average of these metrics should suffice to give an idea of the average quality of the system.

4.1 FlossAr Metrics Evolution

In this section we analyze the evolution of FlossAr source code metrics. At regular intervals of two weeks, the source code has been checked out from the CVS repository and analyzed by a parser that calculates the metrics. The parser and the analyzer have been developed by our research group as a plug-in for the Eclipse IDE.

Number of Classes. This metric measures the total number of classes (including abstract classes and interfaces), and is a good indicator of system size. The number of classes generally increases over time, though not linearly. As reported in Fig.1, the project started with 362 classes – those of jAPS release 1.6. At the end of the project the system had grown up to 514 classes, due to the development of new features implemented by the specialized system.

Besides the class number, we analyze in detail the evolution of CK and LOC metrics, that are very useful for understanding the complexity of the system developed, and to assess the quality of the product built and how the agile practices used during the project affected the metrics in the different phases. All of the three metrics considered should be kept low for having a system of "good" quality. The basic statistics of these metrics (mean and standard deviation) are reported in Table 1 for each relevant phase of the project, that is for all phases but phase 1. Note that, when these metrics are computed every other week, they refer to an average of the CK metrics over all

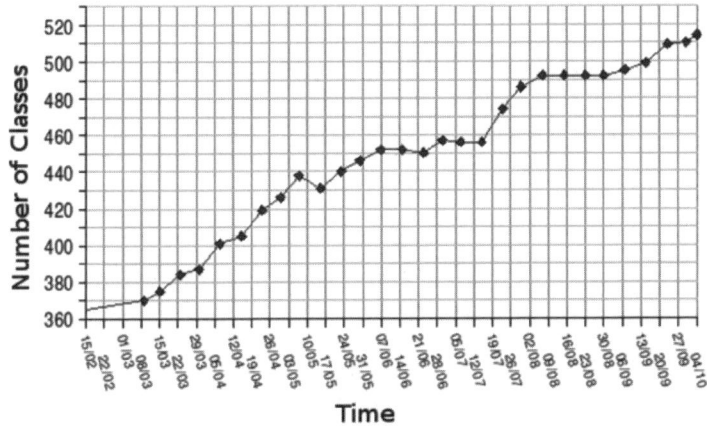

Fig. 1. The evolution of the number of classes

Table 1. Statistics related to measured metrics, for the relevant project phases

Metrics	Phase 2		Phase3		Phase 4		Phase 5	
	mean	st.dev.	mean	st.dev.	mean	st.dev.	mean	st.dev.
LCOM	25.3	0.4	30.0	5.2	34.7	1.3	33.0	0.4
RFC	14.5	0.34	16.0	0.43	15.3	0.16	15.1	0.11
MLOCs	9.53	0.15	10.7	0.27	10.8	0.05	10.9	0.07

the classes of the system, or of the method LOCs over all its methods. The statistics shown in Table 1, on the other hand, show the mean and the standard deviation of these (average) metrics computed in the sampling days, over a phase of the project.

LCOM: The evaluation of LCOM average value, reported in Fig. 2 in conjunction with other metrics and the process phases, shows a stable behavior during the second phase, with an average value of 25.3, and then a steady increase in the middle of the third phase. The peak occurs at the beginning of the fourth phase (RFC peak happens two weeks before), where it reaches a value slightly less than 36. LCOM shows a subsequent slow decline until it stabilizes at an average value of 33 during the fifth phase. The standard deviation of LCOM values computed during phases 2 and 5 are low compared to those of phase 3 and, to a lesser extent, phase 4. This reflect the strong variations of LCOM occurring in these phases.

RFC is a measure of the complexity level of system classes. The evolution of the average value of RFC is reported in Fig. 2, together with the other considered metrics. RFC shows a fair increase during the first development phase of the project (phase 2), followed by a much higher increase during phase 3, up to a peak with an average value of 16.4 methods callable in response to a generic message sent to an instance of the class. During phase 4, the average value of RFC shows a strong decrease, until it reaches a plateau of about 15 methods callable in response to a message. The standard deviation is relatively high in the second and third phases of the project, when RFC tends to increase, while it is lower in the last two phases, when it stabilizes.

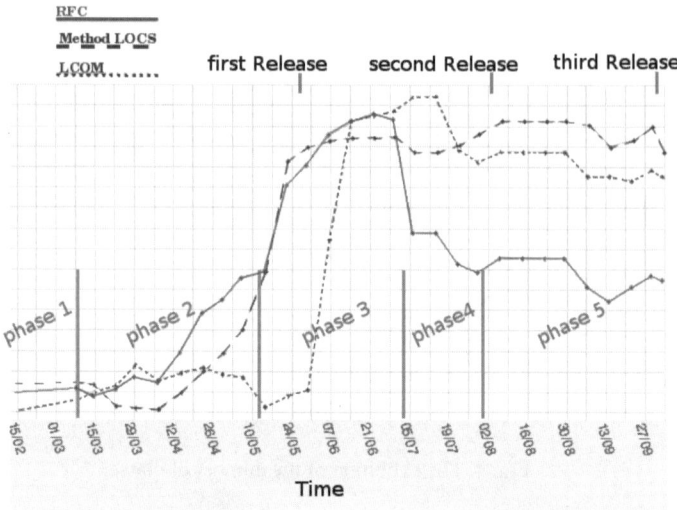

Fig. 2. Development phases and evolution of some key metrics related to software quality

Method LOCs. This metric is the average number of lines of code of a method. The evolution of Method LOCs, reported in Fig. 2, shows an increasing trend during phase 2 and the beginning of phase 3, until just before the first release, and then a relative stabilization, with some minor fluctuations, during the remaining of the project. Also in this case, the measured standard deviation reflects whether the metric is varying, or is relatively stable.

Table 2. Confidence level that the measurements taken in two consecutive phases significantly differ, according to K-S two-sample test

Metrics	Phases 2-3	Phases 3-4	Phases 4-5
LCOM	91.5%	75.0%	**97.0%**
RFC	**99.98%**	**98.1%**	**97.0%**
MLOCs	**99.97%**	90.3%	56.4%

To assess how these measurements differ from a phase to the next one (excluding the first inception phase), we performed a Kolmogorov-Smirnov two-sample test. This KS test determines if two datasets differ significantly, i.e. belong to different distributions, making no assumption on the distribution of the data. For each computed metric, we compared the measurements belonging to a phase to those belonging to the next one[1]. The results are shown in Table 2, showing in bold the cases with

---

[1] Since all the metrics computed at a given time depend also on the state of the system in the previous measurement, the assumption underlying KS test that the samples are mutually independent random samples could be challenged. However, we used KS test to assess the difference between measurements in different phases as if they were independent sets of points, and we believe that at a first approximation the KS test result is still valid.

significance levels greater than 95%. Phase 2 metrics differ very significantly from phase 3 in two cases (RFC and MLOCs), and get a significance higher than 90% also for LCOM. The difference of the metrics of other consecutive phases are lower, though in some cases there is significance greater than 95%. These results in fact confirm the difference in trends and values of the various metrics in the various phases that are patent in Fig. 2.

5 Discussion

As described in section 3, the level of adoption of key agile practices, and namely pair programming, testing and refactoring was highly variable in the different phases of the process. Our first observation is that, since these practices were always applied or not applied together, it is not possible to discriminate among them, or to assess their relative usefulness, using the data gathered in this case study. Consequently, we will talk of "key agile practices" as applied together.

The evolution of the studied metrics in conjunction with the process phases, as shown in Fig. 2, results in significantly different values and trends, depending on the specific phase. Our hypothesis is that this variability is due precisely to the different level of adoption of the key agile practices, because, to our knowledge, this is the only difference among the various phases, as regards external factors that might had an impact on the project. The only relevant internal factor in play is the team experience, both in applying agile practices and about the system itself. Since the project duration was relatively short, we estimate that that the latter factor affected significantly only phase 2. Let us now discuss the metrics trends during the various phases.

Phase 2 is characterized by a growing trend both of RFC and LOCs – denoting a worsening of software quality – and by a stationary trend of LCOM. The starting values of these metrics are those of the original jAPS framework, constituted by 367 classes and evaluated by code inspection as a project with a good OO architecture. Note that phase 2 is characterized by a rigorous adoption of agile practices, but we should consider two aspects:

- the knowledge of the original framework was initially quite low, so the first addition of new classes to it in the initial phase had a sub-optimal structure, and it took time to evolve towards an optimal configuration.
- some agile practices require a time to be mastered, and our developers were junior;

Phase 3 is characterized by a strong pressure for releasing new features and by a minimal adoption of pair programming, testing and refactoring practices. In this phase we observe a growth both in the CK metrics, related to coupling among classes, and in the LOC metric, indicating that in this phase the quality has been sacrificed for adding more new features. All the metrics collected in this phase are quite or very significantly higher than those of the previous phase, denoting a further, clear worsening of software quality.

Phase 4, that follows phase 3, is a refactoring phase where the team, adopting a rigorous pair programming rotation strategy together with testing and refactoring, were able to reduce the values of the most important quality metrics. No new features were added to the system. However, the number of classes increased during this phase, because refactoring required to split classes that had grown too much, and to refactor hierarchies, adding abstract classes and interfaces. In particular, RFC complexity metric was very significantly reduced since the beginning of phase 4, and LCOM was reduced as well, mainly at the end of the phase. Method LOCs was not reduced, but it stopped to grow. Note that the values of the metric at the end of phase 4 seem to reach an equilibrium.

The last development phase (phase 5) is characterized by the adoption of pair programming, testing and refactoring practices, and by the addition of further classes associated to new features. In this phase the metrics don't change significantly – although in the end their values are slightly lower than at the beginning of the phase – maybe because the team has become more effective in the adoption of the agile practices compared to the initial phase 2.

In conclusion, in phase 2 we observed a deterioration of quality metrics, that significantly worsened during phase 3; phase 4 led to a significant improvement in quality, and phase 5 kept this improvement. The only external factors that changed during the phases were adoption of pair programming, TDD and refactoring, that was abandoned during phase 3, and systematic use of these practices during phase 4, aiming to improve the quality of the system and with no new feature addition. As regards internal factors, in phase 2 the team was clearly less skilled in the use of agile practices and in the knowledge of jAPS framework.

Although it is not possible to draw definitive conclusions observing a single, medium-sized project, these observations quantitatively relate software quality metrics with the use of key agile practices, and this relation is positive – when pair programming, TDD and refactoring are applied, the quality metrics improve, when they are discontinued, these metrics become significantly worse.

6   Conclusions

In this paper we presented an agile process – aimed to support the development of FlossAr, a Web application for managing a Register of Research – which was devised having in mind the specificities of the project and of the team. The process uses several agile practices, taken from XP, Scrum and FDD.

During the development. we systematically performed measurements on the source code, using software metrics that have been proved to be correlated with software quality. Moreover, the development itself evolved through phases, characterized by a different adoption level of some key agile practices such a pair programming, TDD and refactoring, and by different team skills in using these practices and in the knowledge of the software framework which the system was built upon. Consequently, we correlated the most relevant quality metrics with the agile practices adoption, showing a significant difference in quality metrics of software developed in the various phases, and a systematic improvement of software quality metrics when agile practices are thoroughly used by skilled developers. Clearly, these results represent just a first step toward a more rigorous and systematic assessment of the effect of the use of agile practices on software quality, as measured using standard metrics.

Future work will be performed measuring other bigger projects, taking into account also the number of bugs and the effort to fix them. We also plan to use metrics more sophisticated than the simple computation of the average of metrics computed on the classes of the system. Such metrics will be related to behavior of the distributions of CK metrics on the class population, especially in the tail of the distribution, or could be complexity metrics computed using the complex network approach [14].

References

1. Haungs, J.: Pair Programming on the C3 Project. IEEE Computer 34(2), 118–119 (2001)
2. Chidamber, S., Kemerer, C.: A metrics suite for object-oriented design. IEEE Trans. Software Eng. 20, 476–493 (1994)
3. Beck, K., Andres, C.: Extreme Programming Explained: Embrace Change, 2nd edn. Addison-Wesley, Reading (2004)
4. Schwaber, K.: Agile Project Management with Scrum. Prentice-Hall, Englewood Cliffs (2001)
5. De Luca, J.: A Practical Guide to Feature-Driven Development. Prentice-Hall, Englewood Cliffs (2002)
6. Bohem, B., Turner, R.: Balancing Agility and Discipline. Addison-Wesley Professional, Reading (2003)
7. Stapleton, J.: DSDM Consortium. DSDM: Business Focused Development. Pearson Education, London (2003)
8. Agile Manifesto, http://www.agilemanifesto.org
9. JAPS: Java agile portal system, http://www.japsportal.org
10. Gyimothy, T., Ferenc, R., Siket, I.: Empirical Validation of Object-Oriented Metrics on Open Source Software for Fault Prediction. IEEE Trans. Software Eng. 31, 897–910 (2005)
11. Li, W., Henry, S.: Object oriented metrics that predict maintainability. J. Systems and Software 23, 111–122 (1993)
12. Basili, V., Melo, L.B.: A validation of object oriented design metrics as quality indicators. IEEE Trans. Software Eng. 22, 751–761 (1996)
13. Chidamber, S., Kemerer, C.: Managerial use of metrics for object oriented software: An exploratory analysis. IEEE Trans. Software Eng. 24, 629–639 (1998)
14. Concas, G., Marchesi, M., Pinna, S., Serra, N.: Power-Laws in a Large Object-Oriented Software System. IEEE Trans. Software Eng. 33, 687–708 (2007)

Historical Roots of Agile Methods: Where Did "Agile Thinking" Come From?

Noura Abbas, Andrew M. Gravell, and Gary B. Wills

School of Electronics and Computer Science, University of Southampton
Southampton, SO17 1BJ, United Kingdom
{na06r,amg,gbw}@ecs.soton.ac.uk

Abstract. The appearance of Agile methods has been the most noticeable change to software process thinking in the last fifteen years [16], but in fact many of the "Agile ideas" have been around since 70's or even before. Many studies and reviews have been conducted about Agile methods which ascribe their emergence as a reaction against traditional methods. In this paper, we argue that although Agile methods are new as a whole, they have strong roots in the history of software engineering. In addition to the iterative and incremental approaches that have been in use since 1957 [21], people who criticised the traditional methods suggested alternative approaches which were actually Agile ideas such as the response to change, customer involvement, and working software over documentation. The authors of this paper believe that education about the history of Agile thinking will help to develop better understanding as well as promoting the use of Agile methods. We therefore present and discuss the reasons behind the development and introduction of Agile methods, as a reaction to traditional methods, as a result of people's experience, and in particular focusing on reusing ideas from history.

Keywords: Agile Methods, Software Development, Foundations and Conceptual Studies of Agile Methods.

1 Introduction

Many reviews, studies and surveys have been conducted on Agile methods [1, 20, 15, 23, 38, 27, 22]. Most of these studies focus on the reaction to traditional methods as a reason behind Agile methods. However, Agile ideas have been around long time ago, and people who criticized the traditional methods suggested alternative approaches which were nothing but Agile ideas. Unfortunately these alternative approaches had not been treated seriously enough, and that is why it took us another 30 years to figure out that this is an effective way to develop software.

In their famous paper "Iterative and Incremental Development: A Brief History", Larman and Basili mentioned that iterative and incremental development was in use as early as 1957 [21]. In addition, they described projects that used iterative and incremental approaches in the 1970s. In this paper we will focus on the historical roots of other aspects of Agile thinking such as the response to change, customer involvement, and working software over documentation.

P. Abrahamsson et al. (Eds.): XP 2008, LNBIP 9, pp. 94–103, 2008.

2   What Does It Mean to Be Agile

The understanding of the word Agile varies in practice. In addition, it is difficult to define Agile methods as it is an umbrella for well-defined methods, which vary in practice. This section will show how this word was explained in literature by its proponents, as well as by other researchers.

Some researchers tend to define Agile as a philosophy. Alistair Cockburn's definition is "Agile implies being effective and manoeuvrable. An Agile process is both light and sufficient. The lightness is a means of staying manoeuvrable. The sufficiency is a matter of staying in the game" [13]. Barry Boehm describes Agile methods as "an outgrowth of rapid prototyping and rapid development experience as well as the resurgence of a philosophy that programming is a craft rather than an industrial process" [7].

Another way to describe Agile methods is by stating the basic practices various methods share. Craig Larman stated, "It is not possible to exactly define agile methods, as specific practices vary. However short timeboxed iterations with adaptive, evolutionary refinements of plans and goals is a basic practice various methods share" [22]. Boehm gives more practice-oriented definition, "In general, agile methods are very lightweight processes that employ short iteration cycles; actively involve users to establish, prioritize, and verify requirements; and rely on tacit knowledge within a team as opposed to documentation" [7]. In an eWorkshop on Agile methods organized by the Centre of Experimental Software Engineering (CeBASE), the participants defined Agile methods as iterative, incremental, self-organizing, and emergent. In addition, they stated that all Agile methods follow the four values and twelve principles of the Agile Manifesto [15]. Boehm provided similar definition as he considered that a truly Agile method must include all of the previous attributes [7].

2.1   The Author's View

The previous reviews and discussions were essential to form our understanding of Agile methods. In this subsection, we will illustrate our understanding by providing our definition of an Agile method. In other words, what makes a development method Agile. An Agile method is adaptive, iterative and incremental, and people oriented

- **Adaptive:** An Agile method welcomes change, in technology and requirements, even to the point of changing the method itself [16]. In addition, it responds to feedback about previous work [22]. Fowler stated that an adaptive process is the one that can give control over unpredictability.
- **Iterative and incremental:** The software is developed in several iterations, each from planning to delivery. In each iteration part of the system is developed, tested, and improved while a new part is being developed. In each iteration, the functionality will be improved. In addition, the system is growing incrementally as new functionality is added with each release. After each iteration (s), a release will be delivered to the customer in order to get feedback.
- **People-oriented:** "People are more important than any process. Good people with a good process will outperform good people with no process every time [8]. In an Agile method, people are the primary drivers of project success [13]. Therefore, the

role of the process in an Agile method is to support the development team determine the best way to handle work [16]. Furthermore, an Agile method emphasises on face-to-face communication within the team and with the customer who is closely involve with the development process rather than written documents.

To summarize: Software development is an unpredictable activity; therefore, we need an adaptive process to control this unpredictability. Iterative and incremental development will be the best controller for this process. In addition, it needs creative and talented people.

3 What Was Behind Agile Methods

Some interesting questions are:

What was behind Agile methods?
Where Agile methods were introduced?
What are the origins of Agile thinking?

We will answer these questions through three points: reaction to traditional methods and business change, reusing ideas from history, and people's experience. Then we will go through each Agile principle to see which one are new and which are not with evidence.

3.1 Reaction to Traditional Approaches and Business Change

Although iterative and incremental approaches were in use a long time ago, unfortunately, many sources still recommend the single pass software development lifecycle which known as the waterfall. However, researchers recognized the problem with the waterfall and suggested another approaches such as the V-Model [9], the Spiral model [6] and then the Rational Unified Process (RUP) [8]. These approaches tried to solve the waterfall problems but they are still heavyweight, document and plan driven approaches. Fowler refers to these approaches as engineering methodologies which may work perfectly for building a bridge but not for building software, as building software is a different kind of activity and it needs a different process [16]. Agile Methods are a reaction to the bureaucracy of the engineering methodologies. Another reason behind Agile methods is the increasing change in the business environment. According to Highsmith and Cockburn, Agile methods were proposed from a "perspective that mirror today's turbulent business and technology change" [13]. The traditional approaches could not cope with this change as they assume that it is possible to anticipate a complete set of the requirements early in the project lifecycle. In reality, most changes in requirements and technology occur within a project's life span.

3.2 Reusing Ideas from History

Many Agile ideas are hardly new. Furthermore, as the following paragraphs show many people believed long age that this is the most successful way of building software. However, these ideas have not been treated seriously, and in addition, presenting them as an approach for developing software is new [16, 22].

Iterative and incremental development is at the top of our list. When we defined an Agile methods we considered IID the heart of any Agile method. People were using these approaches successfully in the 70s and the 80s. Larman and Basili found early roots for (IID) iterative and incremental development since 1950s in NASA and IBM Federal Systems Divisions (FSD) [21]. According to them, NASA's 1961-63 Project Mercury was run with "short half-day iterations". In addition, the Extreme Programming practice of test-first development was applied as tests were planned and written and then the code were written to pass the tests. Furthermore, they use continuous integration as each mini-iteration required integration of all code and passing of the tests.

In 1970, Winston Royce who criticised the sequential model, recommended "five additional features that must be added to the basic approach to eliminate most of the development risks" [29]. These steps had the favour of iterative development. In step two, he recommended an early development pilot model for a 30-month project. This model might be scheduled for 10 months. In addition, in step five, he stated that the customer should be formally involved and he/she have to commit himself/herself at earlier points before the final delivery.

In their famous paper "Iterative and Incremental Development: A Brief History", Larman and Basili described a number of projects were iterative and incremental approaches were in use. These projects were major, government, life-critical systems, involving large numbers of people. In addition, most of the projects used a combination of top down concepts and incremental development. The projects used different iterations' lengths, which were longer than the range recommended by today's iterative methods.

People who criticised the waterfall suggested alternative approaches. In his paper "Stop the life-Cycle, I Want to get off", Gladden suggested a new view of the development process and he called it the Non-Cyclical Hollywood Model. According to Gladden, this model satisfies three propositions [18]:

System objectives are more important than system requirements: this meets the Agile idea of having a general understanding of the system rather than having detailed requirements which will change over the project

- A physical object conveys more information than a written specification: this is noted as the Agile manifesto values: Working software over Comprehensive documentation.
- System objectives plus physical demonstrations will result in a successful product: by successful project he meant that a product that performs the function intended and satisfies the customer's need.

Gladden believed that most users do not have a clear idea about their needs. In addition, he raised the problem of missing and changing requirements.

Another suggestion was from McCracken and Jackson in their paper "Life Cycle Concept Considered Harmful". They suggested two scenarios of system development processes [25]:

Prototyping: They suggested building a prototype extremely early in the development process as a response to the early statements of the user. A series of prototypes or a series of modifications to the first prototype will gradually lead to the final product. This is exactly how development in Agile is meant to be, with short iterations each of which improves the system. In addition, they recommended a close relation with the user: "development proceeds step-by-step with the user, as insight into the user's own environment and needs is accumulated".

The second suggestion was a process of system development done by the end-user and analyst in this sequence: implement, design, specify, redesign, re-implement. Again, to start with implementing the system is the idea of modern iterative development. In addition, they suggested providing the user with an implementing tool and one version of a system. It is a similar idea of the CASE tools, which were used in Rapid Application Development (RAD) the early version on DSDM.

Agile ideas appeared in old development processes as well. In 1985, Tom Gilb wrote "Evolutionary Delivery versus the 'Waterfall model'". In this paper Gilb introduce the EVO method as an alternative of the waterfall which he considered as "unrealistic and dangerous to the primary objectives of any software project".

Gilb based EVO on three simple principles [17]:

- Deliver something to the real end-user
- Measure the added-value to the user in all critical dimensions
- Adjust both design and objectives based on observed realities.

In addition, Gilb introduced his "personal list" of eight critical concepts that explain his method. When he discussed the early frequent iteration, he emphasised the concept of selecting the "potential steps with the highest user-value to development–cost ratio for earliest implementation" [17]. Another important concept in EVO method is "Complete analysis, design and test in each step" where he stated that the waterfall is one of the great time wasters with too many unknowns, too much dynamic change and systems complexity. Gilb stressed being user oriented:

"With evolutionary delivery the situation is changed. The developer is specifically charged with listening to the user reactions early and often. The user can play a direct role in the development process"

And being results oriented, not process oriented,

"Evolutionary delivery forces the developers to get outside of the building process for a moment, frequently and early – and find out whether their ship is navigating towards that port of call many cycles of delivery away"

Obviously, many of Gilb's concepts meet Agile principles. Not only the frequent delivery and the short iterations, but also he stressed the user role in the development process. In addition, he recommended an adaptive process and he gave the developers the power to change the direction of the process.

After Gilb's EVO, in 1988, the DuPont Company presented a methodology called Rapid Iterative Production Prototyping (RIPP). The main goal was to build working prototypes that could be presented to customers regularly to ensure that the finished product is what they wanted. The company guaranteed "Software in 90 days... or your money back" [3].

James Martin expanded this methodology into a large formalized one which became the Rapid Application Development (RAD). The RAD lifecycle has four phases: requirements planning, user design, construction and implementation (Martin 1991). What distinguishes RAD from traditional lifecycles is that in RAD construction phase we do the detailed design and code generation of one transaction after another. Each transaction can be shown to the end users to make adjustments. In addition, the "timebox" applies to the construction phase. The team will be given a fixed timebox within which the system must be constructed. The timebox inputs are the functions and the design framework of the system. The output is the system which will be evaluated to decide whether to put it in production or not. Within the timebox, "continuous iterative development is done" in order to produce a working system by the end of the timebox [24]. Martin recommended 60 days length for the timebox, with a 1-5 person team. The term "timebox" was created by Scott Shultz and was first used in DuPont. Shultz stated that the timebox methodology was successful as all the applications were complete in less time than it would have taken just to write the specification for a COBOL or FORTRAN application [24].

We can see that RAD has almost all Agile ideas. Actually, it formed the base for DSDM, one of the Agile methods [34]. RAD recommended quick delivery, iterative development, a small team of highly trained developers who work together at high speed, and user's involvement at every stage. Clearly, these ideas are the heart of Agile methods. However, the term "timebox" is used differently in Agile. In RAD, it is the whole construction phase and it consists of many iterations, where in Agile the timebox means a fixed iteration. In a fixed iteration, if the requests of the iteration can't be met within the timebox, the scope will be reduced [34,22].

3.3 People's Experience

As has been already mentioned, the manifesto gathered people who needed an alternative to traditional approaches. Importantly, most people involved in the manifesto had experience in software development. Furthermore, they had their own well-defined methods such as Extreme Programming (XP), Crystal and Scrum.

Ken Schwaber, one developers of Scrum, described his experience in the early 1990s when he was running a software company. He mentioned that their requirements were always changing and their customer's methodology did not help, instead it slowed them down. In order to solve the problem, he showed these methodologies to process theory experts at the DuPont Experimental station in 1995. He stated that they were amazed that his company was using an inappropriate process. In addition, they said that systems development had so much complexity and unpredictability that it had to be managed by an "empirical" process control model [32]. Ken's company and other organizations asked another question, which is why empirical development approaches deliver productivity while defined processes such as Capability Maturity Model (CMM) do not. They passed the question to scientists at DuPont Chemical's Advanced Research facility, and the answer was that CMM is treated as a well-understood defined process while it is not, and it is performed without control and therefore it gives unpredictable results [31].

Kent Beck, founder of XP, also had a story. In April 1996, he was hired to help Chrysler, a payroll system. The project was in a state where two months away from production, the development team were not "computing the right answers yet". With the CIO of Chrysler, they decided to start from scratch with a smaller team. With Ron Jeffries, who became the first XP coach, and with the help of Martin Flower with analysis and testing, the first XP project took off. They worked on the base of three weeks iteration, where they implemented stories chosen by the domain expert. In April 1997, the system was live, and it was resalable, cheap and easy to maintain and extend. Beck stated "it was a technical and business success" [4].

Another story is from Alistair Cockburn, one of the Agile Manifesto authors. In 1991, IBM Consulting Group asked him to write a methodology for object-technology projects [12]. He decided to interview the project teams. He found out that their stories were different from what was mentioned in methodologies books. He found that "close communication, morale, and access to end users separated in stark contrast the successful projects [he] visited from the failing ones". Cockburn tried these ideas on a $15 million, fixed-price, and fixed-scope project of forty-five people. He was the lead consultant of the project and he wrote up the lessons learned from the project interviews, and from the project itself. Using these ideas, Cockburn built his Agile method Crystal. Interestingly, unlike most of other authors of the manifesto he stated that he came to Agile principles "through the need for efficiency, not the need to handle rapidly changing requirements".

3.4 What's New (and Not) About Agile Methods

In this section we will go through each Agile principle, and we will try to find the roots of this principle. We will see this section will support our previous argument. This will be illustrated in the next table.

Principle	New or not with Evidence
Our highest priority is to satisfy the customer through early and continuous delivery of valuable software.	EVO first principle: deliver something to the real end-user [17].
Welcome changing requirements, even late in development. Agile processes harness change for the customer's competitive advantage.	Relatively new, the problem always existed but without a real solution.
Deliver working software frequently, from a couple of weeks to a couple of months, with a preference to the shorter timescale.	In EVO the frequent and early delivery is essential, also RAD recommended quick delivery [17, 24].
Business people and developers must work together daily throughout the project.	Relatively new as some approaches recommended good relation with customer, however, the idea of daily communication and on-site customer is new.
Build projects around motivated individuals. Give them the environment and support they need, and trust them to get the job done.	These ideas were raised in the psychology of computer programming book which was published in 1985; the author empathized on the importance of motivation which is the inner directing force (chp10). In addition, he mentioned that the richness of the environment gives it a self–maintaining quality which resists the imposed changes.(chp4) [37].
The most efficient and effective method of conveying information to and within a development team is face-to-face conversation.	The previous book focused on the importance of how the working space can affects the social interaction which in turn will affect the work. The author emphasized on how face to face communication helps transmitting useful information [37].
Working software is the primary measure of progress.	EVO second principle: measure the added-value to the user in all criteria dimensions [17].

Agile processes promote sustainable development. The sponsors, developers, and users should be able to maintain a constant pace indefinitely.	In the Death March book, Edward Yourdon pointed the importance of managing and controlling progress and he suggested the "daily build" concept to succeed that mission [39].
Continuous attention to technical excellence and good design enhances agility.	Probably we could find the same idea of the importance of doing a much better programming job (technical excellence) in Dijkstra's famous article "Humble programmer" [40].
Simplicity the art of maximizing the amount of work not done--is essential.	The famous saying on simplicity of design comes from Antione de Saint-Exupery: "Perfection is achieved, not when there is nothing more to add, but when there is nothing left to take away" [30].
The best architectures, requirements, and designs emerge from self-organizing teams.	We could find the idea of self-organizing team in open source projects which were out roughly at the same time as Agile methods. In the Cathedral and the Bazaar paper, Raymond referred to the developers as people bring their own resources to the table [28].
At regular intervals, the team reflects on how to become more effective, then tunes and adjusts its behaviour accordingly.	The idea of process improvements was presented in CMMI level 5 with different emphasize as in Agile all the team will reflect on improving the process not only the management [36].

4 Discussion and Conclusion

Although Agile methods are new as a whole, their principles and ideas have been around long time ago, and people who criticized the traditional methods suggested alternative approaches which were nothing but Agile ideas. Unfortunately these alternative approaches had not been treated seriously enough. For example Somerville first edition of the software engineering book describes "The Software Lifecycle". At this point the word "waterfall" was not yet in common use: if you assume there is only one lifecycle, you do not need to give it a name. By the time edition 1989 Sommerville states that "one of the reasons for the wide spread adoption of the 'waterfall' model is that it allows for the straight-forward definition of milestones throughout the course of a project. Alternative approaches, such as evolutionary prototyping, are such that milestone definition is a more difficult and less certain process". Even in the most recent edition (the 8th in 2007) Sommerville devotes just one chapter (chapter 17) out of 32 to "rapid" software development. In this chapter it is claimed that "dissatisfaction with these heavyweight approaches led a number of software developers in the 1990s to propose new agile methods" [43]. In this paper we provided historical and anecdotal evidence that a) dissatisfaction with heavyweight approaches existed long before the 1990s, b) non-waterfall projects succeeded as early as 1957 and c) viable alternatives such as EVO, RAD and RIPP had been developed and applied successfully in the 1980s.

We hope that the strong emerge of Agile methods and the pressing need for such development methods these days will convince the software development community that this is the right way to develop software. In addition, we think that the education about Agile thinking history will help understanding as well as promoting the use of Agile methods.

References

1. Abrahamsson, P., Solo, O., Ronkainen, J., Warsta, J.: Agile Software Debvelopment Methods, VTT technical Research Centre of Finland (2002)
2. Ambler, S.: Quality in an Agile World. Software Quality Professional 7(4), 34–40 (2005)
3. Ambrosio, J.: Software in 90 days Software Magazine. Wiesner Publications, Inc. (1988)
4. Beck, K., Andres, C.: Extreme Programming Explained: Embrace Change, 2nd edn. Addison-Wesley Professional, Reading (2004)
5. Boehm, B.: Guidelines for Verifying and Validating Software Requirements and Design Specifications. In: Samet, P.A. (ed.) Euro IFIP 1979, IFIP. North-Holland Publishing Company, Amsterdam (1979)
6. Boehm, B.: A spiral model of software development and enhancement. IEEE Computer 21(5), 61–72 (1988)
7. Boehm, B., Turner, R.: Balancing Agility and Discipline: A Guide for the Perplexed. Addison-Wesley Longman Publishing Co., Inc., Amsterdam (2003)
8. Booch, G.: Object Solutions: Managing the Object-Oriented Project. Addison Wesley Longman Publishing Co., Inc., Amsterdam (1995)
9. Coad, P., de Luca, J., Lefebvre, E.: Java Modeling Color with UML: Enterprise Components and Process with Cdrom. Prentice Hall PTR, Englewood Cliffs (1999)
10. Cockburn, A.: Characterizing People as Non-linear, First-Order Components in Software Development, Humans and Technology Technical Report (1999)
11. Cockburn, A.: Agile Software Development. Addison-Wesley Longman Publishing Co., Inc., Amsterdam (2002a)
12. Cockburn, A.: Crystal Clear A Human -Powered Methodology for Small Teams. Addison-Wesley, Reading (2005)
13. Cockburn, A., Highsmith, J.: Agile Software Development: The Business of Innovation. Computer 34(9), 120–127 (2001a)
14. Cockburn, A., Highsmith, J.: Agile Software Development: The People Factor. Computer 34(11), 131–133 (2001b)
15. Cohen, D., Lindvall, M., Costa, P.: An Introduction to Agile Methods. Advances in Computers, 1–66 (2004)
16. Fowler, M.: The New Methodology (2005), http://www.martinfowler.com
17. Gilb, T.: Evolutionary Delivery versus the "waterfall model". ACM SIGSOFT Software Engineering Notes 10(3), 49–61 (1985)
18. Gladden, G.R.: Stop the Life-cycle, I Want to Get off. 7(2), 35–39 (1982)
19. Highsmith, J.: Adaptive Software Development: a Collaborative Approach to Managing Complex Systems. Dorset House Publishing Co., Inc. (2000)
20. Highsmith, J.: Agile Software Development Ecosystems. Addison-Wesley Longman Publishing Co., Inc., Amsterdam (2002)
21. Larman, C., Basili, V.R.: Iterative and Incremental Development: A Brief History. IEEE Computer Society 36(6), 47–56 (2003)
22. Larman, C.: Agile and Iterative Development: A Manager's Guide. Alistair, C., Jim, H. (eds.). Pearson Education, Inc., London (2004)

23. Levine, L.: Reflections on Software Agility and Agile Methods, Software Engineering Institute, Carnegie Mellon University, Pittsburgh, PA, USA (2005)
24. Martin, J.: Rapid Application Development. Macmillan Publishing Co., Inc., Basingstoke (1991)
25. McCracken, D.D., Jackson, M.A.: Lifecycle Concept Considered Harmful, vol. 7, pp. 29–32. ACM Press, New York (1982)
26. Palmer, S.R., Felsing, M.: A Practical Guide to Feature-Driven Development. Pearson Education, London (2001)
27. Paulk, M.C.: Agile Methodologies and Process Discipline. CrossTalk- The Journal of defence Software Engineering, 15–18 (2002)
28. Raymond, E.S.: The Cathedral and the Bazaar (1999)
29. Royce, W.W.: Managing the Development of Large Software Systems 1970. In: Proceedings, IEEE WESCON, pp. 1–9 (1970)
30. Saint-Exupery, A.D.: Wind, Sand and Stars. Harcourt (1992)
31. Schwaber, K.: Controlled Chaos: Living on the Edge. Advanced Development Methods, Inc. (1996)
32. Schwaber, K., Beedle, M.: Agile Software Development with Scrum. Prentice Hall PTR, Englewood Cliffs (2001)
33. Sommerville, I.: Software Engineering (1st, 3rd, 8th) edn. Addison-Wesley, Reading (1972, 1989, 2007)
34. Stapleton, J.: DSDM: The Method in Practice. Addison-Wesley Longman Publishing Co., Inc., Amsterdam (1997)
35. Thomas, D.: The Essential Unified Process (EssUP) - New Life for the Unified Process Dr. Dobb's Portal: the Worlds of Software Development (2006)
36. Turner, R., Jain, A.: Agile Meets CMMI: Culture Clash or Common Cause? In: Wells, D., Williams, L. (eds.) XP 2002. LNCS, vol. 2418, pp. 153–165. Springer, Heidelberg (2002)
37. Weinberg, G.M.: The Psychology of Computer Programming, p. 304. John Wiley & Sons, Inc., Chichester (1985)
38. Williams, L.: A Survey of Agile Development Methodologies (2004)
39. Yourdon, E.: Death March: The Complete Software Developer's Guide to Surviving Mission Impossible Projects. Paul, D.B. (ed.), p. 227. Prentice Hall PTR, Englewood Cliffs (1997)
40. Dijkstra, E.W.: The humble programmer. Communication of the ACM 15(10), 859–866 (1972)

Seven Years of XP - 50 Customers, 100 Projects and 500 Programmers – Lessons Learnt and Ideas for Improvement

Mike Holcombe[*] and Chris Thomson

Department of Computer Science, University of Sheffield,
Portobello Street, Sheffield, S1 4DP, UK
m.holcombe@dcs.shef.ac.uk

Abstract. Over the last seven years we have been using eXtreme Programming (XP) in two commercial software development settings within the University of Sheffield. The detailed performance of a variety of different project teams has been analysed by the Sheffield Software Engineering Observatory - a joint research project between the Department of Computer Science and the Institute of Work Psychology - during this period, based on empirical data collected from these projects. A number of research questions have been investigated: the comparison between XP and a traditional software development approach in terms of product quality and the impact on quality of the number of XP practices used etc. Problems associated with some aspects of XP have been identified and adaptations and development of the XP methodology have been introduced. Other issues studied in the Observatory include the relationship between methodology and individual well being; the impact of personality on project outcomes; the level of conflict in different groups; the relationships between customers and programmers and issues relating to testing. The possible benefits of XP have been assessed alongside the problems with implementing the methodology in a variety of settings. 'People' issues are a major determinant in successfully adopting the XP approach in a sustainable way. This paper is a brief review of some of this work.

Keywords: XP, empirical software engineering, methodological compliance, human factors.

1 Introduction

The last 7 years or so have seen an explosion of interest in agile development methods and attempts by many software development organisations to adopt these ideas. However, there is little rigorous research data about the long term benefits or otherwise of the adoption of such techniques.

The Software Engineering Observatory at the University of Sheffield[1] exists to examine a variety of issues in modern software engineering practice in controlled conditions and in as a realistic a setting as possible. In order to achieve this we base this

---

[*] Also epiGenesys Ltd. <http://www.epigenesys.co.uk>
[1] http://www.observatory.group.shef.ac.uk

P. Abrahamsson et al. (Eds.): XP 2008, LNBIP 9, pp. 104–113, 2008.

work around a large number of commercial software development projects carried out in University companies. The Observatory is a collaboration between the Department of Computer Science and the Institute of Work Psychology in the University. This means that we can look at a wide number of aspects of software development particularly some associated with 'people' issues such as team cohesion, well-being, conflict and personality and how these factors may impact on software quality.

2 The Observatory Context

Over the last 20 years the curriculum in the Department of Computer Science has included a second year module called the Software Hut. This module, lasting for the whole of the second Semester, involves teams of students developing a software application for an external business client. The way that it is organised involves dividing the students into teams of between 4 and 6 individuals. There are a number of external clients and each client is involved with between 3 and 4 teams. These teams then compete to build a suitable solution for the client's needs and the client then chooses a preferred solution from those delivered and the winning team is rewarded with a small cash prize.

Twelve years ago a new initiative was undertaken, this involved the setting up of a commercial software house that was run by the fourth year undergraduates and the advanced masters students as part of their course. This company, Genesys Solutions has traded successfully during this period and has recently been spun out as a full University company (epiGenesys) with professional full time manager and technical staff, as well as the students who are working in the company as part of their studies.

In both of these activities students are required to spend around 15 hours per week over 12 weeks, in the case of Genesys this is throughout the two Semesters.

An interesting factor in these activities is that the population of students moves on after the end of their involvement – thus presenting us with the problem of both dealing with a major break in development work for those projects that extend beyond the end of the academic year and of maintenance on past projects produced by programmers who have since moved on. These issues focus a spotlight on the type and quality of the documentation that is produced during a project. Over the years this has seen the development of a number of developments in terms of the design approach, infrastructure, management and quality assurance mechanisms that we have developed.

In 2000 we started to use a version of XP. In Genesys XP was adopted as fully as we could and has been the fundamental approach taken for all projects. In the Software Hut we initially divided the class into two halves, one half was asked to use XP and the other the plan based approach using the Discovery methodology (A J H Simons, Object Discovery: A process for developing medium-sized applications, *Tutorial 14, ECOOP 1998 Tutorials*, (Brussels : AITO/ACM, 1998), 109pp). The projects were arranged so that each client worked with teams of the same level of experience, some teams using XP and the others the Discovery method and we were then able to compare the two approaches under realistic conditions to see which approach tended to be the most successful.

As well as the final product we are able to analyse all of the intermediate project material, minutes of meetings of the teams and of client meetings, timesheets, requirements and other documents, test sets, quality assurance reports, program code etc. We sample this material on a weekly basis [17]. This provides a rich resource of information that is unhindered by problems of commercial confidentiality.

A key factor that distinguishes this type of research from much of the available literature in empirical software engineering is that all the projects are *real* ones, have a real client, involve detailed business analysis as well as the delivery of working software and are thus a much better test for measuring the benefits and problems of a complete software engineering process. The fact that we can also run comparative experiments on *real* projects is probably a unique facility (previous studies have only assessed toy projects with professionals and students comparatively, often with a focus on only single XP practices [15, 16, 20].

In terms of the Genesys company we can study the adoption of agile approaches within a realistically operated software house – no comparative studies are carried out in Genesys since it is, essentially, a commercial operation with targets for earning and productivity.

One of the reasons why we adopted an agile methodology was the realization that the type of documentation available during maintenance was often misleading and unhelpful. Although a large amount of design documentation (UML diagrams etc.) was archived it rarely reflected the final state of the code since it wasn't always updated as implementation decisions were made after the initial design phase. This we began to question the purpose of all this documentation. The choice of XP as the agile approach was driven by a number of issues:

1. It was a complete package of techniques (practices) focused on the delivery of high quality software to meet the client's business needs;
2. The emphasis in XP on testing set it apart from another approaches – software testing had, for a long time, been a major research interest of the group.

The idea of using XP was very popular with most – but not all – students who had previously been fed a diet rich in UML and formal methods. The motivation to try to meet the client's requirements as they changed during the elicitation and analysis phases was also an attraction.

3 Problems Associated with Introducing XP

Although the reception of the main tenets of XP were enthusiastically received during the initial training is soon became apparent that it was a very hard methodology to adopt fully. Some aspects were quite easily done, for example the idea of describing requirements a set of stories – although there was some confusion about the size of a story. Iterations tended to be quite large initially until we managed to get enough experience to help the students think in terms of delivering chunks of code on a weekly basis. There was a general problem in that much of the early literature on XP was written for experienced programmers rather than novices. In particular, the emphasis on testing and refactoring was something that few students were prepared for. There was a severe shortage of a texts with real practical examples and advice that would allow students to adopt XP fully. Many of the books were rather theoretical, conceptual and philosophical treatments that did not provide the students with enough practical detail to help them progress.

Over the years we have studied a large number of XP projects and gathered a great deal of detailed data. Many conclusions can be drawn from this information, issues relating to how easy it is to adopt XP, what additional support is needed, how the XP approach compares with a traditional approach? What impact does the personality of individuals have? Does XP engender a more positive attitude to work, and so on? A number of papers discuss the detailed empirical approach, the data and its analysis, for example: 1, 2, 6, 9–14, 17-19, 24. One of the longer term aims of the Observatory project is to provide on-line access to much of this raw data for bona fide researchers – who may have to sign a Non-Disclosure Agreement to protect client confidentiality.

4   Adoption of and Compliance with the XP Methodology

Some of the practices associated with XP are enthusiastically adopted, these include using stories and small increments, continuous delivery as far as it is practical and extensive communication with customers – it is not practical for us to have on-site customers but teams will meet their customers weekly for much of the project. The reduction in design documentation is popular and many students are less than inspired by UML so that an extensive design period is usually counterproductive.

More problematic practices include test first and, for some, pair programming. The evidence from the research literature on pair programming is pretty inconclusive and controversial and rarely carried out under realistic conditions found in a real project. We have found that many students welcome the idea and, after some initial issues settle down well to pair programming – they gain a great deal an learn a lot by working intensively in pairs. Since our main objective is to provide a deep learning environment for students this is a positive aspect. Some students find it extremely hard to do, these are usually those with a particular type of personality – loners and highly introverted types.

Williams [20] presented some evidence for the benefits of pair programming. The approach has been criticised on blogs such as hacknot.info [21] and other experiments by other researchers [7] have produced different conclusions. In practice, pair programming is not for everyone since some people's personality is such that they seem to be unable to cope with the intense relationships with their partners that are needed. Our experience has been that, in the right context, that is, a real project with a real customer and combined with the other XP practices, pair programming works for most people – many of whom become very enthusiastic about it.

Test first has been something of a disaster. It is very rarely done properly, programmers find it very unnatural since they have never met the concept before and their attitudes are rather set from their first programming classes and it is difficult to overcome this. They are happy to write done outline tests at the time of writing their story cards but rarely actually write complete tests – let alone running them on empty code.

The evidence for the benefits of a Test First approach is also mixed. The first thing to say is that it is actually quite difficult to carry out – nearly all of the approaches to teaching introductory programming that are found in universities tend to downplay testing – if it is considered seriously at all. Thus many programmers find the idea of writing a test set before they start coding unnatural. This makes it difficult to carry out comparative experiments without having to undertake some extensive training on the technique.

Janzen [23] found that the design of the software was ‘better’ – smaller and less complex units whereas [22] found that the quality of the design was poorer. There are a number of other examples of inconclusive results e.g. [16].

One comment that is worth making is that the time that tests are written and used is only one of a number of factors that might impact on the benefits of doing Test First, another is the type of tests created – testing is very dependent on the capabilities of the test sets to detect faults and so influences the ultimate quality of the software under test. Simple measures such as test coverage can provide some insight into the quality and effectiveness of a test set but things are more complicated than that.

5 Areas Where XP Needs Strengthening and Supporting

There are a number of things that we have done to try to make the XP processes better. One of these is to focus much more on the architecture and dynamic modeling of the proposed system. We have tried to formalize and document certain aspects of the project in such a way that any document that has been introduced serves a multiple number of uses – in other words it must add value in more than one aspect of the project. An example of this is the stories – these are defined in a simple template which is shown below. Apart from the usual administrative information – story number etc. we have also included some information about what triggers the story – the background information tha it needs to operate correctly (for example data from a database or look-up table etc.) and what the expected results are of this story in operation. This data provides a basis for strong test design. On the reverse we put some more useful information including descriptions of the tests and any non-functional requirements.

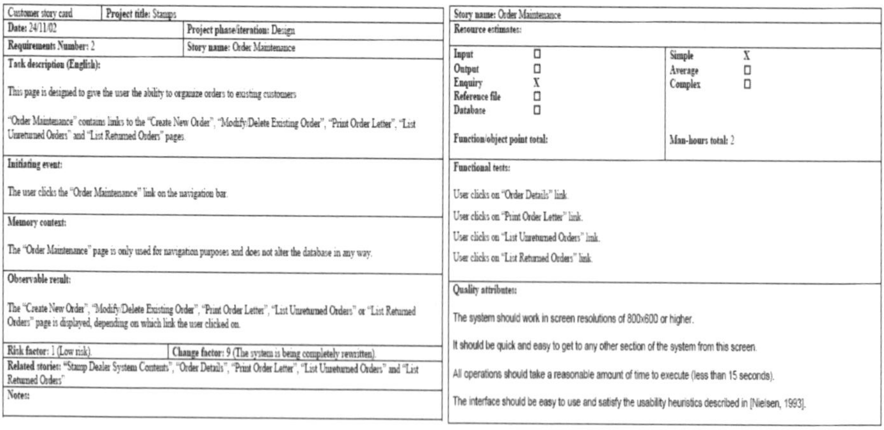

Customer story card	**Project title:** Stamps
Date: 24/11/02	**Project phase/iteration:** Design
Requirements Number: 2	**Story name:** Order Maintenance
Task description (English): This page is designed to give the user the ability to organize orders to existing customers “Order Maintenance” contains links to the “Create New Order”, “Modify/Delete Existing Order”, “Print Order Letter”, “List Unreturned Orders” and “List Returned Orders” pages.	
Initiating event: The user clicks the “Order Maintenance” link on the navigation bar.	
Memory context: The “Order Maintenance” page is only used for navigation purposes and does not alter the database in any way.	
Observable result: The “Create New Order”, “Modify/Delete Existing Order”, “Print Order Letter”, “List Unreturned Orders” or “List Returned Orders” page is displayed, depending on which link the user clicked on.	
Risk factor: 1 (Low risk).	**Change factor:** 9 (The system is being completely rewritten).
Related stories: “Stamp Dealer System Contents”, “Order Details”, “Print Order Letter”, “List Unreturned Orders” and “List Returned Orders”	
Notes:	

Story name: Order Maintenance	
Resource estimates:	
Input ☐ **Output** ☐ **Enquiry** X **Reference file** ☐ **Database** ☐ **Function/object point total:**	**Simple** X **Average** ☐ **Complex** ☐ **Man-hours total:** 2
Functional tests: User clicks on “Order Details” link. User clicks on “Print Order Letter” link. User clicks on “List Unreturned Orders” link. User clicks on “List Returned Orders” link.	
Quality attributes: The system should work in screen resolutions of 800x600 or higher. It should be quick and easy to get to any other section of the system from this screen. All operations should take a reasonable amount of time to execute (less than 15 seconds). The interface should be easy to use and satisfy the usability heuristics described in [Nielsen, 1993].	

Fig. 1. Story card examples from a system developed for a retail company

We also generate some operational descriptions using generalised state machine diagrams [18, 19].

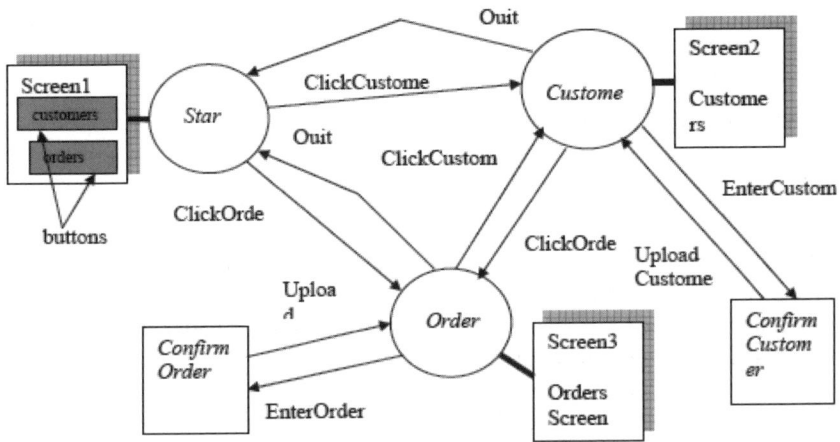

Fig. 2. An eXtreme X-machine (XXM) for a simple orders database

In this diagram the circles represent natural states of the systems – positions where certain functionality is possible and the squares are states where queries will be made in order to complete a process properly. Screens are also displayed where appropriate – these can often be very helpful when discussing the system with a customer. If necessary, the transitions can themselves be replaced by a more complex diagram detailing what is happening at a lower level of abstraction. Thus we have a genuine hierarchical way of describing complex systems which is very easy to understand and use.

Such diagrams will be used to help everyone understand what the overall objective of part of the system is, will be the basis for some analysis – for example, identifying what needs to be done to add suitable robustness to the system – in other words we will have to think through the machine design and ask ourselves – how could each transition fail and what should we do about it?

The diagrams can also be used to generate very powerful functional tests – one simple way is to ensure that every possible path through the machine is triggered at least once. These techniques have been very successful in our projects.

These are examples of how XP can be developed as an agile development approach by addressing those areas that are either not fully defined or could be improved. Further details will be available in [3, 4].

6 People and XP

There is again a problem in identifying conclusive and convincing evidence about the benefits of XP. Carrying out comparative experiments in an industrial setting is always going to be a problem and much of the evidence is based on simple experiments involving students.

Macias [6] found a small benefit in a comparative study involving small industrial projects. The quality of final software delivered was evaluated by the external clients using a systematic measurement process with a maximum value of 50 and Bayes theorem was applied to these data. The average of External quality was 34.95 then a team succeeded if Q > 34.95 and a team failed if Q <= 34.95. With this criteria the following probabilities were obtained:

- Probability that a successful team was XP: 0.5454
- Probability that a successful team was Trad: 0.4545
- Probability that a failing team was XP: 0.444
- Probability that a failing team was Trad: 0.555

This gives a measurable difference but not a significant one between the two treatments (XP and traditional design-led).

Abdullah [2] found that the more XP practices used the better the quality of the software, again in small industrial projects.

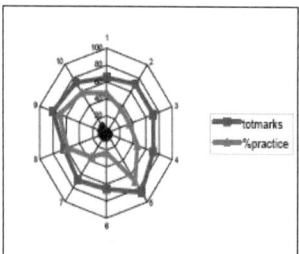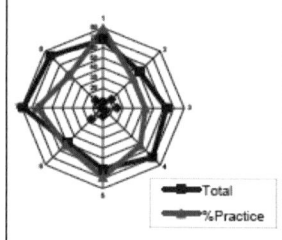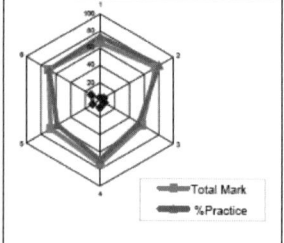

Fig. 3. Spider diagrams comparing product quality with the number of XP practices used over 3 years of projects

The marks were the evaluations of the products by the external clients, there were 7 different clients, 51 teams and 230 programmers in this series of experiments.

The line graphs (Fig. 4) reflect a constant relationship pattern between practices and external quality in all of the cases The Spearman test conducted revealed **a significant positive relationship** between the two variables [n=6, r=0.749, p = 0.086].

Abdullah also found [3] that there was evidence that teams using XP experienced a higher level of well-being than teams using a design-led approach involved in the same projects.

Thomson found that the link between changes as reported by developers and those made to the code was not strong for any teams whatever the method – suggesting that changes occur in the high level design not necessarily in volume – perhaps supporting the use of refactoring [17].

The research on the role of personality and XP performance and compliance has been taken further by Karn and Cowling [9-14]. This work has looked at conflict in teams, how conflicts were resolved, the amount of discussion and openness exhibited by individuals in teams etc. Personality characteristics were also examined using a standard personality test and some conclusions drawn from this about the sort of combinations of personalities that made good XP teams, [9]. Where there were problems it was often caused by developers having very different levels of experience and where the more experienced members resented helping the others. This was a major problem with some pair programming activities.

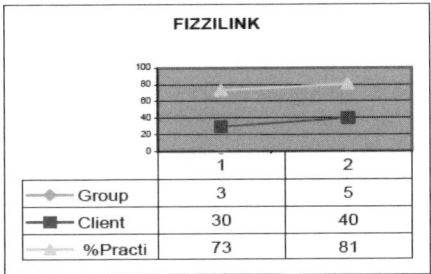

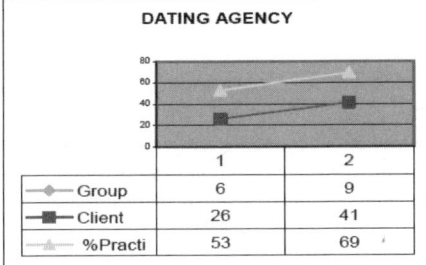
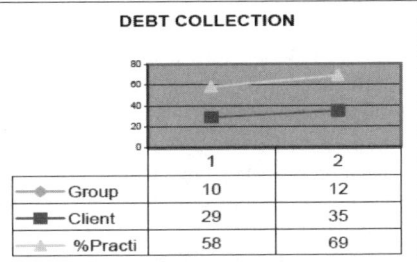

Fig. 4. The influence of the number of XP practices adopted and the quality of the final product taken from [24]

7   Conclusions

There has been a lot of research into whether agile developments actually deliver what is claimed. In particular some of the practices discussed above have been considered to see if they work. In many cases the detailed experiments involve students carrying out tasks in a laboratory setting. Unfortunately these experiments often lack credibility in the sense that it is not possible to generalise their finding to real industrial settings – in other words the results lack external validity. Secondly, by taking the individual practices and considering them in isolation from the other practices may also fail to provide evidence for the benefits of XP and other 'complete' agile methodologies.

Over the past seven years we have gained a lot of experience of using XP in real commercial development projects. In some cases we have been able to run comparative experiments – pitching XP against a design led approach; using test first against test last and so on. We have seen how personalities affect the outcomes of projects, what parts of XP don't work well without some extra development and how it is possible to run a company on an agile basis when the staff turnover is also extreme (everyone leaves together in June and new teams arrive in October!).

References

1. Syed-Abdullah, S., Holcombe, M., Gheorge, M.: Practice Makes Perfect. In: Marchesi, M., Succi, G. (eds.) XP 2003. LNCS, vol. 2675. Springer, Heidelberg (2003)
2. Syed-Abdullah, S., Holcombe, M., Gheorge, M.: The Impact of an Agile Methodology on the Well Being of Development Teams. Empirical Software Engineering 11(1), 143–167 (2006)
3. Holcombe, M., Thomson, C.: 20 Years of Teaching and 7 Years of Research: Research When You Teach SEEFM 2007 SEERC, Thessaloniki, Greece (2007)
4. Holcombe, M.: Running an Agile development Project. Wiley, Chichester (2008)
5. Janzen, D., Saiedian, H.: Test-driven development concepts, taxonomy, and future direction. Computer 38, 43–50 (2005)
6. Macías, F., Holcombe, M., Gheorghe, M.: A Formal Experiment Comparing Extreme Programming with Traditional Software Construction. In: The Proceedings of the Fourth Mexican International Conference on Computer Science (ENC 2003), Tlaxcala, México, September 8-12, 2003, pp. 73–80 (2003)
7. Nawrocki, J., Wojciechowski, A.: European Software Control and Metrics (Escom), (2001),
   http://www2.umassd.edu/SWPI/xp/pairprogramming/Nawrocki.pdf
8. Williams, L., Kessler, R.R., Cunningham, W., Jeffries, R.: Strengthening the case for pair programming. IEEE Software 17, 19–25 (2000)
9. Karn, J.S., Cowling, A.J.: An Initial Observational Study of the Effects of Personality Type on Software Engineering Teams. In: The Proceedings of the 8th International Conference on Empirical Assessment in Software Engineering (EASE 2004), Edinburgh, pp. 155–165 (2004)
10. Karn, J.S., Cowling, A.J.: A Study into the Effect of Disruptions on the Performance of Software Engineering Teams. In: The Proceedings of the 4th International Symposium on Empirical Software Engineering (ISESE 2005), Noosaheads, Australia, November 17-18, 2005, pp. 417–427 (2005)
11. Karn, J.S., Cowling, A.J.: Using Ethnographic Methods to Carry Out Human Factors Research in Software Engineering. In: The Proceedings of the Measuring Behavior, Wageningen, Holland, pp. 505–508 (2005)
12. Karn, J.S., Cowling, A.J.: A Follow Up Study of the Effect of Disruptions on the Performance of Software Engineering Teams. In: Proceedings of the 5th International Symposium on Empirical Software Engineering (ISESE 2006), Rio de Janeiro, September 21-22 (2006)
13. Karn, J.S., Cowling, A.J.: Using Ethnographic Methods to Carry Out Human Factors Research in Software Engineering. Journal of Behavior Research Methods (in press)
14. Karn, J.S., Cowling, A.J., Holcombe, M., Syed-Abdullah, S., Gheorghe, M.: The Positive Effect of the XP Methodology. In: Baumeister, H., Marchesi, M., Holcombe, M. (eds.) XP 2005. LNCS, vol. 3556, pp. 218–222. Springer, Heidelberg (2005)
15. Muller, M., Tichy, W.: Case study: extreme programming in a university environment. In: Software Engineering, ICSE 2001. Proceedings of the 23rd International Conference (2001)
16. Muller, M., Hagner, O.: Experiment about test-first programming. Software, IEE Proceedings- [see also Software Engineering, IEE Proceedings] 149, 131–136 (2002)
17. Thomson, C.: Defining and Describing Change Events in Software Development Projects, PhD Thesis, University of Sheffield, UK (2007)

18. Thomson, C., Holcombe, M.: Applying XP ideas formally: The story card and extreme X-machines. In: Drandis, D., Tigka, K. (eds.) 1st South-East European Workshop on Formal Methods, pp. 57–71. South-East European Research Centre, Thessaloniki, Greece (2003)
19. Thomson, C., Holcombe, M.: Using a formal method to model software design in XP projects. Annals of Mathematics, Computing and Teleinformatics 1(3) (2006)
20. Williams, L., Kessler, R.R., Cunningham, W., Jeffries, R.: Strengthening the case for pair programming. IEEE Software 17, 19–25 (2000)
21. [hacknot2004] http://www.hacknot.info/hacknot/action/showEntry?eid=50 (18/12/07)
22. Siniaalto, M., Abrahamsson, P.: Does test-driven development improve program code? Alarming results from a comparative case study. In: CEE-SET 2007, the Central and East-European Conference on Software Engineering Techniques (2007)
23. Janzen, D.: An Empirical Evaluation of the Impact of Test-Driven Development on Software Quality. Thesis, University of Kansas (2006)
24. Syed-Abdullah, S.L.: Empirical study of Extreme Programming. PhD thesis, University of Sheffield (2005)

Applying XP to an Agile–Inexperienced Software Development Team

Liana Silva, Célio Santana, Fernando Rocha, Maíra Paschoalino, Gabriel Falconieri, Lúcio Ribeiro, Renata Medeiros, Sérgio Soares, and Cristine Gusmão

Department of Computing and Systems – University of Pernambuco
R. Benfica, n. 455 – 50.720-001 – Recife – PE – Brazil
{lsos,cas,fafr,mpf,grff,lr,rwm,sergio,cristine}@dsc.upe.br
http://www.dsc.upe.br

Abstract. Agile Methods are becoming each day a more and more frequently used alternative among software developing organizations producing high-quality products in real-world projects. Despite this growth in industry, few academic institutions provide courses related to this new software development approach. This paper describes an initiative of introducing agile method concepts through a Master's Degree course where the students had not experienced XP before. In spite of being MSc students they had previous software development background in industry environment. In this work we present how the issues found over the process may and have been handled as well as the benefits found; how the XP practices have been adapted and applied in a project with time, personnel, and skill constraints and what hindered some principles from being fully effective. We also present real results and open problems for further studies from this experience. The study used a real-life application taken from a need of a real software development company.

Keywords: Agile Methods, XP-Inexperienced, Adaptation, Teaching.

1 Introduction

In the last years, Agile Software Development has been successfully adopted by Companies in different market segments like Airlines Companies [1], Banking [2] and Railways [3], Universities [4,5], Research Institutes [6,7,8], and Government Agencies [9]. Many agile methods like Scrum [10], XP [11], Crystal [12], and Lean [13] are now used in worldwide organizations.

However, most of the undergraduate, graduate, and post-graduate courses still use traditional methods to teach software engineering. Usually, the software engineering courses are based on tools, heavy documentation, follow a previous plan, and use waterfall-based lifecycles when one project is assigned to the students.

There are many worldwide initiatives using Extreme Programming as the main approach in academic courses that show the students how agile methods work. We can find these initiatives in several countries, like in Brazil [5], Germany [4], New Zealand [14], and USA [15]. Academic initiatives to evaluate new methods and techniques are very important, since experimentation in industrial environment is extremely expensive, and therefore, more difficult.

P. Abrahamsson et al. (Eds.): XP 2008, LNBIP 9, pp. 114–126, 2008.

Following this line, a Software Engineering course in a Master's program has been oriented to perform agile software development approach. The course consisted in working on a project employing the agile practices as much as possible to develop a real-life application. It is important to mention that despite being Master's students at the moment, the team came from the software development industry, which implies in experienced software developers, but with no experience in agile techniques.

The proposal context is a real software development project where agile practices were introduced to the developers in theoretical classes of a Software Engineering course. The results also show lessons learned from this process. Besides this introduction section, there are six other sections. Section 2 shows how the course has been organized, what project has been chosen, and how it was planned to be executed. Section 3 explains how the restrictions have influenced throughout the development and outcome of the project. The XP practices that have been used and how these practices have been adjusted to the project are presented in Section 4. The problems occurred during the development and what was the impact on the process and the results achieved are indicated in Section 5. Section 6 aims to present the lessons learned from the whole project and the course. Finally, Section 7 brings the conclusions of this work.

2   The Study Context

This section shows how the MSc course has been organized, the project that has been chosen, and the execution planning.

2.1   Methodology

The course had two goals: the first was to introduce the concepts of agile software development to the students using Extreme Programming as a method to conduct a project. Working on a real-life application development using agile practices as much as possible can provide more realistic information than performing a theoretical study. The second goal consists in evaluating if a team having few experience in agile techniques could apply some of them in a real project.

To reach the goals mentioned above, the study was conducted in two phases. The first definition was to analyze the course with the purpose of teaching in the context of M.Sc. students. At the end of the course the students would prepare a workshop to discuss the final results.

The second definition was to analyze the course with the purpose of evaluating the effectiveness of the experience from the faculties' point of view. This particular result should be used as data to improve the course for the next semesters.

2.2   The Course

The course lasted one semester and contained a total of 60 hours of classes, distributed in 4 hours a week. It was divided in two parts. The first one, which lasted about 12 hours, was supposed to present the main points of agile methodologies by reading specific papers and discussing them. The second part, which was supposed to last about 48 hours, was dedicated to apply the agile practices to the software development, based on what the students have learned on the previous classes. However, as the students worked from home, more than 48 hours were employed to do the job.

On the first 12 hours the course provided fundamentals of Agile Software Development and the students had to present workshops about them. These workshops were used to train the students on the following techniques: XP [11], Scrum [10], Test Driven Development (TDD) [16] and Refactoring [17]. After the workshops were presented, the students chose one real-life application and Extreme Programming as a methodology to develop the system that would solve it.

The next phase was dedicated to the project development, which is more detailed in the next section. At the end of the project, the students presented a workshop showing the status and conclusions of the project, pointing out problems, enhancing the lesson learned, constraints and, last but not least, the positive aspects of the project.

2.3 The Project

The project consisted in developing a system to automate tests cases generation from use cases entries on a web environment. The software requirements were given by a real software development company that had the need for such a tool, but no resources to develop it. The main goal of it was to save time on creating test cases. As advantage, the tests personnel could be assigned to other tasks like increasing test coverage, for example.

The development was divided into components, which represent use cases as follows:

- Project record: responsible to keep the project registration;
- Requirement record: responsible to keep the project requirements;
- Actor record: responsible for the actors registration of each use case in the system;
- Field record: responsible for the I/O fields registration of each use case;
- General flow record: responsible for general flow registration that may be applied to many use cases;
- Use case record: most important functionality of the system, where all the other previous modules are related. It is responsible to keep the use case registration of each project;
- Test case generation: responsible for the automatic test cases generation from the selection of use cases.

The project development lasted three months and was divided into a planning phase and five iterations according to the schedule described on Table 1.

Table 1. Macro Schedule

Planning	23/Aug/07 to 30/Aug/07
Iteration 01	04/Sep/07 to 13/Sep/07
Iteration 02	18/Sep/07 to 04/Oct/07
Iteration 03	09/Oct/07 to 25/Oct/07
Iteration 04	30/Oct/07 to 15/Nov/07
Iteration 05 (Final)	20/Nov/07 to 29/Nov/07

The planning took three classes (6 hours) to be completed and defined roles, scope of the project, estimation of how long the iterations would last, practices to be used, deadlines, technology, and the writing of the first stories was performed, defining the main stories and the planning of the first iteration.

The first iteration was shorter than the others with two weeks because it was used to provide background information to the members who had little knowledge about the technology. This iteration was also used for one of the programming pairs to try coding some stories and provide background knowledge about the possible problems and the size of the project, and also fix few technology issues.

The iterations 2, 3 and 4 were used to code and plan the next iteration. At the end of each one, a release with valuable software was delivered.

The last iteration was supposed to cover some possible delays. Since the project had both scope and deadline set, some sort of safeness was supposed to be provided by this short iteration, if needed. This practice is known as "Slack" in [19].

The infrastructure used in the project was the university laboratories and free tools that were required. A configuration and a database server were created by the students and their services were available on the internet. The work in laboratories was not mandatory and the students could work remotely. The developed software was cutting-edge, using technologies as Java 1.5, JSP & Servlets, Eclipse, Ant, Subversion, MySql and Mantis.

2.4 The Team

The team was composed by seven students and two faculties. The students have been organized in three programming pairs and it was necessary to assign a special role for one student: the *Libero* [5] The Libero was supposed to support the programmers creating the product web screens and continuously test the releases that were being delivered, contributing to refactoring, improvements and representing the client since the student on this role worked in the company which actually demanded the software.

The faculties initially assumed the role of clients, but they were exchanged by real users of the system before the beginning of the project development and they assumed the chicken [10] role. The faculties were inexperienced in the practice of agile software development and, among the students, only one had more solid experiences with XP. This particular student volunteered to be the coach and tracker of the project, but since that the team was small and inexperienced in both technology and methodology, the team decided to keep him on the programming role and follow the project without coach, tracker, and specific tester roles.

The details of the project status were frequently posted at the project's wiki Page (http://engsw-mestrado-2007.pbwiki.com/). The documents are in Portuguese at the moment because this was the real communication channel used by the team on the project.

3 Project Constraints

Conventional practices usually focus on commercial environment where the work load is usually up until forty hours a week and sometimes more. In spite of some non-agile environments have attributes similar to agile ones, such as the work environment structured according to the project to be executed, the skilled team, customer and process to be handled, agile environments focus on team work where everyone may play different roles. The academic environment, where the project started at, stressed out some restrictions that directly influenced not only the project results, but the way to be and actually was executed as well. The most important constraints are explained as follows.

3.1 Development Environment

University laboratories were used for the pair programming as well as the domestic environment for the remote work. Using the university facilities were perhaps of the most dangerous constraint in the beginning of the project, since some privileges access and network securities were not in charge of the students.

3.2 Workload

It has been determined that the project should be worked on four hours a week, which is equivalent to the Software Engineering course defined working hours. This has been scheduled for the whole project (planning, coding, and testing – although testing has not been devoted much attention to). The fixed fourteen weeks, four hours a week actually would result in about 48 hours of work to complete the project, however, more work than these hours were delivered by the team.

3.3 Customer Involvement

The clients, initially represented by the Software Engineering faculties, were not present in every moment of the project. Thus, the rest of the team itself had been in charge of all project's rc-planning like: scope redefinition, deadlines, and costs. The final users here represented by two employees from a private IT company which could potentially be a client to use the system, have made the validation at the end of each iteration but they were not present on the project development either.

3.4 Leadership

The professors acted as project supervisors together with one of the members from the development team who had a more XP practical experience. Thus, there has definitely been no coach role developed by any one on this project.

3.5 Team

Most of the members of the team did not have full domain of the used technology for the project development and agile methods experience either. As this project did not take place in a corporative environment, it was not possible to hire skilled personnel for all necessary training. Thus, each member was responsible for his/her own required learning.

The number of people in the team was also restricted to seven, since that was all enrolled to the course. Other problem was the pairing. The pairs for the programming were set in a way that they could work together, even though one was a very skilled programmer and the other not so experienced.

The small number of students also brings to the team the issue of lack of roles. Some of them very important, like coach and trackers, could clearly have its absence noticed.

3.6 Tracking

Once again, since the team was not expert on the methodology, it was not possible to have a well defined tracking system for the project development training. This constraint has drawn some modifications on the original XP features which will be detailed on the next section.

4 XP Practices

Some of the agile practices have been successfully adopted and used throughout the project; while others were neglected due to some specific reason detailed below and still few remaining ones have only been partially used. Here are our findings:

- Pair Programming – This practice has been partially followed. In spite of initial planning has defined that the team was supposed to be divided in pairs as it should be, the practice has been corrupted. Two out of three pairs have decided to switch the programmer pair in some times of the iterations in a matter of sparing each other from getting tired or addicted to doing the work and perhaps not watching the activity or watching out for errors. That way, both of the workers could play the role of watching the programming and not just programming itself. The pairs have also remote and/or individually worked. Due to local infrastructure issues and restrictions explained on the previous section, all the members came to finding best to work individually in some days. It was needed to set the environment at their homes and work remotely; hence the pairs were working separately from each other. This practice has been adjusted according to the working pace of the project. Considering the project was not being done in industry and there were a lot of factors interfering on the pairs working together the whole time, it was known that this practice would be affected. However, the pairs communicated as much as possible when they were working remotely from home, which, stimulated to reach the objectives of the practice.
- Sustainable Pace – This practice consists on the team keeping a feasible working pace, enough to complete the projects with no delays. It has not been followed thoroughly though. The idea was to work on the project the defined hours of the classes in a week, which was four hours. One of the pairs has worked around fifteen hours a week during the last three iterations while the other two pairs have been idle on the same period though. On the previous weeks, the two mentioned pairs were working around six to eight hours a week. This discrepancy was due to the dependency between the stories. One pair was in charge of a story and another pair could not start another story until that first one is ready. The extreme long time to finish one story by the first pair and not let the work continue was because

the pair decided to remodel the whole code structure too on the same iteration and they had to integrate the changes. As there was no coach and the two faculties did not watch out for this hold up, the pace has been compromised. The team did not find itself in a muddle; it was rather stuck and idle, with no one to manage the situation and re-address activities. The team did what they thought it was best for their tasks on the iteration and did not worry about the others. It is known that in XP one may have more freedom on working regarding process, but that does not mean the people can do whatever they want to. This is another evidence of the inexperience of the team on the methodology.

- Refactoring – This practice is about remaking the code in order to improve it by removing redundancy, eliminating unused functionalities, adapting it to patterns or even trying to make the software work in an acceptable way. Refactoring throughout the entire project life-cycle saves time and increases quality [18]. Here, it was practiced in three iterations:
    o   On the second one to standardize the screens;
    o   On the third one to make the database stand for multi-connections and;
    o   On the one before the last one, to place the entities in the project pattern determined by this database change.

In fact, of course refactoring helped on the code perspective. It is known that this is not an only XP practice, but rather much of a general development good practice.

- Planning Game – A project starts with a short exploratory phase in which the customer expresses the requirements [5] and the development team helps creating stories to fulfill a release plan detailing which story should be implemented in each iteration. This practice has been partially accomplished. The requirements were defined by a real client, a company which had the need of implementing the system but did not have enough resource to do it.. So the team learned the requirements from the customer and created an idea. Then the planning began. The idea was broadcasted to all and the whole team participated on the creation of the stories which turned into iterations. The planning of each iteration was performed by the whole team. Each programming pair chose the stories to implement based on dependency between one another. On the Planning Game, a brainstorming happened so that the meaning of each story to be developed was clear. It was not possible to implement a tracking system to monitor the development of the stories because of the lack of experience of the team on the practice. The faculties did not become available for this. Even with the possibility to use methods such as Story Points or Pair-Hours [11], the team did not find itself in a homogeneous pace to work with desired production estimates.

- Stories – They work as use cases but are distinct from long requirements. They are more closely to user scenarios detailing only enough to build a reasonable low risk estimate, but not restricted to user interface implementation. This practice has been almost all accomplished. Stories were created during the Planning Game and well understood by the team. The stories together with one another are supposed to result on the system desired. One small detail that has been modified and probably did not influence in the job was that the stories have been kept in a wiki repository created by the team and not manipulated in story cards as recommended. That way, they were still pretty visible to all. Another interesting thing to be pointed out is that user stories may be used to create acceptance tests for using in the end of the development as checklist.

- Short Iterations – The development team is supposed to deliver small releases instead of big amounts of codes at a time. Whatever is planned to every iteration should be completed with the ones next to it. On the current project, this has been performed. The iterations lasted three weeks and all of them have generated functional software versions with new functionalities, even if they have not completely met the scope, they were delivered with observations to be followed on the next iteration. This was considered a good practice. The workers have a short deadline and are forced to be productive most of the time. In a traditional methodology development software process, the deadlines for the developers are too far and it is common to see them starting working on a pace and finishing working extra time. Here, with a tight date, it was necessary to watch the results at the end of each day and have a better and closer monitoring of their own activities, which helped on a more stable and smooth kind of a work.

- Face to face Communication – XP requires direct communication among all members and this may be a limitation. This has been partially used; only when everyone was at the same site (lab). As previously mentioned, a considerable part of the project has been developed remotely, hindering this practice from being effectively performed. The course schedule used to be twice a week and that was the time the students really had to attend the classes. They did not belong to the academic activities or board that made them stay at the university for longer time. Other Masters activities were usually performed by their local jobs, homes or whatsoever. However, the team did not face serious issues on communication. With all resources available such as instant messaging, email, mobile and Voip technology, the team was always communicating and exchanging information during the development. This would have been completely different if this project had been executed in industry. As the workers were supposed to be paid for working on a project like this, in industry, they would spend most of the hours of their days at the office working on it. Thus, face to face communication would definitely not be a problem.

- Collective Code Ownership – This topic indicates that the code created by a programming pair may be modified by any other pair. Or still that it is shared and owned by all. Everyone is able to edit it and see the changes made by others. But it still remains as a unique code. The project had its configuration management based on Subversion tool (SVN). Thus, the code was available to all the programmers. This actually helped the workers, in a way that if a pair had changed something in a specific class or whatever part of the code and tried to upload it through the tool to attach it to the rest of the code when some other worker had checked it out, a warning would pop up and let know somebody else is working on it. The changes may and probably will affect the code if that warning is ignored, since the other worker is currently working on the same code, so this practice must be taken a closer look.

- Coding Standards – It indicates that the developers must agree on a common set of rules enforcing how the system shall be coded. This turns the understanding easier and helps on producing a consistent code. Java was the chosen programming language for coding. Aside of that, the team did not gathered to discuss a common pattern. However, maybe for a regional reason when everyone is used to program in a way or maybe just luck, there was not any problem found regarding this issue and the coding was pretty homogeneous.

As the team was mostly inexperienced with the methodology, there was a strong desire to follow the XP practices rigorously. However, this was not possible and the team learned about the rule *"Fix XP When It Breaks"*, which was to adapt the practice trying to be developed to the project's restriction. The rules must follow until the team has changed them [18]. The team wanted to adapt to the changes and it is important to point out that, maybe, some adaptation may have gone to a different path from agility. For instance, the face to face communication is a great impact practice on the project and as it could not be followed, the workers adapted it to the way they thought it was best. And this might have been not agile, in spite of the communication has been kept or tried through other ways.

5   Achieved Results

On this section, the problems found throughout the project execution are described as well as the achieved results in the end of it and how they have been handled.

5.1   Problems

In the beginning of the course, the first iteration has been planned and then the first problem of the whole project was detected: the lack of infrastructure. The team did not have its own laboratory, sometimes needed to share the lab with other students and the environment configuration had some limitations and also took some time to be set every time that would use a different computer. Hence, this problem resulted in a schedule delay.

Another problem was the lack of knowledge in the development methodology. None of the professors had the necessary knowledge in the used methodology and this caused some management failures. Since the only person with some insight in XP could not assume the coach role, the project had no real management and this factor contributed to the project delay.

The lack of familiarity with the used technology on the development was another identified problem. Then, an inconsistent plan was resulted, since it was not possible to exactly determine the timing of each activity and this led to failures on the project chronogram. To minimize this difficulty, a whole iteration was needed to provide training on the technology. However many other serious failures emerged, for instance, in the beginning the team had little idea about the size and effort of the project and this led the team to break the sustainable pace to deliver the releases in time.

Still another problem found was the dependency among functionalities, which hindered some pairs from working simultaneously. Then, some pairs were not able to finish their tasks waiting for other pairs to finish a required functionality. Besides, the code needed refactoring for small fixes, to fix a problem in the user access on the application that was not identified at the beginning. This activity consumed one of the pairs a lot. Hence, the development needed to hold until the refactoring was finished.

The interaction between the programmers has been affected throughout the project, since not everyone was able to keep regular face-to-face meetings. The solution found when the geographic distance became an issue was having virtual meetings. This strategy was not fully effective because there was not enough infrastructure at the residence of the programmers to keep the iteration close to a real one. Often these virtual meetings were ineffective because the people who had knowledge about the problem were not available at the moment of these virtual meetings.

The course schedule used as time reserved to develop the Project – four weekly hours – was below the necessary for the desired scope and available schedule. In fact one project where both scope and deadlines are set, agile loses its main advantage, which is embracing changes.

Even with one of the pairs working about fifteen hours a week, which is almost four times more than the general available time, the team knew that the initial scope was not going to be reached at the end. Hence, the team decided to reduce the scope during the development process in order to be able to delivery some product in the end of the course.

Finally, the motivation of the team was strongly influenced by activities outside the project, as other courses from the Masters. Not everyone had full time available to the Masters course. This lack of motivation can be pointed as one of the main causes of the project failure. One particular factor that had considerably discouraged the team work was that after a heavy loaded iteration and concluded stories, the job was still behind schedule and there was still need of refactoring. Then, it was detected that the project would not successfully reach its end in time and the team needed to keep the work pace.

5.2 Results

Goldman [5] states that the best way to learn XP is putting it in practice in some active project. Hence, a Masters Course tries to teach their students this modern technology by letting them manage themselves in a development of a project. This forced the students to apply some XP activities, as defining stories based on the idea of the product, planning the development of each iteration and working with a metaphor or part of it in every release.

Even with the difficulties, some XP practices could be well handled and observed such as the pair programming, stories and the planning game. Considering that not everyone in the team had worked with the idea of programming in pair before, they had the opportunity to exchange experience between themselves in a beneficial way. At the end, all the programmers agreed that working in pairs was more productive. Unfortunately it was not possible to measure how much better the productivity has been improved, how good the mutual help was or how much of the bug finding happened when the pairs were working together because the entire development process was using this methodology.

The stories and the planning game were executed at the very beginning of the process. The stories were defined and the team decided who would integrate the release of that iteration. But what was most visible was that even with more than forty percent of the project already implemented (final of third iteration), everyone knew that it was not going to be possible to conclude the whole project with success in time. This reflects that everyone in team had knowledge about the entire project size and development.

In spite of the expectation to finish the project according to the scope and planned deadlines, the modules were not all fully developed. Test case generation, Field Record and part of Use Case Record modules have remained pendent. This scope reduction was caused by the lack of experience of the team in not previously realizing that the plan was way larger than what could possibly be accomplished in the defined schedule and size of the team.

The study conducted by the faculties finished inconclusive because other factors such as infrastructure and lack of technical knowledge would be a bias if they were not considered, once they had strong influence in the final result of the project.

6 Lessons Learned

Some lessons could be observed during the project development as follows:

- Infrastructure – One needs to be built before project starts. Kent Beck [11] says that some months before XP team starts a project, they need to create a reasonable environment so that the team can work with a good productivity pace. On this particular project, the poor infrastructure took precious hours of the process and has helped on not delivering the complete project in the end.
- Technical Skills – The technical skills of the team must be evaluated before planning the project. This issue was considered one of the main reasons for the team not to complete the project with success.
- Planning – The lack of experience of the team in the technology and in the methodology took to a mistaken planning at first. Also the lack of a tracker to estimate and measure productivity led to uncontrolled empiric means, which, though, did not avoid the delays on delivering stories, dependency in one another and consequently, an incomplete project delivery.
- Pair Programming – It may work better when the pairs have a nice understanding of the system and technology. It was shown to be more productive when a pair with its most experienced member watching and the less experienced one programming because every mistake used to be observed right away and instructed to correct it.
- Extreme Programming – Considering every listed difficulty, the methodology has shown to be very useful in three special aspects: the first one shall be the learning of the team who did not have previous knowledge in the practice and the learning process has been accelerated with the pair programming. The second aspect to be considered is the visibility that XP provided throughout the development, even with no traceability the team was aware of the delays. The last one is how close the stories were from one another as well as the system functionalities, and how the metaphor could leave abstraction and reach a lower level which was the stories.
- Course – The team has realized that even with all the drawbacks in using XP, its teaching exclusively inside the classroom with exposing lectures is not recommended as the best way to teach Software Engineering course focused on Agile Methods.

According to Goldman [5], the best way to understand how the method works is to work on a project as closest as possible from agility.

7 Conclusion

A new way of system development has been proposed with the rise of agile methodology. The idea to bring this knowledge to post-graduate students is important and reasonable and has been accomplished throughout a project that was proposed to be resolved using agile practices.

Due to some factors that came in the way during the course development, the project has not been entirely concluded in time and not every Extreme Programming practice has been able to be used by the team. The students then learned about *"Fix XP When It Breaks"* rule, where they changed agile practices that did not fit, adjusting them to the project's specifications.

However, there was a clever perception by every member of the staff that XP brings a different view with its practices and the experience has been considered a good and valid one to be adopted in other contexts as well. The particularities, differences from ordinary methods and limitations that characterize this methodology certainly seal agility rules and space in Software Engineering.

It has been considered of great value the feedback related to the course and that the teaching must continue considering observations and suggestions pointed out in this particular course. The experience of teaching Agile Methods is also considered important in this process and the learning process needs to be done differently from the conventional way with boards and students in a classroom everyday hearing how the practices work from the teachers and not living it themselves.

References

1. Gary, H.A.: Sabre takes extreme measures. Computer World (March 2004) (1995), `http://www.computerworld.com/softwaretopics/software/story/0,10801,91646,00.html`
2. Perguliano, B.: eXtreme Programming applied: a case in the private banking domain. In: Proceedings of OOP, Munich (2003), `http://www.quinary.com/pagine/downloads/files/Resources/OOP2003Paper.pdf`
3. Anderson, J., Bache, G., Sutton, P.: XP with acceptance-test driven development: A rewrite project for a resource optimization system. In: Marchesi, M., Succi, G. (eds.) XP 2003. LNCS, vol. 2675, pp. 180–188. Springer, Heidelberg (2003)
4. Miller, A.R.: Extreme Programming in a university project. In: Eckstein, J., Baumeister, H. (eds.) XP 2004. LNCS, vol. 3092, pp. 312–315. Springer, Heidelberg (2004)
5. Goldman, A., Kon, F., Silva, P.J.S.: Being Exteme in the ClassRoom: Experiences Teaching XP. Journal of the Brazilian Computer Society 10(2), 1–17 (2004)
6. Fuqua, A.M., Hammer, J.M.: Embracing change: An XP experience report. In: Marchesi, M., Succi, G. (eds.) XP 2003. LNCS, vol. 2675, pp. 298–306. Springer, Heidelberg (2003)
7. Manarro, K., Melis, M., Marchesi, M.: Empirical analysis on the satisfaction of it employees comparing xp practices with other software development methodologies. In: Marchesi, M., Succi, G. (eds.) XP 2003. LNCS, vol. 2675, pp. 166–174. Springer, Heidelberg (2003)

8. Pelrine, J.: Modelling infection scenarios – a fixed-price eXtreme programming success story. In: ACM OOPSLA Companion Proceedings, pp. 23–24. ACM Press, New York (2000)
9. Santana, C., Gusmão, C., Vasconcelos, A., Timóteo, A.: Implantação de um Processo de Estimativas de Tempo Utilizando Pontos por Estória em uma Instituição Pública. In: First Workshop on Rapid Application Development, Ninth Brazilian Symposium of Software Quality (2007)
10. Schwaber, K., Beedle, M.: Agile Software Development with SCRUM. Prentice-Hall, Englewood Cliffs (2001)
11. Beck, K.: Extreme Programming Explained – Embrace Change. Addison-Wesley, Reading (2000)
12. Cockburn, A.: Agile Software Development. Addison-Wesley, Reading (2002)
13. Poppendieck, M., Poppendieck, T.: Lean Software Development: An Agile Toolkit. Addison-Wesley, Reading (2003)
14. Mugridge, R., MacDonald, B., Roop, P., Tempero, E.: Five Challenges in Teaching XP. In: Marchesi, M., Succi, G. (eds.) XP 2003. LNCS, vol. 2675, pp. 1013–1021. Springer, Heidelberg (2003)
15. Kessler, R., Dykman, N.: Integrating traditional and agile processes in the classroom. In: Technical Symposium on Computer Science Education Proceedings of the 38th SIGCSE technical symposium on Computer science education, vol. 39(1), pp. 312–316 (2007)
16. Beck, K.: Test Driven Development by Example. Addison-Wesley, Reading (2002)
17. Fowler, M., Beck, K., Brant, J., Opdyke, W., Roberts, D.: Refactoring: Improving the Design of Existing Code. Addison-Wesley, Reading (1999)
18. Extreme Programming, http://www.extremeprogramming.org
19. Beck, K.: Extreme Programming Explained – Embrace Change, 2nd edn. Addison-Wesley, Reading (2004)

Investigating the Usefulness of Pair-Programming in a Mature Agile Team

Irina Diana Coman, Alberto Sillitti, and Giancarlo Succi

Free University of Bozen-Bolzano, Center for Applied Software Engineering,
Piazza Domenicani 3, 39100 Bolzano, Italy
{IrinaDiana.Coman,Alberto.Sillitti,Giancarlo.Succi}@unibz.it

Abstract. Pair-programming (PP) is one of the key practices of Agile Methods and there are various claims regarding its benefits. However, the empirical evidence to sustain these claims is insufficient, often coming from studies with students as participants. Moreover, the results are sometimes contradictory. Nevertheless, there are already mature agile teams that currently use PP, pairing on an "as needed" basis. We investigate the dynamics of the pairing process in a mature Agile team to understand when practitioners consider PP useful and to compare this with the claimed benefits of PP. In this paper we present the results of a 3 months study of PP in an Agile team of 16 developers.

Keywords: Pair-programming, PP, XP, Agile Methods.

1 Introduction

Pair-programming (PP) is a programming technique that requires two programmers to work together at solving a development task while sharing the monitor, the keyboard, and the mouse [9]. PP has received significant attention and interest, partially due to the increased adoption of eXtreme Programming (XP) [2], in which PP is one of the key practices.

There are many studies that investigate the potential benefits and pitfalls of pair-programming. The main claims are that PP improves productivity [6], [7], the quality of the solution [5], and job satisfaction [5]. Moreover, it reduces the time needed for task completion [3], [5], it is particularly useful in complex tasks [10], and it is useful for training [4]. A detailed review of the studies on PP is beyond the scope of this paper, but we refer to the work of Hulkko and Abrahamsson [4], which contains such a review for works on PP (excluding those focusing on educational aspects of PP) up to June 2004.

Nevertheless, the previously stated claims regarding PP are not supported by all empirical evidence. For instance, some studies have found that there is no significant difference between development time for XP groups working in pairs and working alone [7] or between quality for code produced by pairs and by solo programmers [4].

In this paper, we propose a new approach to understanding in what cases the pair programming is useful. We propose to study the occurrence of PP in teams that already have a vast experience with this practice and use it on an "as needed" basis. Thus, we can understand when skilled practitioners perceive PP useful.

P. Abrahamsson et al. (Eds.): XP 2008, LNBIP 9, pp. 127–136, 2008.

In this paper, we explore this approach by studying the occurrence of pair programming in a mature Agile team of 16 developers over approximately 3 months. We investigate whether PP occurs more in training situations and whether there are variations in the amount of PP during various iterations or parts of the iteration.

The paper is organized as follows: section 2 introduces the related work; section 3 and subsections present our study; sections 4 and 5 present and discuss the results; section 6 describes the limitation of our study; finally, section 7 draws the conclusion and introduces future work.

2   Related Work

Although there are many studies on PP, few of them report the amount of PP that takes place in a team. Hulkko and Abrahamsson [4] have monitored 4 projects (3 of them commercial) lasting 8 weeks each. The development teams considered were made of master students, research scientists, and practitioners. The developers had no previous experience with PP and the practice was not occurring entirely on an "as needed" basis.

The study in [4] reports that the percentage of PP is quite similar for the various projects during the first three iterations and showed different trends starting with the fourth iteration. Moreover, the effort spent in PP is the highest in the first iterations of the project and in the last iteration.

Hullko and Abramsson [4] also interviewed the members of the teams in order to find out the "rationale for pair-programming". They report that the developers considered PP most useful for learning and for solving complex tasks.

Cockburn and Williams present in [11] the results of the usage of PP in a web programming class at the University of Utah. They report that the students had minimal questions for the teaching staff and that a survey revealed that 74% of the students wrote "between my partner and me, we could figure everything out". Moreover, in their study, 84% of the students agreed that they learned faster and better because of always working with a partner.

McDowell et al. [12] present a study on approximately 600 students attending a university course. They report that the students that used PP scored better on programming assignments and had higher course completion rates. A comparison of the equal percentages of pairing and non-pairing students that attempted the class revealed higher scores in the final for the pairing students. Thus, they conclude that PP is useful for learning.

Williams et al. [13] present the results of a survey administered to professional software developers. Based on 30 responses, they report the average values for assimilation (12 days with pairing vs. 27 days without pairing) and for mentoring of new team members (26% of day with pairing vs. 37% of day without pairing).

3   The Study

The goal of our study is to investigate the way in which PP occurs in a mature Agile team to identify the cases when developers perceive it useful. We investigate the trends of PP in this team and the claim that PP is useful for knowledge transfer between developers. To this end, we collect data on the time spent by developers at their computer working alone and in pairs.

3.1 Environment

Our study takes place in a large Italian company (that prefers to remain anonymous). The study spanned a period of 84 days (approximately 3 months), out of which 59 working days. Initially, the team was composed of 14 developers but 2 more joined the team, at the beginning of the second month of our study.

The developers are all Italians with ages between 30 and 40 years. They all hold university degrees in computer-related areas and have from 10 to 15 years of programming experience.

The team works on several projects, mainly in C#. They are an Agile team, using a customized version of XP. In particular, they use weekly iterations, PP, user stories, and the test-first approach. They use PP on an "as needed" basis. The team has been using XP for more than two years previously to our study. The members of the team were not aware of the actual purpose of our study.

The working space of the team consists in an open space, where each member has her own personal space. Therefore, informal communication between the developers is easily possible.

3.2 Data

For our study, we collected data on all the activities of developers at their computers, regardless of the software that they were using, by means of a non-intrusive data collection tool, PROM [1]. The data have granularity of 1 second and consist in a timestamp, the name of the currently focused window (for all software applications) or the name of the current method, class, and file (for code accessed in the usual IDE), and the name of the currently used software application.

When PP occurs, the developers start a small user interface and enter the names of the members of the team. This user interface runs in the background during PP. Developers can stop it manually whenever they finish the PP session.

Thus, we collect extended information on the software application they use, the locations they access, and the composition of the pairs for PP.

The developers had several months of experience with the data collection tool and the interface for PP previous to our study.

To address the privacy concerns inherent to the use of these kinds of data collection tools, we first explain in detail how the tool works and what data it collects; than, we ensure that each person (including upper management people) has access only to her own data and to an aggregated summary of the data of all developers in the team. Moreover, the participation in the study is on a voluntary basis. Developers are also allowed to look at anytime at the data collected on their own machine and decide if the data can be sent to the central database or if they have to be deleted.

Although the developers were allowed to suspend their data collection at any given time, all 16 developers collected data throughout all the study.

The conditions described above are needed to protect the privacy of the developers and to ensure their collaboration. We address the possible impacts of these conditions on our study in section 6.

4   Results

The total time spent by each developer at the computer is on average 6.84 hours a day with a median of 7.58 hours. We have data for all developers during all days when they are present. However, not all of them are present during all the working days. Therefore, the number of days for which we have data varies for each developer.

Regarding PP, there are days when all the developers programmed alone. The average number of days when a developer PP is 10.44 and the mean is 10.5 days. On average, a developer PP for 2.83 hours a day, with a median of 2.24 hours (not considering days in which they program only alone).

Percentage of PP. For the analysis on the trends in PP, we discard the data of the two newcomers and consider only the data from the 14 veteran members of the team. We do this mainly because we consider the two newcomers, during their first month of work, not being representative of the team and because they are not present at the beginning of the study.

The veteran members of the team do PP on average for 2.75 hours a day each, with a median of 2.16 hours. On average, each veteran member of the team does PP for 10.21 days (median of 9.5 days). In the days when developers do PP, they spend on average 47.81% (median 43.48%) of their time in doing it.

To understand possible trends in the amount of PP, we investigate whether there are significant differences between the beginning and the end of iteration (weekly iterations in this case). Usually, the team spends the Mondays for non-coding activities, including stand-up meeting, planning of the iteration, and design. Therefore, there is no PP and we focus only on the remaining of the week (and thus of the iteration).

We consider PP on Tuesdays and Wednesdays as PP at the beginning of the iteration (group 1) and PP on Thursdays and Fridays as PP at the end of the iteration (group 2) and we compute the amount of time spent in PP for each day and each developer. We are interested in finding out whether there is a significant difference between the amount of PP in the team during the beginning and the end of the iteration, and not in the amount of PP of each individual developer. Therefore, we compute for each week and each group the average time spent in PP. Thus, we have the average time spent by a developer in PP at the beginning and the end of the iteration. While the averages of the two groups are slightly different (14.65% of time is spent in PP at the beginning of the iteration and 15.17% at the end of the iteration), a Welch t-test (to account for possible different standard deviations of the two groups) does not offer evidence for rejecting the null hypothesis ($p=0.923$). Thus, we do not have enough evidence to consider significant the difference between the average percent of time spent in PP at the beginning and the end of the iteration.

Considering iterations as a whole, the percentage of PP seems to vary from one week to another. The average percentage of PP during various iterations varies from 0 to 26.26% with an average of 14.53% and a median of 12.81%. At present, we do not have enough data to investigate possible trends in this variation.

The percentage of total PP of the veteran members of the team during various iterations varies from 0 to 26.58% with an average of 14.53% and a median of 12.81%. Fig. 1 shows such values for the different iterations: there are no clear general trends and the values vary quite a lot from one iteration to another.

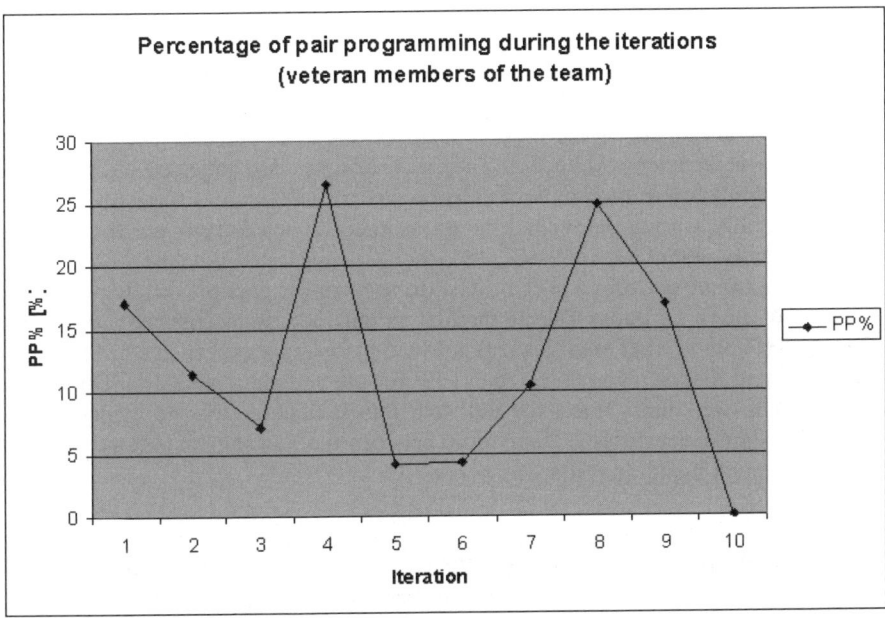

Fig. 1. Total percentage of PP (only veteran members considered) during each iteration

PP for training. There are claims that PP is an efficient way of training. To investigate whether developers themselves perceive PP as needed in situations when training through a transfer of knowledge is needed, we investigate PP of developers that are new to the team compared to PP of developers that are veteran members of the team.

We consider the developers new to the team as newcomers during their first month in the team. We expect that after this month, they have already acquired enough knowledge so that there is no need anymore for a massive knowledge transfer between developers. Therefore, we focus on comparing the average amount of PP of the newcomers during their first month to the average amount of PP of veterans during the same month. We also compare the average amount of PP of the newcomers after the first month with the average amount of PP of the veterans in the same period of time.

We compute for each day and each developer the amount of time spent in PP as a percentage of the time spent at the computer that day. Then, we compute for each day and for each of the two groups (newcomers and veterans) the average percentage of PP (Table 1). On average, the newcomers do PP during their first month for 74.33% of their time and for 29.31% during their second month. On average, the veterans do PP during the same first month for 52.68% of their time and for 43.55% during the second month.

Table 1. Average PP of a veteran and a newcomer developer during the first and second month

Group	Avg. PP of a developer in the first month	Avg. PP of a developer in the second month
Newcomers	74.33%	29.31%
Veterans	52.68%	43.55%

To investigate whether the difference between the means is statistically significant, we compare the means of the two groups during the first month and during the second month. Fig. 2 shows the average percentage of daily PP per user during the first month of the newcomers, while Fig. 3 shows the same data collected after the first month. During their first month, newcomers seem to do PP more (except for one day) than the veterans. During the second month, neither the newcomers, nor the veterans do PP constantly more.

In both cases, we perform a Welch t-test (to account for possible different standard deviations of the two groups). During the first month, there is a statistically significant difference (at 0.05 level of significance) between the average percentage of PP for the newcomers and the average percentage of PP for the veterans (p = 0.01). During the second month, we cannot reject the null hypothesis, thus there is no evidence of a statistically significant difference anymore between the newcomers and the veterans during the second month (p = 0.1359).

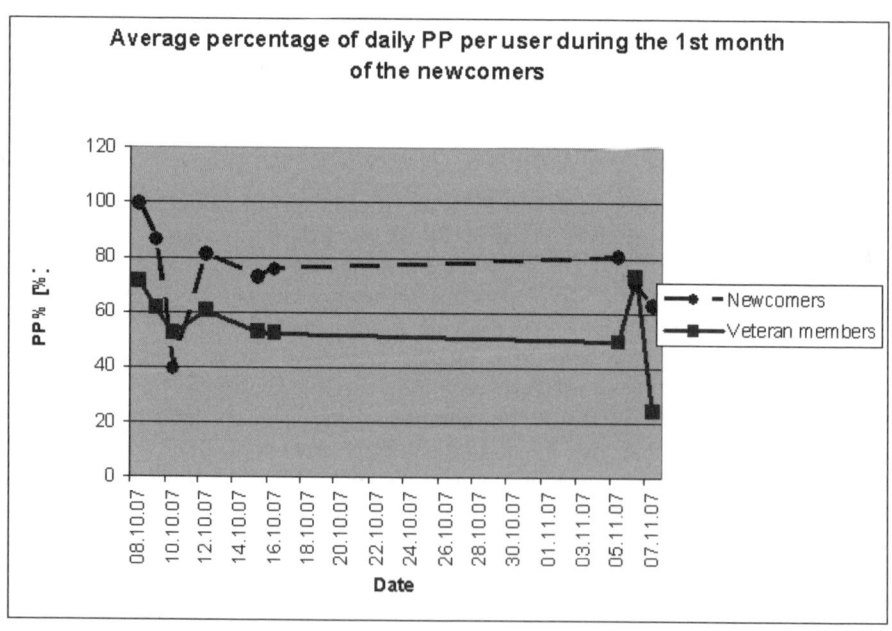

Fig. 2. Average percentage of daily PP for a developer during the first month of the newcomers

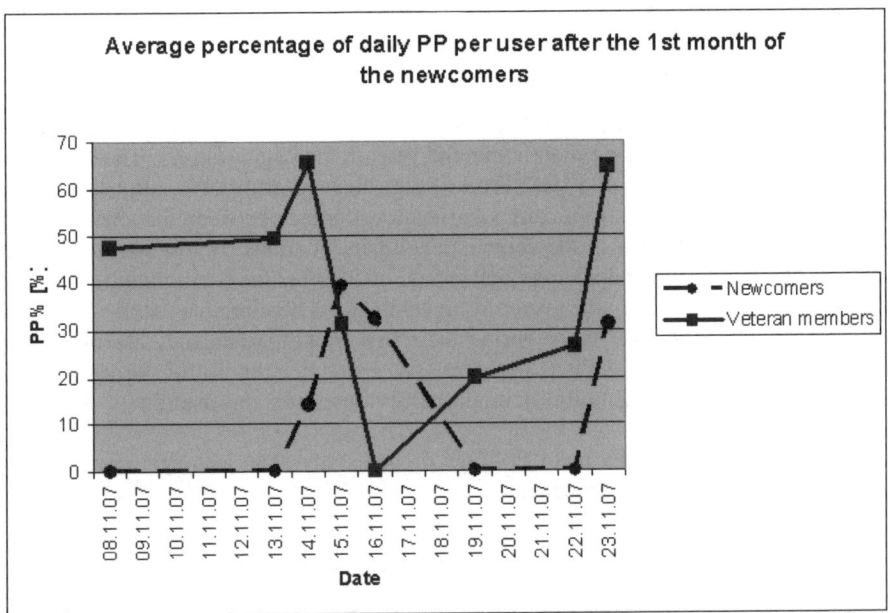

Fig. 3. Average percentage of daily PP for a developer during the second month of the newcomers

5 Discussion

Percentage of PP. During all the iterations, the overall percentage of PP is lower than 30% (Fig. 1). This suggests that developers do not use PP very often. Moreover, the percentage of PP for each developer during each day (Fig. 2 and Fig. 3), reveals that there are days when developers do not use PP at all. This has a clear influence on the overall low value of PP for the entire team.

Although the developers do not use PP every day, the percentage of PP during the days when it is used is quite high for each developer (Fig. 2 and Fig. 3). These values are closer to those reported in [141], although constantly lower. However, in [141], PP was imposed during some parts of the development, thus the percentage of PP is expected to be higher. Moreover, the members of the team in our study constantly spend about 20% of their time on email and other communication activities at their computer. Obviously, such activities are done alone.

The actual amount of PP varies quite much in the various iterations but without showing any clear trend. Moreover, there are also iterations during which the overall percentage of PP is extremely low (less than 5%). We cannot relate these variations between iterations with stages of a project to compare our results with those in [141], given that throughout the study, the developers were performing maintenance work on an existing project. One possible explanation for these variations among iterations relates to the existing claim that PP is more useful on complex tasks. Thus, if there are significant differences of complexity between the user stories implemented in each iteration, PP could be used more during the iterations with more complex user stories or where more difficulties have been encountered. However, more investigation into the actual characteristics of the user stories during each iteration is needed in order to support or refute this possible cause of variations in amount of PP during iterations.

PP is valuable for training. Our data shows that the newcomers in a team constantly do PP more during their first month than the veteran members (Fig. 2). The difference is statistically significant at a 0.05 level of significance. Moreover, after the second month, there doesn't seem to be any significant difference between the amount of PP of the newcomers and that of the veteran developers. A statistical test could not reject the null hypothesis that the average percentage of PP after the first month is the same for the newcomers and the veteran developers. Therefore, it seems that the newcomers indeed use PP more during their first month, when they are practically training. We conclude that PP is perceived by developers as useful during training. This adds to the existing body of empirical evidence on the usefulness of PP for training.

Table 2 summarizes the main findings of our study. The findings are compared with the existing empirical evidence.

Table 2. Summary of our empirical results

Issue	Existing Empirical evidence	Findings of the Present Study
• Evolution of percentage of PP during various iterations of a project.	• Mainly above 60%. • Highest during the first and the last iterations of a project. • Ascendant or descendant trends during the life of a project.	• Around 60% for veteran members on the days when they pair programmed and above only for newcomers during their first month. • Overall constantly below 30%. • No clear trends.
• Evolution of percentage of PP during various stages of the iteration.	• No evidence	• No support to sustain significant variations of the percentage of PP during various stages of the iteration.
• PP is valuable for training	• Support from developer interviews	• Support (p=0.01) that the newcomers PP more during their first month than the veterans.

6 Limitations

The study presents several limitations. The most important ones are listed here below.

To ensure the privacy rights of the participants, they have the possibility of stopping the data collection at any time, temporary or definitively, without giving any explanation. Moreover, they can choose not to collect data on specific software tools.

These options are available to each of the participants on their own machine and are transparent to us.

During our study, none of the developers decided to entirely stop the data collection. This is obvious, since we have data for each developer on each day (when present at work). Moreover, the developers were interested in the data collection and in the daily summaries available to them regarding their activities at the computer on the previous day.

The average total time at the computer for each developer is 6.84 hours per day. This time does not include the meetings or any other activities that the developers do without using their computer. Since the developers had several meetings during the week, we think that 6.85 hours of computer interaction per day, per developer is a reasonable amount. Moreover, developers stated to us during informal meetings that they never stopped the data collection.

There is also an internal limitation of the tool that collected data. While the tool is able to discern for long idle periods at the computer and eliminate them from the total time recorded (thus, from the data considered in our study), it is not able to discern for short interruptions (seconds or a few minutes). This type of interactions can be easily generated since the developers work in a shared environment where informal communication is common.

The external limitations of our study are related to the limited size (1 team of 16 developers) and to the specificities of our sample. However, our study does not aim at generalizing from these results, but at adding a new piece of evidence, from a new angle, and from a real-world industrial setting to the body of empirical evidence on PP.

7   Conclusions and Future Work

The main contribution of this work consists in the empirical results on the usage of PP in a mature Agile team. We investigated the actual amount of PP performed and its variations, as well as the support for the claim that PP is useful for training and knowledge transfer. The empirical results provide actual, quantitative, and concrete information on the practical usage of PP in industry and add to the body of empirical evidence regarding PP and claims on its potential benefits. However, more studies are needed to generalize from the results. As future work, we would like to replicate this study in other teams.

Our empirical results show support for the claim that PP is useful for training. However, there are other claims regarding PP benefits, such as improved productivity, improved quality of solution, reduced task completion time, and usefulness for complex tasks. As future work, we plan to apply our approach to evaluate these claims by investigating the actual PP of industry teams and the characteristics of their tasks and code.

Moreover, we consider as future work the investigation of the trends in the PP in industry teams over a more extended time frame and the relations between such trends and various stages of the projects.

Acknowledgements

We would like to thank the developers involved in this study for their participation and availability and Prof. Enrico Di Bella of the University of Genoa (Italy) for his suggestions about the statistical analysis of the data.

References

1. Sillitti, A., Janes, A., Succi, G.: Collecting, Integrating and Analyzing Software Metrics and Personal Software Process Data. In: Proc. Of EUROMICRO (2003)
2. Beck, K.: Extreme Programming Explained. Addison-Wesley, Reading (1999)
3. Nosek, J.T.: The Case for Collaborative Programming. Communications of the ACM 41, 105–108 (1998)
4. Hulkko, H., Abrahamsson, P.: A Multiple Case Study on the Impact of Pair Programming on Product Quality. In: Proc. Of ICSE, pp. 495–504 (2005)
5. Williams, L., Kessler, R., Cunningham, W., Jeffries, R.: Strengthening the Case for Pair Programming. IEEE Software 17, 19–25 (2000)
6. Lui, K.M., Chan, C.C.K.: When Does a Pair Outperform Two Individuals? In: Proc. Of XP (2003)
7. Nawrocki, J., Wojciechowski, A.: Experimental Evaluation of Pair Programming. In: Proc. Of ESCM (2001)
8. Williams, L., Shukla, A., Anton, A.I.: An Initial Exploration of the Relationship Between Pair Programming and Brook's Law. In: Proc. Of Agile Development Conference (2004)
9. Beck, K., Andres, C.: Extreme Programming Explained: Embrace Change. Addison-Wesley, Reading (2005)
10. Arisholm, E., Gallis, H., Dyba, T., Sjoberg, D.I.K.: Evaluating Pair Programming with Respect to System Complexity and Programmer Expertise. IEEE Transactions on Software Engineering 33(2) (2007)
11. Cockburn, A., Williams, L.: The Costs and Benefits of Pair Programming. In: Proc. Of XP 2000 (2000)
12. McDowell, C., Werner, L., Bullock, H., Fernald, J.: The Effects of Pair-Programming on Performance in an Introductory Programming Course. In: Proc. Of SIGSE technical symposium on Computer science education, pp. 38–42 (2002)
13. Williams, L., Shukla, A., Anton, A.I.: An Initial Exploration of the Relationship Between Pair Programming and Brooks' Law. In: Proc. Of Agile Development Conference (2004)

Just Enough Structure at the Edge of Chaos: Agile Information System Development in Practice

Karlheinz Kautz[1] and Sabine Zumpe[2]

[1] Copenhagen Business School, Department of Informatics, Howitzvej 60, DK-2000 Frederiksberg, Denmark & University of New South Wales, School of Information Systems, Technology & Management, Sydney NSW 2052, Australia
Karl.Kautz@cbs.dk
[2] The University of Queensland, UQ Business School, Business Information Systems, Brisbane QLD 4072, Australia
S.Zumpe@business.uq.edu.au

Abstract. Agile information systems development is not well understood and suffers from a lack of sustainable theories, which are based on empirical research of practice. We use a framework that focuses on the 'edge of chaos' as the area, where agile information systems development takes place to fill in this gap. Our study identifies for a concrete project under investigation, where the beneficial balance between stability and instability lies. It discusses the circumstances, which influence this balance and the relationships of the elements, which constitute it.

Keywords: Edge of chaos, complex adaptive systems theory.

1 Introduction

The field of information systems development (ISD) is still not well understood and suffers from a lack of sustainable theories which are firmly based on empirical research of ISD practice [1]. This is also true for agile information systems development or, to use the more established term, agile software development (ASD[1]). The concept ASD serves as an umbrella for a number of pragmatic approaches which have emerged out of a critique of traditional, document driven development approaches [3]. ASD is guided by 4 values, which are contrasted with 4 other, competing values, namely (1) individuals and interactions over processes and tools (2) working software over comprehensive documentation (3) customer collaboration over contract negotiation and (4) responding to change over following a plan.

What this however means more concrete in practice and how it relates to a theoretical understanding of ASD as well as to ISD in general has only to a limited extent been systematically investigated and reported beyond text book descriptions and stories often provided by the authors of the methods themselves. The research

---

[1] The abbreviation ASD as used in this article should not be confounded with the same abbreviation, which Highsmith [2] uses for his agile development method called Adaptive Software Development.

P. Abrahamsson et al. (Eds.): XP 2008, LNBIP 9, pp. 137–146, 2008.

presented in this paper contributes to further filling in this gap by providing an independent study based on scientifically collected and analysed empirical data.

For this purpose, understanding ISD as a complex adaptive system (CAS), it utilises a framework first introduced by Wang & Vidgen [3] that focuses on the investigation of the 'edge of chaos' in such a system as the area where ASD takes place.

The paper is structured as follows: The next section contains the theoretical framework, which is applied in our research. Section 3 includes both a brief description of our research approach and the case setting which built the background for our study. Section 4 analyses the collected data by applying the theoretical lens and presents our findings. The last section concludes and summarises the paper.

2 Theoretical Background and Framework

Some authors of ASD methods ([4], [5]) put forward that ASD has a theoretical grounding, namely in complex adaptive systems (CAS) theory. However, research ([6], [7], [8], [9]) has shown that this claim is largely a post-rationalization: the theory is, if at all, used in a very relaxed way to justify what is done in practice. Consequently the large amount of literature available on ASD is of anecdotal and descriptive character. While these are useful reports, they do not provide any deeper analysis or theoretical underpinning for a thorough understanding of ASD.

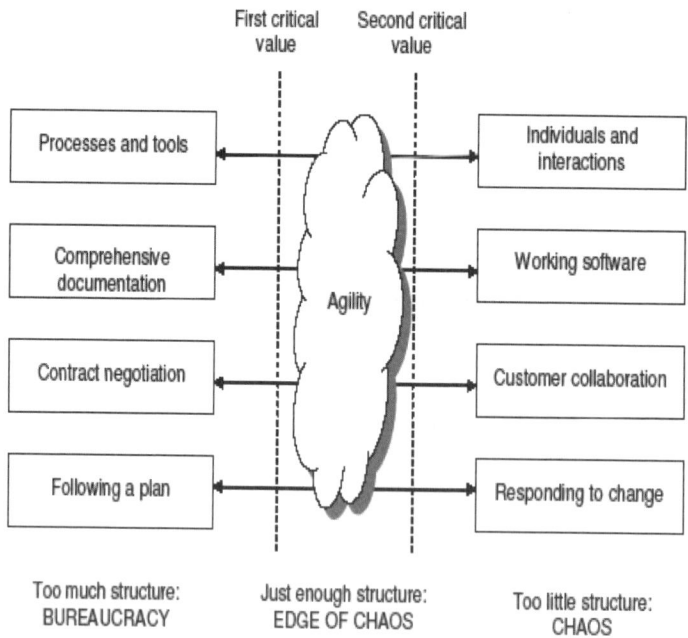

Fig. 1. The edge of chaos (Wang & Vidgen [3])

CAS theory, however, can be an insightful grounding for understanding complex systems such as ISD endeavours in general and ASD projects in particular. The key concept in CAS is the poise at 'the edge of chaos'. Wang & Vidgen [3] use this concept and provide a conceptual framework to study ASD as structured chaos. In their framework the edge of chaos is characterised by both being at the same time stable and unstable [10], it is the part of a system, which never quite locks into place, yet never quite dissolves into turbulence [11], it is the place, which provides organisations with both the stimulation and freedom to experiment and to adapt and with the sufficient frameworks and structures to avoid disorderly disintegration [12]. This gives them a competitive advantage: systems that are driven to the edge of chaos out-compete those which are not ([13], [14]). Thus, it is the place where the really interesting behaviour occurs [3]. Two critical boundaries demarcate the edge as the area of having 'just enough structure'. For the eight values, which direct ASD, this means: too much structure leads to bureaucracy with too rigid process and rules, too much documentation, too much emphasis on contracts and their negotiation, and too much focus on following the project plans; on the other hand, too little structure leads to chaos with too loose, if at all defined processes and rules, too much emphasis on working software, too much focus on collaboration, and too much response to change requests. Agility and agile processes lie some where in between, they are neither static nor chaotic. Figure 1 presents the framework and visualises these relations.

In the following we will use the framework to analyse a large ASD project. In doing so, we want to show in an independent study that the framework is useful. At the same time we want to contribute to the small, but growing existing body of scholarly research on ASD in practice. Before doing so, we introduce our research approach and the case setting.

3   The Research Approach and Case Setting

The research presented in this paper is qualitative. It is based on an empirical case study of an ASD project in a large German public sector organization, called WaterWorks, performed by a German software company, called AgDev, which has specialised on ASD. The empirical data for the case study was collected in semi-structured, open-ended interviews, which were conducted by a team of two researchers in a three days period. The research team performed 12 interviews with 11 individuals - the AgDev project manager was interviewed twice. This included nearly a third of the development team and a representative sample of key players and future users in the customer organisation. The interviews were tape-recorded and subsequently transcribed. For the qualitative data analysis a software tool (NVIVO7) was used. The interview data was supplemented with company and project documents such as method, requirements and release descriptions, as well as project plans.

The data collection, the coding of the data and the data analysis have been guided by the eight values underlying ASD and a theoretical framework developed and applied earlier by [15] to provide a better understanding of ISD in practice. This framework distinguishes between a structuralist, an individualist and an interactive process perspective, which together provide a holistic understanding of ISD projects. For the purpose of this paper we have used the structuralist perspective consisting of the information system under development, the formalised method to be used (if any), the structural characteristics of the involved development team and its members, as well as the project's structural context, to identify the structural profile of the investigated project. This perspective helps us to structure the description of the case setting, which is summarized in table 1:

The project under investigation was concerned with the development of an operations management system (OMS) for the WaterWorks of a large German city. Founded 150 years ago the organization is now partially privatised with the city council holding 50.1% of the ownership. The system was developed with a web-based graphical user interface and a backend to interface the technical infrastructure as defined by an underlying ERP system.

The project was organized in 4 subprojects to provide IT support ranging from customer management to the maintenance of the sewer system. After several attempts of traditional ISD based on a standard ERP system, which had not led to the desired results, the organization opened a tendering process. It was won by a small software company, AgDev.

Table 1. The structural Profile of the OMS Project

Information System	Operations management system (OMS) with web –based GUI user interface and ERP back end
Formalized Method	xP: short releases and iterations of 3-6 months/3-6 weeks planning games, user stories, story cards, onsite users pair programming, collective ownership, stand-up meetings continuous integration, testing, re-factoring
Involved Development Team and Developers	2 overall project managers (1 AgDev, 1 WaterWorks) AgDev: up to 12 staff with multiple roles: project manager, analyst, customer contact, and developer highly motivated and educated, limited xP experience 4 subproject development leaders also as customer contacts, analysts, developers with xP experience WaterWorks: 4 customer subproject leaders also as user representatives at least 1 additional user representative for each subproject; not the whole time onsite
Structural Context	ASD method had been clearly communicated to customer AgDev: No experience with large ASD projects WaterWorks: 1. ASD project project team onsite in a WaterWorks building general requirements document as basis for contract failed ERP implementation

AgDev consisted of about 25 employees, 20 of them being developers, and based its development approach on the agile method xP [16]. The formalized method includes planning techniques for releases and iterations called planning games, user stories and story cards to specify user requirements, onsite customers to support customer-developer communication, daily meetings (stand-up meetings) of the whole project team to support team communication, pair programming, re-factoring, collective ownership, continuous integration and testing to develop the software proper and tuning workshops to improve the development processes regularly. They have extended the method with some project management processes to cater for larger projects such an elaborate overall project plan, formal reporting mechanisms and a formal contract based on a requirements specification produced by the customer. In the tender process AgDev had convinced the management of WaterWorks that their approach was viable and would deliver the OMS as requested.

The project was organised in 2 phases. In a first 12 months exploration phase prototypes catching requirements and possible solutions were developed. This led to the development of a comprehensive requirements document by the customer organisation and their decision to contract AgDev also for the development of the OMS proper.

In this main development phase a team of about 12 development staff with multiple roles such as project manager, analyst, customer contact, and developer worked onsite in a building owned by WaterWorks. The project team also consisted of a varying number of users with at least one representing one of the subprojects. These users were by and large, however not the whole time onsite as well. A sophisticated management structure with one subproject manager also acting as contact person from AgDev and one subproject manager also acting as onsite-customer from WaterWorks for each individual subproject was, in addition to two overall project managers, established.

The developer team consists largely of highly educated and motivated, young staff and only the project managers have experience with ISD using an agile method, but none of them had ever participated in such a large project.

When this study was performed phase one had been successfully closed and after a break of over a year due to internal politics at WaterWorks phase two had been going on for 4 months. Responding to an inquiry call during our analysis the AgDev project manager stated that the project ended 10 months later on time and budget with all parts of OMS being operational. Despite some challenges (see section 4) from beginning to end the project was considered a success by all stakeholder groups involved.

The ASD method to be used had been clearly communicated to WaterWorks, which had been the main reason why AgDev won the tender. The project champion, an influential member of staff, who did not directly participate in the project team, but who was involved in most of the important decisions remembered: *"They presented a method, they explain it, and could convince us to get soon user feedback and a working solution."* Thus it became WaterWorks' first ASD project and the largest ASD project for AgDev at that point in time. With this structural profile in mind, we will now analyse the project in more detail.

4   Analysis and Discussion

The eight values are not just related to each others in pairs, but are highly interrelated. Processes and tools f. ex. beyond individuals and interactions, are also related to working software, customer collaboration, and responding to change; and individuals and interactions are also related to comprehensive documentation, contract negotiations and following a plan. Due to the space limitations we will in the following stick to the pairing of values as put forward by the promoters of the agile manifesto to structure the presentation of our analysis and discussion and we will only use selected aspects of each value to demonstrate the usefulness of the 'edge of chaos' framework.

4.1 Individuals and Interaction over Processes and Tools

xP provides quite a number of processes and tools such as short releases and iterations, planning games, user stories, story cards, onsite users, pair programming, collective ownership, and stand-up meetings to structure ASD. In the OMS project pair programming is a prominent process to support the interaction of the individuals of the development teams by working in shifting pairs of developers in front of a screen while implementing the requirements written down as user stories on story cards as executable code. Two sub-processes or mechanisms here are important: 1) to regularly shift a partner and 2) to regularly shift possession of the keyboard within a team.

In the project the developers find it difficult to find the appropriate synchronization points at which to change a partner in the teams of 4 developers. No common practice exists. However they do not follow an overly bureaucratic rule such as shifting partner every morning regardless of the status of a story card. To avoid both too much red tape and too much chaos some developers prefer to stay with a partner until a card is closed. *"... changing a partner was always a problem, it still is as changing in the middle of a card seems foolish to me and I don't really like doing it ..."* says one developer.

This of course can lead to limited interaction, spread of knowledge and dead ends. Thus, although some uncertainty regarding the mandate exists, a subproject leader might intervene if a pair has worked together for too long, say 3 days. In doing so, a balance, 'just enough structure' is created between shifting too often and not shifting at all.

The developers started out with a practice which did not really support the objectives of interaction, namely that one developer exclusively held the keyboard and programmed, while the other watched and sometimes commented. To avoid such situations a process was introduced where using a stopwatch after 20 minutes the keyboard had to switch. This was however abandoned as too bureaucratic and not fruitful in a creative work environment. The teams found their own rhythm. *"We don't do that anymore. It didn't function. Well, now it also functions without any explicit rule."* was how one developer commented the emerged practice.

This has also been the case with stand-up meetings. They are performed by all teams together everyday before lunch with the purpose to keep everyone up to date with the current status of the project and to exchange useful information. These sessions originally were quite detailed and long, but they have been refined and were then acknowledged as very helpful. One AgDev subproject manager describes: *"In the beginning we did this all together, but we found out that it can become too much, as some are doing something that is not of interest for other teams. But it is good to know what others do. It does not have to be in detail. And that is what the teams do now, all teams, but we keep it short."*

Other intensive interaction takes place in the beginning of each iteration, where all story cards are jointly discussed. Despite the fact that these mechanisms can not totally provide the intended collective ownership as the project leader regrets and explains with the size of the teams, they apparently provide enough structure for the project to be successful: they keep the project teams informed and decrease the need for documentation, a topic which will be discussed in the next subsection.

4.2 Working Software over Comprehensive Documentation

In the OMS project working software is the measure of progress. Each iteration produces operational software, but also minor advancements are demonstrated to the customers. The WaterWorks project manager stated: *"... I have never experienced a project that could generate output so fast."* and continues *"The major benefit is that we do not work so abstract, but rather focus on the real thing."* One of his subproject managers adds to this *" ... this way we have seen that we are on the right way, as we can use 95% of what has been developed this way, and just the last 5% we have to do something with again ... ".* This is confirmed by one developer by saying *"Yes that functioned well, we made all 3 weeks a short presentation of the running software."* and another one extended this: *" ...we got very quick feedback when we showed what we had done."* Thus, the short feedback cycles provide the necessary structure for the development of the working software. On the other hand, structure is also provided through documents.

Quite a number of different documents exist, but they are all comparably short and concise. From a customer perspective these are related as follows: *"Well, we have the overall realization concept as the basis for the contract and as a refinement hereof the requirements lists. These lists govern what should be the outcome of an iteration. For me this is the basis for my acceptance test: has been achieved what is on the list? And on the level below there are the story cards, these, so to speak, represent the detailed specifications and plans for the developers' process."* The developers share this perception and confirm that the documents, both in length and in number, are adequate. One of them says: *"Absolutely sufficient"* and is acceded by a colleague: *"I flipped through the realization document in the beginning and never touched it afterwards ... the requirements change anyway every 2. week."*

The developers, however, also admit that they need and produce further internal documents, fragments of functional and technical specifications, in the form of an open Wikipedia and that there is a necessity to interact with the customers as part of their collaboration to clarify the contents of story cards. Together with these measures the utilized documents afford the balance between too little and too much structure.

4.3 Customer Collaboration over Contract Negotiation

Customer collaboration in the OMS project comes in different ways. It takes the form of onsite customers and users, as well as telephone contact and email correspondence, especially to clarify requirements as specified on story cards. The planning games, the presentations of working software and the acceptance tests are as well crucial elements, which structure the collaboration.

The planning games are partly based on the overall realization concept, a document which was produced by the customer as a basis for the contract. Another foundation of the planning game are the requirements lists. These are largely produced by AgDev, both their project leader and some of the subproject leaders, who also work as contact persons for their counterparts at WaterWorks and as developers. They develop these documents with input from the onsite customers. The story cards are solemnly produced by the developers in team work sessions, where they also estimate them. The developers and the customers then together prioritise these cards.

This can be considered a quite limited form of customer collaboration, however, as one subproject leader expressed it, there can be a number of reasons for this: *"Here we have users, who have to take their working gloves off before they go to the keyboard ... in contrast to projects I've been involved in before, where the customers were wearing ties, here the subproject leaders are partly folks, who have done something quite different before, they have a different education and that becomes apparent with regard to their abstraction capabilities and their abilities to write down some texts."* However, this form of customer collaboration apparently provides some of the necessary structure to cope with the complexities of a comparatively large ASD project, which was performed by quite a number of inexperienced staff, while leaving room for less structured collaboration as well.

That is to say, when implementing the story cards, it became obvious that some additional collaboration was needed. One subproject manager estimates that user contact is necessary for nearly every story card. He puts forward that maybe 60% of a card's contents is clear. When no user is onsite available the communication process is as follows: *"Certain users want to be contacted by phone to be reached straight away, while others prefer to get their requests via email, but answer timely."*

The overall collaborative spirit of the project showing that the limited customer collaboration was not replaced by formal contracts and negotiations is also expressed by the project champion, who after having been involved in the original contract negotiations states: *" ... we decided not to be tough on change requests and back-up formalities, but rather to work constructively with them to make progress. And my good feelings have been confirmed."* The AgDev project leader confirms this and describes the context of requirement changes: *"The customer is quite relaxed. In such situations they look where they can cut expenses planned for other requirements or we discuss if we can make the implementation simpler to meet the budget planned."*

The balance between stability and instability is brought about by different kinds of customer collaboration and by acknowledging, but not privileging the important role of contract negotiations, which also extends to the handling of change requests, which brings us to the last 2 values.

4.4 Responding to Change over Following a Plan

As described above, in the OMS project change, especially change of requirements is an accepted fact of life. Many change requests are detected through the scheduled acceptance test sessions for an iteration with a customer representative onsite and are then dealt with in the next iteration. The customer representatives also regularly perform 'road shows' in the user departments to collect feedback and ideas and proposals for improvements.

But change requests are also brought forward by the users on a shorter time scale. There are weekly and bi-weekly feedback loops built into an iteration. The AgDev project manager explains: *"And then after a week the customer rep is back and wants to see what happened during the week and he gets the first feedback and this then continues ... ."* They have the following consequence: *" ... often we show the customer rep something once a week and then he's going 'well, I thought this would be different' ... thus there are always small changes ... "* as one developer puts it.

These frequent feedback loops also have the effect that minor misunderstandings are caught and dealt with as changes early before they can grow into something larger, as the same developer explains *"Until now it has not happened that everything was totally wrong; there are of course some refinements or a bug is found or something similar. There is always something."* The feedback is taken seriously and immediately responded to with action: *"Through the feedback we got, we could react directly ... ."* as it is described by one developer.

The different feedback mechanisms provide some structure to handle the changes, but plans and planning although not impeding more spontaneous actions are playing an important role as well. Even the weekly sessions are to some extent planned, as are of course the acceptance tests. As one WaterWorks subproject leader relating to the size and complexity of the project says *"Planning is essential in such kind of projects."*

Therefore, the project also has an overall long term plan covering an 14 months period anticipating 3-6 releases depending on the subprojects. A more fine-grained plan is developed for the individual iterations, which make up a release detailed to single weeks. The planning game and the story cards then offer the devices to perform planning on the most detailed level for very short periods of time. The frequent planning sessions embedded in a 'larger' and coarser plan together with the different means to handle change provide just enough structure for the project to move forwards.

5 Conclusions

We have applied Wang & Vidgen's [3] framework to give a detailed description and analysis of how the edge of chaos provides just enough structure to perform a successful ASD project in practice. The framework takes both the preferred, and the less preferred values of the founders of the agile development movement into account. It shows that they are not opposites, but fundamental and interconnected elements, which, when balanced appropriately, present the ground for successful ISD endeavors. This balance will be different for different projects and more such studies are needed to identify common patterns, if there are any, beyond what has been found in this research.

Our study also shows how the 4 pairs of values are interrelated and how an analysis of these relationships provides a richer picture of practice as a prerequisite for understanding it and for building a sustainable theory of ASD and ISD.

References

1. Kautz, K.: The Enactment of Methodology – The Case of Developing a MultiMedia Information System. In: Proceedings of ICIS 2004, Washington, D.C., USA, December 12-15 (2004)
2. Highsmith, J.: Adaptive Software Development – A Collaborative Approach to Managing Complex Systems. Dorset House Publishing, New York (1999)

3. Wang, X., Vidgen, R.: Order and Chaos in Software Development: A Comparison of two Software Development Teams in a major Company. In: Proceedings of the 15th ECIS, St. Gallen, Switzerland, June 7-9 (2007)
4. Highsmith, J.: Agile Software Development Ecosystems. Addison-Wesley, Boston (2002)
5. Highsmith, J., Cockburn, A.: Agile Software Development: the Business of Innovation. Computer 34(9), 120–122 (2001)
6. Kalermo, J., Rissanen, J.: Agile Software Development in Theory and Practice, M.Sc. Thesis in Information Systems Science. University of Jyväskylä, Finland (2002)
7. Turk, D.R., France, R., Rumpe, B.: Limitations of Agile Software Processes. In: Third International Conference on eXtreme Programming and Agile Processes in Software Engineering, Alghero, Sardinia, Italy (2002)
8. Conboy, K., Fitzgerald, B.: Toward a Conceptual Framework of Agile Methods. In: Zannier, C., Erdogmus, H., Lindstrom, L. (eds.) XP/Agile Universe 2004. LNCS, vol. 3134, pp. 105–116. Springer, Heidelberg (2004)
9. Vidgen, R., Wang, X.: Organizing for Agility: a Complex Adaptive Systems Perspective on Agile Software Development Process. In: Proceedings of the 14th ECIS, Göteborg, Sweden, June 12-14 (2006)
10. Stacey, R.D.: Strategic Management and Organisational Dynamics: The Challenge of Complexity, 4th edn. Prentice-Hall, London (2003)
11. Waldrop, M.M.: Complexity: The Emerging Science at the Edge of Chaos. Penguin Books, London (1994)
12. McMillan, E.: Complexity, Organizations and Change. Taylor & Francis Group, London, Routledge (2004)
13. Anderson, P.: Complexity Theory and Organization Science. Organization Science: A Journal of the Institute of Management Sciences 10(3), 216–232 (1999)
14. Kauffman, S.: At Home in the Universe: The Search for Laws of Self-Organization and Complexity. Oxford University Press, New York (1995)
15. Madsen, S., Kautz, K., Vidgen, R.: A framework for understanding how a unique and local IS development method emerges in practice. European Journal of Information Systems 15(2), 225 238 (2006)
16. Beck, K., Andreas, C.: Extreme Programming Explained: Embrace Change, 2nd edn. Addison Wesley Professional, Boston, Mass. (2004)

A Preliminary Conceptual Model for Exploring Global Agile Teams

Jason H. Sharp[1] and Sherry D. Ryan[2]

[1] Department of Computer Information Systems, Tarleton State University
Box T-0170, Stephenville, TX 76402 USA
jsharp@tarleton.edu
[2] Department of Information Technology and Decision Sciences, University of North Texas
P.O. Box 305249, Denton, TX 76203 USA
ryans@unt.edu

Abstract. The combination of agile methods and global software development via virtual teams represents an emerging approach to addressing the challenges typically associated with software development projects. The prevailing viewpoint has been that agile methods are not applicable in global settings. However, some current research is challenging this assertion. Therefore, we pose the following research question: How can agile teams be successfully configured in globally distributed environments? Drawing upon configurational theory, work group design research, virtualness concepts, and the software agility literature, the purpose of this paper is to construct a preliminary conceptual model for exploring three proposed dimensions necessary for successful configuration of global agile teams: structure, agility, and virtualness. This paper contributes to the information systems field by providing a starting point towards theory building in the area of globally distributed agile teams and by suggesting three dimensions for measuring and characterizing global agile team configuration.

Keywords: Global agile teams, agile methods, global software development, conceptual model.

1 Introduction

A long-standing challenge in software development has been the completion of projects on-time, within budget, and suited to the requirements of users. Agile methods, which represent an emerging set of software development methodologies based on the concepts of adaptability and flexibility, are currently touted as a way to alleviate these reoccurring problems and pave the way for the future of development [3].

However, the increasing movement toward global software development and the formation of virtual teams poses a potential dilemma for organizations who have adopted agile methods. A fundamental principle underlying agile methods stresses the necessity for colocated teams in order to facilitate daily, face-to-face interaction between stakeholders [23]. Within the context of global software development, virtual teams must rely to varying degrees on technology-mediated communications and in some cases team members never meet in person [25]. This raises the question of

P. Abrahamsson et al. (Eds.): XP 2008, LNBIP 9, pp. 147–160, 2008.
© Springer-Verlag Berlin Heidelberg 2008

whether it is possible to successfully adopt agile methods for use in global software development projects. A growing stream of research suggests that, although it is sometime difficult and takes great care, it is possible [36], [51], [55]. The key is to modify the agile method to fit the global setting. The concept of tailoring agile practices to fit the development context has been suggested by others as well [21].

Team configuration in global settings is a complex phenomenon. While it is true that globally distributed teams encounter many of the same challenges as colocated teams, these are often exacerbated by physical distance [37]. Thus, the actual configuration of agile teams in globally distributed environments appears to be a significant area of research that has currently received little attention. Drawing upon configurational theory, work group design research, team virtualness concepts, and the software agility literature, we propose that it is possible to successfully configure a global agile development team, but that there are a number of issues that must be well thought-out. The purpose of this paper is to construct a preliminary conceptual model for exploring the dimensions involved in the successful configuration of global agile teams. Our contribution is to highlight key aspects of a global agile team when building a team for this environment. This is important not only to help academics understand the relationship among the dimensions of a global software development team, but also to assist managers in their efforts when constructing these teams. The proposed theoretical model is the first phase of a multi-phase research program that will investigate agile software development teams operating in a global distributed environment.

2 Literature Review

This paper reviews multiple streams of literature including agile software development methods, global software development, virtual teams, agile methods in distributed environments, and work group and team design research in its efforts to explore the configuration of global agile teams

2.1 Agile Software Development Methods

With the volatile nature of business environments, rapidly changing requirements, emerging technologies, and the traditionally high rates of project failure, the development of software in a timely and cost-effective manner which meet the needs of an organization continues to be a significant concern [5], [19]. One of the current proposed solutions to this challenge has been the creation of agile software development methods. Highsmith and Cockburn [30] contend that agile methods "view change from a perspective that mirror today's turbulent business and technology environment" (p. 120). The term agile methods grew out of a meeting of scholars and practitioners in 2001 who were interested in establishing common ground among various development methodologies originating from the 1990s. Initially, agile methods were called "light-weight methods," to describe ways of producing software in a lighter, quicker, more people-centered way. However, the Alliance member decided on the term "agile" rather than "light-weight" because the later might be interpreted as insignificant or trivial. The outcome of this meeting was a statement entitled the "Manifesto for Agile Software Development" which summarized the core values as well as established a set of twelve guiding principles [23].

Agile methods represent a group of methods built upon the concepts of flexibility and adaptability rather than a single approach to development [3]. Extreme Programming (XP), Scrum, Feature-Driven Development and Adaptive Software Development are examples of current agile methodologies. Although numerous agile methods exist, working code and effective people lie at the heart of all of them. The completion of projects on time and within budget requires creativity, team work, customer participation, and continuous feedback, all of which are stressed by agile methods [30]. To support the claims of its proponents, recent empirical studies have suggested that agile methods can improve the software development process [1], [2].

2.2 Global Software Development

With the rise in the globalization of business and the advancement of information and communication technologies, organizations are increasingly adopting global software development as a strategy to meet the traditional budgetary and time constraints of software projects. According to Damian and Moitra [16], it is "becoming the norm in the software industry" (p. 17). Carmel [13] defined global software development as teams working together to accomplish project goals from different geographic locations. Many factors are identified which are contributing to this movement. These factors include: a large, talented global resource pool, proximity to the market, quick formation of virtual teams, "round the clock" development, cost advantages, and the need for flexibility [14], [16]. The result is that, "software development is increasingly a multisite, multicultural, globally distributed undertaking" [29, p. 17].

In spite of its potential benefits, as development work becomes increasingly more virtual and distributed the challenges of working effectively in this environment will continue to increase as well. Multiple challenges exist including strategic, cultural, communication, knowledge management, project and process management, geographic, and technical [8], [29].

2.3 Virtual Teams

Related to the implementation of global software development is the formation of virtual teams. Almost a decade ago, Townsend, DeMarie, and Hendrickson [54] wrote of the development of a new workplace that would be "unrestrained by geography, time, and organizational boundaries"; it would be "a virtual workplace, where productivity, flexibility, and collaboration will reach unprecedented new levels" (p. 17). This new virtual workplace would be facilitated by the formation of virtual teams, those "groups of geographically and/or organizationally dispersed coworkers that are assembled using a combination of telecommunications and information technologies to accomplish an organizational task" (p. 18). With the advancement of these information and communication technologies, significant progress has been made in the utilization of virtual teams. However, the use of collaborative tools that enable virtual teams is not without problems. Too often, these technologies are viewed as a "cure all" and inadequate attention is paid to the processes that support the use of these tools.

The rise of virtual teams parallels the reasons behind interest in global software development: ever increasing flat or horizontal organizational structures; the need for inter-organizational cooperation and competition; changing expectations of organizational participation by workers; a shift from production to service/knowledge work environments; and increasing globalization [54]. Virtual teams share many of the challenges associated with global software development such as logistics, culture, technology, and communication [17], [34].

It is important, therefore, to specifically identify the multiple constraints and factors experienced by both agile and more traditional teams. First, logistical issues related to the scheduling of meetings, the arrangement of possible travel, taking advantage of a 24-hour workday, and the act of handing off work from one team member to another [29], [35], [50]. Second, cultural issues involving challenges in communication and coordination, language, holiday schedules, and attitudes toward work in general [35], [41]. Third, communication issues not necessarily related to cultural settings. Interestingly enough, two studies found that virtual teams actually communicated more often than colocated teams [20], [24]. Other factors such as relationship building, coordination, trust, and cohesion are all predicated on effective communication between team members (e.g., [32], [33], [39], [40]). Finally, technical issues must be accounted for. As noted by Townsend et al. [54], "the real challenge of virtual team effectiveness is learning how to work with these new technologies" (p. 22).

Although global software development and virtual teams constitute two distinct areas of research, the two are becoming more and more intertwined. With the move toward global software development by many organizations, the pairing of virtual teams and globally distributed projects is becoming more common [7], [15], [50]. Virtual teams enable greater organizational flexibility and the ability to respond quickly to changing global business environments.

2.4   The Use of Agile Methods in Globally Distributed Environments

In line with this move toward global software development and the use of virtual teams in order to facilitate greater flexibility and adaptability there appears to be a growing interest in the issue of whether distributed software development as a whole can be agile [4], [48] and whether or not specific practices such as pairing programming can be effective among globally distributed teams [22]. The debate regarding the combination of agile and distributed development approaches centers on the significant difference in their key tenets. According to Ramesh et al. [48], agile methods tend to follow more informal processes, while distributed development relies heavily on formal mechanisms. Consequently, the prevailing viewpoint has been that agile methods cannot be applied in global software development projects [31].

A further reason contributing to this view is that proponents of agile methods insist that agile practices must be used in their entirety in order to be effective [21]. One of the overriding practices is the use of colocated teams and the argument that the "most efficient and effective method of conveying information to and within a development team is face-to-face conversation" [23]. Obviously, this poses an immediate problem to the application of agile methods in globally distributed environments. However, as mentioned above there is some research that is challenging this assertion (e.g., [36], [38], [51], [55]).

3   Conceptual Model

Meyer, Tsui, and Hinings [42] defined a configuration to "denote any multidimen-sional constellation of conceptually distinct characteristics that commonly occur together" (p. 1175). Simply put, configurations are patterns or characteristics that describe an entity. Although much work on configurations has been conducted at the organizational level [43], [44], [45], much less has been done at the group level. Teams in particular are representative of group level configurations. Therefore, we pose the following research question: How can agile teams be successfully configured in globally distributed environments? To address this question we construct a concep-tual model consisting of three dimensions drawn from the extant literature: team structure, virtualness, and agility (see Figure 1.).

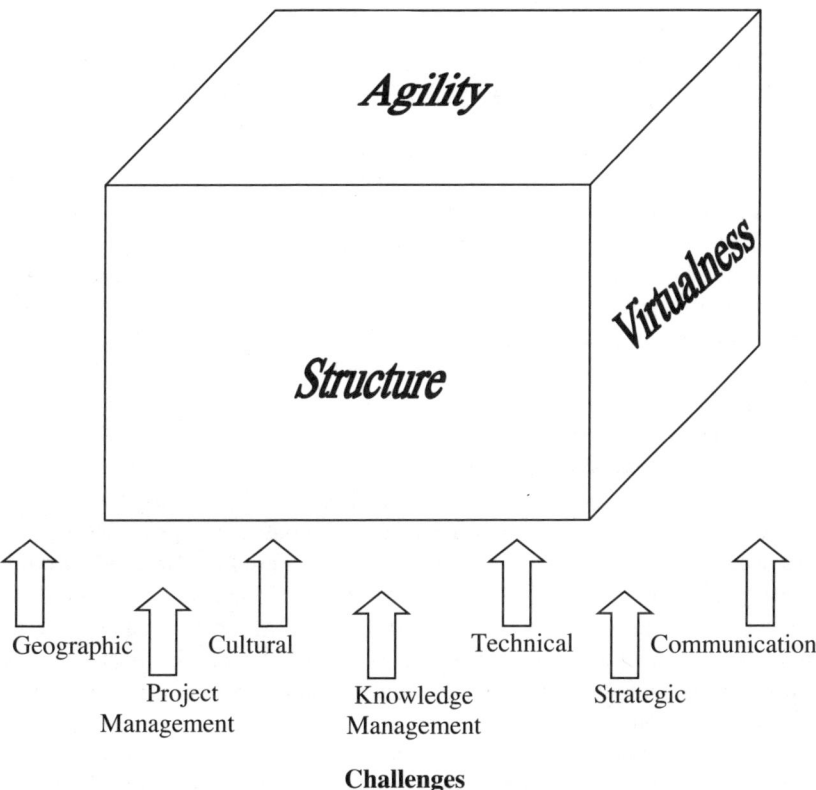

Fig. 1. Conceptual Model of Global Agile Teams (Adapted from [52])

3.1   Team Structure

Meyer et al. [42] suggested that work group design represents a possible group level configurational approach [26], [27], [28]. In work group design research, the structural elements play an important role in the effectiveness of the team. Hackman [26] stated, "it is a fantasy – a tempting and pervasive one, but a fantasy nonetheless – that it is possible to have great teams without the bother of creating enabling team structures" (p. 13). Although work group design research addresses teams in general, "the structural conditions that foster effectiveness of face-to-face teams are just as critical for virtual teams – but with one caveat: *it is much harder to create those conditions in virtual teams*" [26, p. 131]. Unfortunately, the design of the structural characteristics of virtual teams often appears as if it were only an afterthought [46]. As a dimension of the proposed conceptual model, team structure includes the sub-dimensions of task design, core norms of conduct, team composition, and team processes. In sum, Powell et al. [46] stated, "we believe that investigation of team structure in the virtual environment holds significant promise for research and practice because it represents perhaps the most controllable and influential aspect of virtual team design" (p. 16).

3.1.1 Task Design

Task design deals with the construction of the work itself. Team structure is dependent on the work performed [47]. According to Powell et al. [46], significant attention has been paid to the design of virtual team interaction, but much less attention has been given to the design of the work unit itself. The overall goal of a well constructed design is to facilitate collective internal work motivation. In order to reach this goal, task design seeks to provide the team with a meaningful challenge, to allow the team to practice significant autonomy, and to offer the team regular performance feedback [26].

According to Hackman [26], "the ability to create work that is challenging, complete, and significant – and therefore meaningful to those who carry it out – is one of the major advantages of designing work for teams" (p. 99). This is important due to the fact that the division of work across geographically distributed sites represents a strategic challenge of global software development through the use of virtual teams [29]. In distributed work, an element of task design is to carefully divide work in such a way that team members perceive that they are working together on a significant part of the whole project, rather than an on isolated parts. A second aspect for fostering collective internal motivation is to provide "team members a large measure of autonomy to decide how they will use their human and material resources in carrying out the work" [26, p. 100]. Ideally, in global software development, the members at each distributed site would to a large degree work independently while maintaining regular communication to keep the entire project in focus [29]. It is crucial for those individuals chosen for the team to be both independent and self-directing, but at the same time able work interdependently [54].

Third, collective internal motivation is increased by regular performance feedback. As noted by Hackman [26] a team cannot evaluate and learn unless it has data about how it is doing. Subsequently, without learning, there is no improvement. One of the issues regarding performance feedback in globally distributed teams is their ad hoc nature. Because virtual teams are often formed for short-term projects, they may be disbanded before the feedback loop can be completed. Managers and project leaders should be conscious of providing the needed feedback while the team is in existence.

Task design attempts in some way to address the issues of communication and collaboration in distributed work. However, it is often difficult to assess whether or not team members are truly collaborating in a meaningful way or simply employing a divide-and-conquer strategy where work is done in isolation and then pieced back together. From the perspective of the authors, the overall understanding of distributed work needs further examination and at the moment may not be sufficient to what is and what is not sufficient in this type of environment, especially when it is global in nature.

3.1.2 Core Norms

Core norms of conduct indicate the acceptable and unacceptable behaviors of the team [26]. An important element of virtual team design is the establishment of a shared set of norms which direct the individual and corporate behavior of members [49], [54]. During the formation of the team there may be much ambiguity about member roles, overall goals, and the rules which will govern the actions of the team. As such, the team leader or project manager will be called upon to begin the process of defining these areas. It is important that each team member positively internalizes this set of rules and in essence "buys-in" to their use [49]. Hackman [26] suggested that not all norms are equal and that primary and secondary norms should be established.

Primary norms are fundamental and outward looking. As such, primary norms call for the team members to "take an active, rather than reactive, stance toward the environment in which the team operates, continuously scanning the environment and inventing or adjusting their strategies accordingly" [26, p. 106]. Primary norms should establish those things that must "always" be done and those things that must "never" be done within the team. It is important that these two core norms be deliberately created as a part of the team's structure.

Secondary norms constitute additional norms that address those behaviors which the members deem as important enough to regulate. These norms may address such issues such as punctuality, participation, communication, and conflict management [26]. In global settings, the establishment of secondary norms may help alleviate conflicts caused by cultural diversity, language barriers, and communication differences. In addition common goals and strategies should be established [34], [53].

3.1.3 Team Composition

Team composition addresses the elements of size, mix, interpersonal skills, and task-related knowledge and skill. Because task-related knowledge and skill is extremely important most organizations do not err when considering this element. However, it is common for organizations to make mistakes in regard to the others [26].

Hackman [26] advocated having as few team members as possible to accomplish the task, in fact, "a team may function better when it has slightly fewer members than the task actually requires" (p. 118). Hackman cited evidence that while initial productivity does actually increase as size increases, it eventually levels off, and actually begins to decrease for very large groups. Determining the size of the team, therefore, is dependent on the complexity of the task. Powell et al. [46] stated that to their knowledge no specific study to date has been conducted that explicitly examined virtual team size as a variable during the team design phase.

According to Hackman [26], "a well-composed team strikes a balance between having members who are too similar to one another on the one hand and too different on the other" (p. 122). Hackman further cited evidence that there is little proof that homogenous teams outperform heterogeneous teams. In globally distributed teams it is reasonable to expect decreased similarity between team members. This is one reason why cultural and communication issues pose such a challenge. It is important for managers to carefully examine the characteristics of successful virtual teams to inform their decision when choosing virtual team members. Currently, little research has been conducted to examine the personality types which are more amenable to working in virtual teams. However, one study did examine the personality characteristics of agile software development teams specifically. Balijepally, Mahaptra, and Nerur [6] cited several personality issues important to the composition of agile teams such as the ability to work together in creative teams, a willingness to become a generalist rather than a specialist, and a bent toward collaboration and shared ownership. Basing their study on the Five-Factor Model of Personality, the authors emphasized that the personality traits of emotional stability, extraversion, agreeableness, conscientiousness, and openness to experience are helpful measures to explore when assigning team members to an agile project. Further research in this area may also provide further insight when configuring global agile teams.

Ideally, teams should be composed of members who meet a predefined standard for interpersonal skills, "some people just are not cut out to be team players" [26, p. 125]. Similarly, Suchan and Hayzak [53] argued that virtual team members must possess excellent interpersonal and conflict management skills. The importance of addressing interpersonal skills within the context of team structure cannot be overstated. Hackman [26] contends that in an appropriately structured team the number of interpersonal conflicts will be less than in a team for which the task, norms, and composition were given little or no thought.

3.1.4   Team Processes

In regard specifically to global virtual team structure, Prasad and Akhilesh [47] also suggested that team processes are an important structural element and consist of several considerations. The first deals with the mechanism for making decisions. This authority to make decisions might be centralized or decentralized. It may be more formal in which decisions lie with the manager or project leader. Or it may less formal in that the team members are given more control over the decisions that must be made. The decision-making process dovetails with task design and the autonomy of the team. The second process addresses the degree of information sharing between the members of the team and their participation in the long-range planning of projects. The third process deals with the modes of control and communication and coordination.

As mentioned previously all three of these represent a challenge for globally distributed teams. Interestingly enough, Holmstrom et al., [31], found that agile practices appear to actually help reduce the problems of communication, coordination and control caused by the temporal, geographic, and sociocultural distance engendered in global software development projects. The mode of dealing with these three issues may be very systemized, based upon a strict set of procedures and standards on one extreme or left to the actual team to develop their own mode of achieving the overall goal and dealing with behaviors and interactions of the team members. Or, the mode may be somewhere in between, where guidelines as opposed to stringent rules or little direction. Finally, the last process involves the degree of commonality in work process and technology infrastructure. This is an important process due to the potential problems caused by strategic issues such as division of work, time zone differences, and technological inconsistencies between distributed sites.

3.2 Team Agility

The second dimension of the conceptual model represents team agility which may be defined as how closely the team aligns with the general values and principles of agile methods as well as with practices of a specific method. The values and principles are drawn from the Agile Manifesto [23].

The Agile Manifesto ascribes the following values to agile methods: individuals and interactions, working software, customer collaboration, and responding to change. Plan-driven teams, on the other hand, emphasize processes and tools, comprehensive documentation, contract negotiation, and following a plan [23]. Additionally, twelve specific principles have been established to guide agile development. These principles emphasize the need for early and continuous delivery of software, openness to changing requirements, delivering working software on a frequent basis, strong interaction between stakeholders, supporting and motivating team members, promoting sustainable development, fostering technical excellence, and regular feedback. The practices are related to the specific agile methods being employed. For example, Extreme Programming (XP) is built around twelve specific practices. Proponents of agile methods have consistently argued that in order for agile methods to be successful and bring the best benefits, they must be implemented as a whole [9].

However, some research suggests that agile methods can be tailored and that specific values and practices can be chosen and used with benefit (e.g., [21], [36], [38], [51], [55]). This tailoring may allow for teams to adhere to fewer values, principles, and practices and still maintain a high level of agility.

3.3 Team Virtualness

The third dimension of the conceptual model is premised on the concepts of team "virtualness". According to Bell and Kozlowski [10] in the same way that traditional, colocated teams are distinct from virtual, distributed teams, not all virtual teams are exactly the same either. Virtual teams can be placed on a continuum where one extreme represents the "ideal" type while the opposite extreme represents a type of virtual team that closely resembles a traditional team. The "ideal" type can be defined as follows: "it is distributed across time, spans numerous functional, organizational, and cultural boundaries; it is short lived; and is composed of members who each possess multiple roles in different virtual teams" as opposed to the more "traditional" type which is "temporally entrained, has less permeable boundaries, has a continuous lifecycle, and is composed of members who have singular roles" [10, p. 28-29]. This typology serves to characterize teams as more or less virtual based on the combination of the characteristics which includes temporal distribution, boundary spanning, lifecycle, and member roles.

Temporal distribution denotes that a virtual team is distributed across time [10]. Virtual team members may be colocated in time, separated by only a few hours, or separated by many hours. Members may also be temporally synchronized, e.g., located in different time zones, but are still working off of the same time reference.

Boundary spanning indicates that virtual teams not only cross the boundaries of space and time, but also functional, organizational, and cultural boundaries as well. Boundary spanning allows virtual teams to exhibit the characteristics of adaptability, flexibility, and responsiveness that are desired by many organizations. Due to their ad hoc, flexible nature, virtual teams can be formed quickly, but may only be in existence for a short period of time depending upon the project to which they are assigned. As such, virtual teams do not follow the traditional life cycle that occurs in traditional teams. Additionally, depending on the nature of the task, different virtual teams may go through different life cycle stages than other virtual teams. Lastly, virtual teams provide for the selection of members from a substantial pool of workers with a diverse set of skills. Ideally members participate in multiple roles within multiple teams [10].

Based upon these characteristics, the basic argument is that "virtual teams need to adopt different characteristics to successfully operate within the constraints that are imposed by the complexity of their collective task" [10, p. 16]. All of these characteristics are directly affected by the team task, which is one of the reasons it is so important to carefully consider its design [26]. With the move toward global software development, the formation of agile development teams within a globally distributed environment calls for an alternative and more agile configuration. Although the assumption could be made that as agility increases, virtualness decreases, the constant advancements being made in the area of information and communication technologies may allow for globally distributed agile teams to possess a greater degree of both agility and virtualness.

3.4 Challenges

Based upon a review of the literature, many of the challenges associated with the individual use of agile methods, global software development, and virtual teams overlap and represent possible hindrances to the successful configuration of globally distributed agile teams. For this reason, the following common or overlapping challenges have been included in the conceptual model to indicate the potential impact they may have on successfully configuring globally distributed agile teams. Strategic challenges may involve deciding how to divide work across distributed sites as well as dealing with the overall resistance to implementing globally distributed agile teams. The schedule of work, meeting times, and deadlines as well as the cost of travel between sites must also be taken into consideration. Because team members are dispersed across the globe, many cultural challenges exist including differences in language, attitudes toward work structure, values, conflict management, and competencies. Related to culture are the communication issues both formal and informal, development of mutual knowledge and understanding and the building of relationships, trust, and cohesion. A given in these teams are the geographic challenges related to distance, time zone differences, coordination and control and vendor support. Knowledge management also poses a challenge as teams develop mechanisms for collecting and sharing knowledge across sites. Project management concerns such as the synchronization of work and techniques employed must be examined. Finally, the technical aspects revolving around network capability, software, compatibility, and information and communication technologies are of utmost significant for the success of the team (e.g., [8], [29], [35], [37]).

4 Research Methodology

A case study as defined by Yin [56] represents "an empirical inquiry that investigates a contemporary phenomenon within its real-life context especially when the boundaries between phenomenon and context are not clearly evident" (p. 13). Thus, case study research would be an appropriate extension to further investigate this work. One of the most important aspects of building theory from case study research is that the research should begin "as close as possible to the ideal of no theory under consideration and no hypotheses to test" [18, p. 536]. However, Eisenhardt [18] admitted that "it is impossible to achieve this ideal of a clean theoretical state", thus suggesting that the "a priori specification of constructs can also help the initial design of theory-building research (p. 536).

Due to the complex nature of this topic, the need to examine the phenomenon within its natural setting, and the limited amount of research that has been conducted in this particular area, this study will adopt an embedded multiple-case research design utilizing both theoretical and literal replication logic and a pattern-matching analytic strategy [11], [12], [18], [56]. According to Eisenhardt [18] the overall goal of theoretical sampling in regard to literal replication logic is to "choose cases which are likely to replicate or extend emergent theory" [18, p. 537]. Conversely, theoretical replication logic is based on the rationale of selecting cases based on the expectation of contrasting results [56]. Thus, this study will attempt to identify similarities as well as differences between cases which may contribute to the successful configuration of global agile teams. Analysis of the data will serve to identify patterns or emerging themes based upon the three dimensions of the conceptual model as well as the possibility of additional dimensions.

The primary data collection method will consist of semi-structured interviews involving members of globally distributed agile teams within two multinational organizations with team members located in distributed sights and one U.S. organization utilizing an offshore contracting company. It is hoped that these three organizations will provide a rich set of data of differing configurations which can be examined. An interview protocol has been developed and 25 initial interviews have already been completed. Overall, it is estimated that two teams from each of the three organizations will participate representing approximately 50 team members. Additional data will be collected through various forms of documentation and archival records. Within-case and cross-analysis will be used to analyze and evaluate the data that is collected using MaxQDA, a qualitative data analysis software package. The major focus of the initial empirical research will be on the three major dimensions of the conceptual model: team structure, virtualness, and agility. Subsequent research will more thoroughly explore the challenges that impinge upon these dimensions.

5 Conclusion

Based upon the literature exploring agility and distribution and initial interviews conducted with numerous members of global agile teams, it is the belief of the authors that agile methodologies can be successfully applied in global software development projects. If research on the configuration of global agile teams is not conducted, researchers and practitioners alike will not have a clear understanding if there are truly significant differences between how agile teams and non-agile teams are designed in globally distributed settings. As such, we believe that this paper contributes to the information systems field by providing a preliminary conceptual model based on extant literature for exploring the dimensions which may lead to the successful configuration of globally distributed agile teams. This conceptual model may serve as a starting point towards theory building in the area of globally distributed agile teams. This model makes a contribution in that it provides suggested dimensions for measuring and characterizing global agile team configuration. As of this time no known research framework exists which incorporates the dimensions of team structure, agility, and virtualness. The utilization of globally distributed agile teams has the potential to significantly impact the field of software development. As such, our hope is that this framework will serve as a building block for further research in this important area.

References

1. Abrahamson, P.: Extreme Programming: First Results from a Controlled Case Study. In: Proceedings of the Euromicro (2003)
2. Abrahamson, P., Koskel, J.: eXtreme Programming: A Survey of Empirical Data from a Controlled Case Study. In: Proceedings of the ACM-IEEE International Symposium on Empirical Software Engineering, pp. 73–82 (2004)
3. Abrahamson, P., Warsta, J., Sippon, S.T., Ronkainen, J.: New Directions on Agile methods: A Comparative Analysis. In: Proceedings of the 25th International Conference on Software Engineering, pp. 244–254 (2003)
4. Agerfalk, P.J., Fitzgerald, B.: Flexible and Distributed Software Processes: Old Petunias in New Bowls? Communications of the ACM 49(10), 27–34 (2006)
5. Augustine, S., Payne, B., Sencindiver, F., Woodcock, S.: Agile Project Management: Steering From the edges. Communications of the ACM 48(12), 85–89 (2005)
6. Balijepally, V., Mahapatra, R., Nerur, S.: Assessing Personality Profiles of Software Developers in Agile Development Teams. Communications of the Association for Information Systems 18, 55–75 (2006)
7. Barkhi, R., Amiri, A., James, T.L.: A Study of Communication and Coordination in Collaborative Software Development. Journal of Global Information Technology 9(1), 44–61 (2006)
8. Battin, R.D., Crocker, R., Kreidler, J., Subramanian, K.: Leveraging Resources in Global Software Development. IEEE Software 18(2), 70–77 (2001)
9. Beck, K., Andres, C.: Extreme Programming Explained: Embrace Change. Addison-Wesley, Boston (2000)
10. Bell, B.S., Kozlowski, S.W.J.: A Typology of Virtual Teams: Implications for Effective Leadership. Group & Organization Management 27(1), 14–49 (2002)
11. Benbasat, I., Goldstein, D.K., Mead, M.: The Case Research Strategy in Information Systems. MIS Quarterly 11(3), 369–386 (1987)
12. Bonoma, T.V.: Case Research in Marketing: Opportunities, Problems, and a Process. Journal of Marketing Research 22(2), 199–208 (1985)
13. Carmel, E.: Global Software Teams: Collaborating Across Borders and Time Zones. Prentice-Hall, Upper Saddle River (1999)

14. Carmel, E., Agarwal, R.: Tactical Approaches for Alleviating Distance in Global Software Development. IEEE Software 18(2), 22–29 (2001)
15. Crampton, C.D., Webber, S.S.: Relationships Among Geographic Dispersion, Team Processes, and Effectiveness in Software Development Work Teams. Journal of Business Research 58, 758–765 (2005)
16. Damian, D., Moitra, D.: Global Software Development: How Far Have We Come? IEEE Software 23(5), 17–19 (2006)
17. Dube, L., Pare, G.: Global Virtual Teams. Communications of the ACM 44(12), 71–73 (2001)
18. Eisenhardt, K.M.: Building Theories From Case Study Research. The Academy of Management Review 14(4), 532–550 (1989)
19. Erickson, J., Lyytinen, K., Siau, K.: Agile Modeling, Agile Software Development, and Extreme Programming: The State of Research. Journal of Database Management 16(4), 88–100 (2005)
20. Eveland, J., Bikson, T.: Work Group Structures and Computer Support: A Field Experiment. ACM Transactions on Office Information Systems 6(4), 354–379 (1988)
21. Fitzgerald, B., Hartnett, G., Conboy, K.: Customising Agile Methods to Software Practices at Intel Shannon. European Journal of Information Systems 15, 200–213 (2006)
22. Flor, N.V.: Globally Distributed Software Development and Pair Programming. Communications of the ACM 49(10), 57–58 (2006)
23. Fowler, M., Highsmith, J.: The Agile Manifesto (2001),
    http://www.agilemanifesto.org
24. Galegher, B., Kraut, R.E.: Computer-Mediated Communication for Intellectual Teamwork: An Experiment in Group Writing. Information Systems Research 5(2), 110–138 (2004)
25. Gibson, C.B., Cohen, S.G.: In the Beginning: Introduction and Framework. In: Gibson, C.B., Cohen, S.G. (eds.) Virtual Teams That Work: Creating conditions for Virtual Team Effectiveness, Jossey-Bass, San Francisco (2003)
26. Hackman, J.R.: Leading Teams: Setting the Stage for Great Performances. Harvard Business School Press, Boston (2002)
27. Hackman, J.R., Oldham, G.R.: Work Redesign. Addison-Wesley, Reading (1980)
28. Hackman, J.R., Walton, R.E.: Leading Groups in Organizations. In: Goodman, P.S. (ed.) Designing Effective Work Groups, Jossey-Bass, San Francisco (1986)
29. Herbsleb, J.D., Moitra, D.: Global Software Development. IEEE Software 18(2), 16–20 (2001)
30. Highsmith, J., Cockburn, A.: Agile Software Development: The Business of Innovation. IEEE Computer 34(9), 120–122 (2001)
31. Holmstrom, H., Fitzgerald, B., Agerfalk, P.J., Conchuir, E.O.: Agile Practices Reduce Distance in Global Software Development. Information Systems Management, 7–18 (2006)
32. Jarvenpaa, S.L., Knoll, K., Leidner, D.E.: Is Anybody Out There? Antecedents of Trust in Global Virtual Teams. Journal of Management Information Systems 14(4), 29–64 (1998)
33. Jarvenpaa, S.L., Leidner, D.E.: Communication and Trust in Global Virtual Teams. Organization Science 10(6), 791–815 (1999)
34. Kayworth, T.R., Leidner, D.E.: Leadership Effectiveness in Global Virtual Teams. Journal of Management Information Systems 18(3), 7–40 (2001-2002)
35. Kayworth, T.R., Leidner, D.E.: The Global Virtual Manager: A Prescription for Success. European Management Journal 36(6), 183–194 (2001)
36. Kircher, M., Prashant, J., Corsaro, A., Levine, D.: Distributed eXtreme programming. In: Marchesi, M., Succi, G., Wells, D., Williams, L., Wells, J.D. (eds.) Extreme Programming Perspectives, Addison-Wesley, Reading (2001)

37. Komi-Sirvio, S., Tihinen, M.: Lessons Learned by Participants of Distributed Software Development. Knowledge and Process Management 12(2), 108–122 (2005)
38. Lee, G., De Lone, W., Espinosa, J.A.: Ambidextrous Coping Strategies in Globally Distributed Software Development Projects. Communications of the ACM 49(10), 35–40 (2006)
39. Lipnack, J., Stamps, J.: Virtual Teams: People Working Across Boundaries with Technology, 2nd edn. John Wiley & Sons, New York (2000)
40. Lurey, J.S., Raisinghani, M.S.: An Empirical Study of Best Practices in Virtual Teams. Information & Management 38(8), 523–544 (2001)
41. Maznevski, M.L., Chudoba, K.M.: Bridging Space Over Time: Global Virtual Team Dynamics and Effectiveness. Organization Science 11(5), 473–492 (2000)
42. Meyer, A.D., Tsui, A.S., Hinings, C.R.: Configurational Approaches to Organizational Analysis. Academy of Management Journal 36(6), 1175–1195 (1993)
43. Miles, R.E., Snow, C.C.: Organizational Strategy, Structure, and Process. McGraw-Hill, New York (1978)
44. Mintzberg, H.T.: The Structuring of Organizations. Prentice-Hall, Englewood Cliffs (1979)
45. Mintzberg, H.T.: Structure in Fives: Designing Effective Organizations. Prentice-Hall, Englewood Cliffs (1983)
46. Powell, A., Piccoli, G., Ives, B.: Virtual Teams: A Review of Current Literature and Directions for Future Research. The DATA BASE for Advances in Information Systems 35(1), 6–36 (2004)
47. Prasad, K., Akhilesh, K.B.: Global Virtual Teams: What Impacts Their Design and Performance? Team Performance Management 8(5/6), 102–112 (2002)
48. Ramesh, B., Cao, L., Mohan, K., Xu, P.: Can Distributed Software Development Be Agile? Communications of the ACM 49(10), 41–46 (2006)
49. Sarker, S., Lau, F., Sahay, S.: Using an Adapted Grounded Theory Approach for Inductive Theory Building About Virtual Team Development. DATA BASE for Advances in Information Systems 32(1), 38–56 (2001)
50. Sarker, S., Sahay, S.: Implications of Space and Time for Distributed work: An Interpretive Study of US-Norwegian Systems Development Teams. European Journal of Information Systems 13, 3–20 (2004)
51. Schummer, T., Schummer, J.: Support for Distributed Teams in eXtreme Programming. In: Succi, G., Marchesi, M. (eds.) Extreme Programming Examined. Addison-Wesley, Reading (2001)
52. Sharp, J.H., Ryan, S.D.: A Research Framework for Investigating the Successful Configuration of Globally Distributed Agile Teams. In: Proceedings of the Thirteenth Americas Conference on Information Systems, pp. 1–7 (2007)
53. Suchan, J., Hayzak, G.: The Communication Characteristics of Virtual Teams: A Case Study. IEEE Transactions on Professional Communication 44(3), 174–186 (2001)
54. Townsend, A.M., DeMarie, S.M., Hendrickson, A.R.: Virtual Teams: Technology and the Workplace of the Future. Academy of Management Executive 12(3), 17–29 (1998)
55. Xiaohu, Y., Bin, X., Zhijun, H., Maddineni, S.R.: Extreme Programming in Global Software Development. In: Canadian Conference on Electrical and Computer Engineering, vol. 4, pp. 1845–1848 (2004)
56. Yin, R.K.: Case study research: Design and methods, 3rd edn. Sage Publications, Thousands Oaks (2003)

Scrum Implementation Using Kotter's Change Model

Sinéad Hayes[1] and Ita Richardson[2]

[1] Cadence Design Systems (Ireland) Limited,
Eastpoint Business Park, Dublin 3, Ireland
sinead@cadence.com
[2] Lero – the Irish Software Engineering Research Centre,
Department of Computer Science and Information Systems
University of Limerick, Limerick, Ireland
ita.richardson@ul.ie

Abstract. Developing reliable software is a complex task which is becoming even more challenging as customers put overwhelming demands on software companies to produce high quality products in shorter time frames. Scrum is an agile, lightweight software development process that can be used to manage and control software projects using iterative, incremental practices. Scrum aims to increase productivity and improve quality in complex environments. Experts claim that this is a simple process whose aims are effortlessly achieved. The reality is that successful implementation is far from easy and requires significant training and plenty of practice. The case study presented in this paper investigates the use of Kotter's Change Model to support the implementation of Scrum in a software company.

1 Introduction

Software development organisations can improve the quality of software products through the implementation of improved processes and development models. For the implementation of such improvements to be successful, there is a requirement for individual employees – from software engineers to management - to embrace the change that is occurring in the organisation. Companies implementing process change can benefit greatly from using a change management model. However, published change management models and frameworks normally relate to organisational changes as opposed to process related changes. This paper presents research carried out to investigate the use of an organisational change model while changing the company's software development process.

2 An Ever-Changing Software Development Industry

The underlying notion presented in literature that *"change is constant"*, is particularly true in the software development sector [1]. To maintain a competitive advantage, software companies must continually deliver innovative products. This is a complex task which becomes more challenging as customers put increasing demands on them to produce high quality products in shorter time frames.

P. Abrahamsson et al. (Eds.): XP 2008, LNBIP 9, pp. 161–171, 2008.
© Springer-Verlag Berlin Heidelberg 2008

While the R&D teams strive to continuously change and improve their products, they must also change their development processes and procedures. This helps to ensure that effective and efficient techniques are being used to produce the highest quality products possible. Without concrete processes and procedures the end product could be below the accepted quality level, delivered late or over budget.

2.1 Agile Development

The latest software process to gain recognition is agile development. Having introduced concepts such as Scrum, Test Driven Development (TDD) and Extreme Programming (XP), it is distinctly different to linear development. Traditional models adopt a structured approach, where large teams follow a specific plan and adhere to stringent processes to produce a completed product at the end of a cycle. The agile approach thrives on the lack of stable requirements and uses small self-managed teams to frequently produce reliable software that meets customer requirements.

When agile development first emerged the reported success of its use was instantaneous [2]. The key benefits reported included the faster delivery of higher quality products that better matched customer requirements due to their close involvement throughout the project. Leszak et al. [3] have argued that the transition to agile methodologies was initiated as a way of achieving a positive return on investment in quality early in the development life cycle.

However, not all reports of these agile development techniques described positive experiences [1]. Despite the fact that they are *"simple"* and *"quick"* [4], most are very difficult to get right and require extensive training, discipline and managerial support. The ever increasing number of agile methods that are available also presents a problem: not every technique is suitable for every type of project. This factor must be given serious consideration before a specific development methodology is chosen for a project.

Although it can be argued that the traditional and agile approaches to developing software are founded on the same principles, Goldman et al., [5] maintain that when it comes to large, complex and uncertain projects, the flexibility of the agile approach is more employable. More traditional approaches (e.g. waterfall [6], spiral [7]) are best applied to predictable projects that are safe and the likelihood of change is low.

2.2 Scrum Model

The Scrum process recognises that *"these changes are unavoidable and must therefore be explicitly accommodated in the life cycle"* [8]. To control continuous requirement changes, the Scrum model (Figure 1) uses a Product Backlog to maintain a log of all items and issues to be completed during a project. The Product Owner, representing the stakeholder interest, maintains and prioritises the backlog.

Teams work for fixed periods of time called Sprints (short iterations) which last from five to thirty working days. The Sprint Backlog lists more manageable and visible tasks from the Product Backlog and makes the Sprint objectives clear from the outset, keeping the team focused and promoting teamwork. The Burndown Chart graphs the amount of work remaining in the Sprint, which gives management a dynamic view of progress and allows the team to respond quickly if daily commitments are not met.

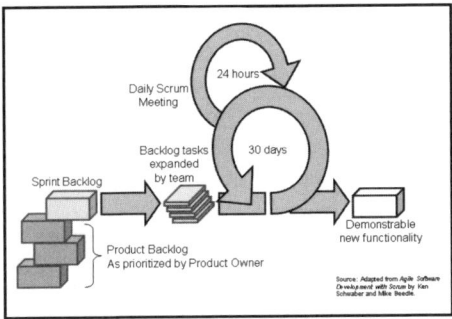

Fig. 1. The Scrum Model [9]

The team is driven by a Scrum Master, who chairs the Daily Scrum Meetings and removes impediments encountered by team members. At the end of each Sprint, a high quality functional product is delivered on time to customers, who use this executable as a way of refining and re-prioritising the Product Backlog. Consulting with customers early and often is the essence of Scrum. Allowing them to add, remove or modify requirements improves their confidence in the product as well as in the development team. It also ensures the delivery of a product that exactly meets customer requirements. Another advantage of Scrum is that if the team decides it is best to abandon a Sprint for valid technical or business reasons, the time wasted (maximum 30 working days) is minimal in comparison to the amount lost during waterfall model implementation.

3   Implementing Organisational Change

Successful growth for any company depends critically on their ability to rapidly improve their processes and extend their product base in response to market demands [10]. Management often fail to realise that when implementing change, if not handled correctly, even the simplest change can have a detrimental effect [11]. Introducing a change should be a formalised planned process, and, although some may be tempted to consider the process for managing change as an overhead, change management techniques have proved to be successful [10].

Each change management initiative is unique, and it is imperative that managers have a clear understanding of required changes. As the rate of change in organisations accelerates, the need for change management becomes increasingly important [12]. Managing a change in an organisation means that there is a greater chance that it will be successfully implemented and as this realisation has become clearer to organisations more change management models have become available.

Planning models, such as those defined by Kotter [13] and Lippit et al. [14] are based on the principle that changes that occur in organisations are planned changes. These models prescribe steps that should be executed sequentially to guarantee a successful change. The 8 steps described by Kotter [15] are:

1. Establish a Sense of Urgency
3. Create a Vision
5. Empower Others to Act on the Vision
7. Consolidate Improvements and
   Produce Still More Change

2. Form a Powerful Guiding Coalition
4. Communicate the Vision
6. Plan for & Create Short-Term Wins
8. Institutionalise new approaches.

4   Case Study at Rhythm Ltd.

Focusing on the transition from traditional to agile development, this paper investigates the hypothesis that Kotter's "Eight Steps to Transforming your Organisation" [15] is a suitable framework for such a change. The change was implemented within a software development team at Rhythm (Ireland) Ltd., a subsidiary of Rhythm International, an American-based electronic design automation company who employ 5000 worldwide in 63 subsidiaries.

Until September 2005, the primary mission of the software development team was the maintenance and support of a product called RhythmDoc. RhythmDoc projects were implemented using the waterfall development methodology [6]. The cumbersome nature of the process meant the team spent more time trying to keep documentation up to date than coding which resulted in projects being consistently late and over budget. This inevitably led to dissatisfaction among customers who were frustrated with the level of support they were receiving due to: low turnaround time of bugs, requirements creep and delayed time to market. In September 2005, the parent company decided that the maintenance of RhythmDoc would cease. Resources in Dublin would develop a superior replacement product called RhythmHelp. Delivery of RhythmHelp was mandatory within 18 months, within budget and with a high level of quality.

Subsequently, past project performance and results were scrutinised, highlighting that the waterfall development methodology no longer suited the Rhythm environment. It was decided that the Scrum process [9] was to be implemented while developing a production version of RhythmHelp by March 2007.

5   Research Methodology

This paper presents a pre-structured case study involving the observation and analysis of the software development team in Rhythm while implementing the Scrum process using Kotter's change model, which was chosen by Rhythm management as a suitable change model prior to instigating this change within the organisation. While one of the researchers was an employee in the company, she was not part of the group that implemented the change. To collate data, a combination of participant observation, semi-structured interviews, workshops and questionnaires, and the collection and analysis of project data and statistics, were used. Miles and Huberman [16] encourage the use of triangulation (application of a combination of different research methods) as a means of corroboration and validation of information. It was important to involve a number of methods in order to ensure the elimination of any bias. It also assisted in ensuring a correlation between the information gathered from the different sources.

6 Implementation of Kotter's Change Model

Step 1: Establish a Sense of Urgency
Prior to any planned change taking place, the need for the change must be communicated to everyone in the organisation. Management should be completely behind the change and the development team must be motivated to realise the change. There must be an evident pressure to change and employees must realise that the company cannot maintain the status quo [17]. Kotter suggests that the best way to do this is to create or identify a crisis which forces leaders to have a better handle on the problem. The absence of such urgency is a reason why so many fail to succeed when implementing a change.

The initial step taken at Rhythm was to investigate existing project artefacts. Through analysis of project data and customer satisfaction surveys, development groups recognised that projects were being delivered consistently late (by up to 400% in some cases [18]), and with poor quality. The team were mired in documentation and unable to handle the relentless changes to requirements. There was a lack of shared knowledge among the developers. At this point, people had begun to realise the seriousness of the situation – failure to deliver could result in the company moving the development of this product to an alternative location. A different development methodology was required, and Scrum was to be implemented.

Step 2: Form a Powerful Guiding Coalition
Kotter describes the need to involve different members of the organisation in the change on a gradual basis and to form a project team. This should begin with one or two individuals and as the project gains momentum and more resources are required the team grows to assist in the change implementation. This approach works well in situations where organisations may wish to use pilot projects [19]. According to Small and Downey [20] it is imperative that there is adequate support from senior management and a dedicated change manager that will drive the team. Kotter recommends that characteristics of team members should include: power, position, leadership and credibility.

The senior management team at Rhythm International were *"delighted to see some positive and pro-active steps being taken to resolve a now critical issue"*. The development team leader was very enthusiastic. He had the influence to encourage and reassure his team during the change process. While senior management in Dublin agreed that *"performance within the team"* was *"an obvious problem"* they failed to understand why processes *"that work perfectly well for the rest of the organisation could not be applied to the Dublin Team"*. Despite their reservations, they agreed to lend their support so that a united front could be presented – this was critical to the success of the project.

Step 3: Create a Vision
At this point, important decisions need to be made regarding the specifics of the change and how it should be enforced [21]. Success can happen if there is a clear strategy and implementation plan for implementing the change. A clear and concise vision, while also being realistic and attainable, should be defined. Otherwise, management run the risk of people getting disheartened and further adding to resistance to change. Jones et al., [22] recommend that the vision should be created in three steps:

1. Confront reality and articulate the need for change
2. Demonstrate faith that the company has a future and the leadership to get there
3. Provide a road map to guide behaviour and decision making.

At Rhythm, the vision for the change project was *"To become successful in the application of agile development methods, particularly Scrum, and leverage these techniques to improve product quality, reduce the time to market, and increase customer satisfaction"*. An implementation plan was written which stated the objective of the change project, project scope and schedule, project completion criteria and measurements, potential risks and mitigating factors.

Step 4:   Communicate the Vision

Kotter [13] suggests that communication of the vision should come from senior management, giving employees relevant timely information and soliciting their feedback. Relevant input received from employees should be fed into the overall project plan [22]. They believe such communication is invaluable in guaranteeing leadership-team alignment. Furthermore, change advocates such as Gremba and Myers [23] and Senior and Fleming [11] promote the creation of a work plan or schedule, as it is in keeping with project management techniques. This can also provide valuable information regarding individual responsibility. It can also detail how the change will affect different people. It can educate people about the change which assists in reducing the level of resistance that can arise due to unfounded rumours and incorrect information [24].

Within Rhythm, a meeting which included a presentation and discussion about the change project and the proposed Scrum process was held to launch the new RhythmHelp project. Senior managers from the United States were in attendance. The implementation plan, including the training plan, roll-out schedule, project risks and mitigating factors and project goals and measurements was also presented. In general, the development team were positive: *"I like the fact that there is more emphasis on taking responsibility for development work"*. Due to attendance by senior management, the attitude of the Dublin management team became more positive. Subsequently, the vision and strategy were distributed and internal meetings were held to ensure team members were clear about the new process. At this point no team member had any formal experiences of any agile methodologies.

Step 5:   Empower Others to Act on the Vision

To ensure a successful change project, Kotter [13] argues that obstacles, such as organisational structure and narrow job categories, should be removed. Borjesson and Mathiassen [19] present the notion of setting up a process action team to implement the change. Kotter [13] agrees with this approach but also believes that the team must have the authority to remove or eliminate obstacles as they arise, especially those that have the potential to cause a project failure. Borjesson and Mathiassen [19] also consider the concept of a pilot project to be useful in providing the basic concepts of the new process. It gives people the opportunity to experience new and challenging aspects of the process, raise questions about how it will work and iron out any confusion. It can help convince management and others of the new process benefits. Problems encountered in the pilot project, such as training, can be resolved before the new process is officially rolled out.

At Rhythm the basic concepts of the Scrum process were implemented in a pilot project, which consisted of 10 requirements. A Sprint Backlog was created, and time and responsibilities were assigned to each requirement. Short daily Scrum meetings were held and the burndown was monitored. The team embraced the opportunity to be self-organised and self-managed and although only the fundamentals of the Scrum principles were applied, the project was 100% successful (Figure 2, [18]). Previously, the same team had taken up to 4 times longer to complete a project with a similar amount of requirements.

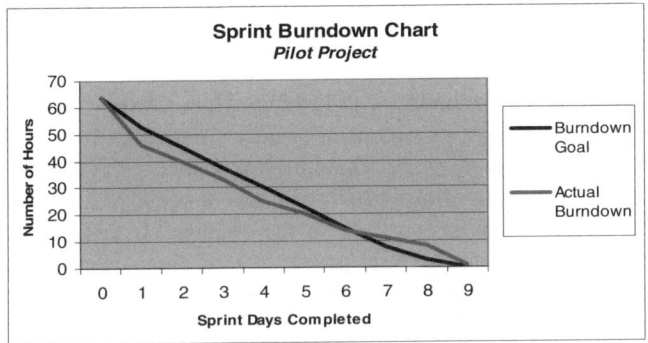

Fig. 2. Burndown Chart for Pilot Project

Pilot team members reported that they preferred using the Scrum process and would like to implement it in future projects. They also highlighted aspects of the process with which they were not familiar. This resulted in Scrum Master training being organised for some team members and general Scrum training for the entire team. Consequently, the team were equipped with the essential information and technical ability when the Rhythm Help project was officially launched.

Step 6: Plan for and Create Short-Term Wins
Kotter argues that it takes time to successfully implement significant change and momentum can be lost without evidence of progress. Therefore, change should take place in small steps, each having clear goals and objectives. Completing goals communicates a clear message, keeping people motivated, maintaining a sense of urgency and ensures that change agents regularly assess progress and revise plans.

Implementing Scrum means that short term wins for a software development project are inherent in the process. As each 4 week Sprint has a clear goal and results in a demonstrable product it was easy to assess what was achieved in the Sprint, acknowledge how much has been accomplished in a particular phase, and realise what work remains to be completed.

Measuring success is not something that Kotter [13] emphasises greatly at this stage but other advocates such as Mathiassen et al., [21] recommend the use of methods to monitor the improvements that have been made. There are many benefits of having such measurement criteria in place. Firstly, measurements can be used as a means of keeping those directly involved in the change project motivated. Secondly, positive results reassure management that the change project is evolving in the right direction. Thirdly, the measurement results show a direct correlation between the effort being invested and the result being achieved. This visible progression in the change project clearly results in further promoting the commitment to the change from staff and management alike.

Within Rhythm, having clear goals, objectives, project completion criteria and process measurements explicitly stated in the implementation plan was advantageous. Measurements were gathered and documented at the end of each successive Sprint allowing comparison of results were comparable and recognition of progress and process improvement. These included fault density, turnaround times of product change requests, task effort estimates and burndown rate.

Step 7:   Consolidate Improvements and Produce More Change
Given the length of a change management project it can often happen that the team celebrates victory prematurely [13]. Once the immediate crisis has been addressed there is a temptation to relax efforts which will have a negative impact on the project as well as the morale of those working on the change. If this happens, it can be difficult, if not impossible, to motivate people to start again. For this reason Senior and Fleming [11] argue that it is necessary to revisit the original plan on a regular basis and revise it in accordance with current situations and circumstances and Kotter suggests that management or change advocates be even more involved in the process to ensure that the changes are continued.

At Rhythm, the Scrum process was consistently implemented and each Sprint introduced a new and improved element of the process. At the end of each Sprint a retrospective meeting was held and the team decided what elements of the process needed to be added, removed or tweaked to improve performance in the subsequent Sprint. The advantage of Scrum meant that the suggestions raised at the retrospective meeting were translated into tasks, added to the Backlog and assigned a deadline for completion during the following Sprint. Consistently assigning time to process improvement in the Sprint Backlog avoided 'premature victory' pitfall.

Step 8:   Institutionalise New Approaches
The final state is what Kotter calls *"anchoring new approaches in the culture"*. If the change has been implemented so that it is now part of the organisations culture then the change has been successful. The required change must be reinforced on a regular basis and this can be done by building the change into career development plans and reward systems [11].

This step is beyond the scope of this case study as; according to the ISO/IEC 15504 Process Assessment Model [25] the process has not yet reached the level of maturity to be considered part of the culture at Rhythm. However, using Sprints is now an accepted and expected approach among the Dublin team members. Colleagues across the world are now requesting help and advice as they implement similar processes. In this regard, it is imperative that the Dublin team perfect their performance as they are fast becoming a "Centre of Excellence" in this area.

7 Discussion

Adopting an agile development practice is a process of continuous learning and improvement [2] and the transition from sequential development requires intense focus and strict discipline. The steps outlined by Kotter were beneficial when implementing the Scrum process at Rhythm. However, there were aspects relating to agile development and software engineering in general that were either overlooked or not given enough consideration. Likewise, there were elements of the framework that were unnecessary or did not warrant as much attention as Kotter advised.

Firstly, when Kotter refers to change management, he assumes that the approach is always top-down. At Rhythm, the change project was introduced by middle management. As a result one of the first steps conducted in the change project required gaining the support and approval of senior and corporate management teams.

The sense of urgency required by Kotter was inherent in the RhythmHelp project. The team was aware that change was needed. They were willing to make the adjustments to guarantee success. Kotter's steps of preparing goals and objectives and to have a clear and communicated vision worked well. At Rhythm the team went one step further and documented these goals and objectives in a dedicated implementation plan which proved to be an invaluable document in terms of monitoring schedules and recording project measurements.

A fundamental flaw in Kotter's approach is the absence of any mention of a pilot project – which was a concept that worked extremely well for Rhythm as it helped to eliminate stress and apprehension and allowed the team to become self-organised, self-managed and self-directing. The success of the pilot project also served as a means of convincing senior management that the team was taking the right approach.

Measurements were presented to the team at the end of each Sprint and at key stages during the RhythmHelp project. These provided quick wins and inspired confidence in the development and management teams. They proved that the development and change projects were moving in the right direction. Measurements also helped to maintain focus and sustain the improvement efforts. Currently, in Rhythm, they are concerned with continually improving upon the new performance levels achieved by the group and finding better ways of working.

Following Kotter's model was a beneficial starting point for implementing a change project and although it wasn't entirely suitable; its use prevented the Rhythm team in Dublin from making some of the customary mistakes that organisations often make during change projects. Without using Kotter's model, the organisation may have faced difficulty in implementing agile development. Our research shows that, through following Kotter's structured change model and tweaking it to suit our specific needs, the Scrum process was implemented efficiently.

8 Conclusion

Development teams considering an agile approach should first examine their immediate needs and determine if this is a suitable solution. They should be aware that, initially, agile methodologies work best with smaller groups. We recommend that teams adopting an agile approach should first select the principles that suit them and follow them closely. After initial implementation, other aspects of the process can be introduced. As the team gets more confident during later iterations or even projects, principles and methods can be customised to suit their own needs and the whole process should eventually become second nature to the group.

There are many books and references available on change management and agile development. Reading case studies by companies in similar situations is strongly recommended as they present both realistic and beneficial lessons. Textbooks may concentrate too much on positives and offer only regimented solutions. Case studies on previous experiences will give the researcher a more balanced insight.

Given the Rhythm experience, we recommend that the change from a traditional to agile process should be managed through the use of a prescribed framework. This will ensure that change is implemented thoroughly within the organisation. While Kotter's change model was a good basis in this case, there were specific aspects relating to agile development and software engineering in general that were either overlooked or not given enough consideration. Likewise, there were elements of the model that were unnecessary or did not warrant as much attention as Kotter advised. In this regard we conclude that a more tailored and specific framework is required for software development companies who are moving from sequential to agile development. Research on this aspect is currently underway.

The process at Rhythm has progressed so well that techniques such as Extreme Programming (XP) and Test Driven Development (TDD) were introduced subsequently. Scrum is beginning to be applied in its precise form - as a management and control tool for all engineering practices and standards related to the project. However, the change project is far from complete. There are still aspects of the process that require further improvement. Furthermore, as Global Software Development (GSD) projects are being implemented at Rhythm and across the software industry, it is necessary to research this area further to establish how the agile approach can be successfully implemented across multi-site projects.

Acknowledgement

This research is supported by the Science Foundation Ireland funded project, Global Software Development in Small to Medium Sized Enterprises (GSD for SMEs) grant number 03/IN3/1408C within Lero - the Irish Software Engineering Research Centre (http://www.lero.ie) and the Higher Education Authority through the M.Sc. in Software Engineering, University of Limerick. The authors would like to thank the employees and management of Rhythm.

References

1. Law, A., Learn, S.: Waltzing with Changes. In: Proceeding of the Agile Development Conference (2005)
2. Schatz, B., Abdelshafi, I.: Primavera Gets Agile: A Successful transition to Agile Development. IEEE Software 22(3), 36–42 (2005)
3. Leszak, M., Perry, D., Stoll, D.: A Case Study in Root Cause Defect Analysis. In: 22nd International Conference on Software Engineering (June 2000)

4. Beck, K.: Extreme Programming Explained – Embrace Change. Addison-Wesley, Reading (2000)
5. Goldman, S., Nagle, R., Preiss, K.: Agile Competitors & Virtual Organisations: Strategies for Enriching Customer. Wiley & Sons, New York (1997)
6. Royce, W.W.: Managing the Development of Large Software Systems. In: Proceedings of IEEE WESCON, pp. 1–9 (1970)
7. Boehm, B.: A Spiral Model of Software Development and Enhancement, vol. 21(5), pp. 61–72. IEEE Computer Society Press, Los Alamitos (1988)
8. Laplante, P., Neill, C.: The Demise of the Waterfall Model is Imminent and Other Urban Myths. Queue 1(10) (2004)
9. Schwaber, K., Beedle, M.: Agile Software Development with Scrum. Prentice Hall, England (2002)
10. Forte, G.: Managing Change for Rapid Development. IEEE Software 14(6), 114–123 (1997)
11. Senior, B., Fleming, J.: Organizational Change, 3rd edn. Prentice Hall, England (2006)
12. Mosier, S., Guenterburg, S., Raphael, R.: The Relationship of Technology Change Management to Risk Management. In: Proceedings of the IEEE Engineering Management Society (2000)
13. Kotter, J.: Leading Change. Harvard Business School Press, Boston (1996)
14. Lippit, R., Watson, J., Westley, B.: The Dynamics of Planned Change. Her Court Brace, New York (1958)
15. Kotter, J.: Leading Change: Why Transformation Efforts Fail. Harvard Business School Press, Boston (2005)
16. Miles, M., Huberman, A.: Qualitative Data Analysis, 2nd edn. SAGE Publications, USA (1994)
17. Richardson, I., Varkoi, T.: Managing for Change when Implementing Software Process Improvement Initiatives. In: European Software process Improvement Conference, EuroSPI 2003 (2003)
18. Hayes, S.: Assessing the Suitability of Kotter's Change Model for Software Development Organisations Moving from Sequential to Agile Development, Thesis (MSc.) University of Limerick (2007)
19. Borjesson, A., Mathiassen, L.: Making SPI Happen: The IDEAL Distribution Effort. In: Proceedings of the 36th Hawaii International Conference on System Sciences (HICSS 2003) (2003)
20. Small, A., Downey, E.: Managing Change: Some Important Aspects. In: Proceeding of the Change Management and New Industrial Revolution (IEMC 2001) (2001)
21. Mathiassen, L., Ngwenyama, O., Aaen, I.: Managing Change in Software Process Improvement. IEEE Software 22(6), 84–91 (2005)
22. Jones, J., Aguirre, D., Calderone, M.: 10 Principles of Change Management (2004) (accessed 20th September 2006), http://www.strategybusiness.com/
23. Gremba, J., Myers, C.: The IDEAL Model: A Practical Guide for Improvement. Software Engineering Institute (SEI) Publication, Bridge (3) (1997)
24. Kotter, J., Schlesinger, L.: Choosing Strategies for Change. Harvard Business Review 57(2), 106–114 (1979)
25. Software Engineering Institute; International Standard for Process Assessment (ISC/IEC 15504) (2007) (accessed 12th April 2007), http://www.sei.cmu.edu

Agile Estimation with Monte Carlo Simulation

Juanjuan Zang

Jzang@thoughtworks.com

Abstract. Work estimation is very important for Agile projects, especially for time critical ones. Inaccurate effort estimation can cause over-commitment, scope creep and trust in the team. Though re-estimation sometimes is necessary, it usually doesn't happen due to the time and budget constraints. Moreover, the initial communication and commitment to business users and stakeholders make it more difficult to re-estimate and revise the project plan and launch date. This paper discusses how to manage the estimation uncertainty, reduce the risk of inaccurate estimation, and better communicate to upper management by using Monte Carlo model simulation.

Keywords: Agile, Iteration, Release, Estimation, Velocity, Monte Carlo Model, Simulation, Random number, Frequency.

1 Introduction

Every project needs effort estimation in order to provide useful information on release planning, project progress, work remaining and milestones to be achieved. Every project requires some estimate of how long the project will take. For a typical Agile project, once the list of stories capturing the overall scope of the work comes out, the next step is to estimate all the stories in the backlog list. The estimation, along with story prioritization, is the backbone of release and iteration planning. Once the team finishes the estimation for each story, the team can create the release plan with an estimate of release date, or even a project plan, with a projection of a go live date based on the estimation of total effort, the story priority, and the assumed team velocity per iteration[1]. The release plan and date are communicated to the business users, stakeholders, and upper management, and then the development starts. In most projects, this initial work goes smoothly. But then comes the "estimation itch:" based on new information and knowledge acquired, the team feels the need to re-estimate the stories.

Now what do we do? Regardless of the question whether the team SHOULD and CAN re-estimate the effort of the stories, the key challenge is how the team will communicate the new release plan and date to business users and upper management if the estimates change?

Before answering this question, let's revisit the estimation the team initially did.

---

[1] Usually use historical data, sometimes run an initial iteration and use the velocity of that iteration, or sometimes just take a guess.

P. Abrahamsson et al. (Eds.): XP 2008, LNBIP 9, pp. 172–179, 2008.

An initial estimation is not supposed to be accurate. The exercise of estimation is for the developers to converge on a single estimate for the story based on the best knowledge they have at that time. However the best knowledge they have, according to Philosophers, is called *priori* knowledge, which is knowledge before you experience something. Let's call this *knowledge-before-the-fact*. This is the type of knowledge the team has when they estimate something. Before estimating development of a particular story, say for profile creation, the team thinks it's about 5 story points, because it seems to be about the same total effort as some other story, also estimated at 5 points. But after gaining more knowledge or further information, which is called *a posteriori* knowledge, or after-the-fact[2] the team realizes that the example profile creation story is actually 8 points.

In AMDD (Agile Model Driven Development), the team usually does requirements envisioning in the first week or the first iteration of the project (iteration 0). The goal of the effort is to identify some high-level requirements as well as the scope of the release, or what they think the system should do. The team works closely with business users and end users to explore how users will work with the system. The team usually sketches a domain model which identifies fundamental business entity types and the relationships, and a user interface model which explores UI and usability issues. The objective here is to build a shared understanding rather than to write detailed documentation. Based on the identified high level requirements and all other information during the initial envisioning, the team produces an initial cost estimate and schedule, or the release plan. The team does more than just write stories; they discuss each story with business users and document all the questions, assumptions, the risk factors (the volatility, the complexity and the completeness) associated with each story. Yet the requirements are very high level, and each story has so many uncertainties, the estimation is still just an estimate, not the actual work effort. Regardless of how much envisioning done, it is always expected the team will acquire new information and new knowledge later, the original estimation may deviate and the re-estimation may have to happen.

If we call the knowledge-before-the-fact estimation "apple," and after-the-fact estimation "orange," the dilemma of "comparing apples and oranges" is always present. This means the release plan and release date should be tolerant of imprecision in the estimates and should be allowed to adjust if there is an estimation blowout. Unfortunately, most of time, this is not the case.

2 Background

The first project I finished early last year was a "quasi-fixed bid" project meaning the bid was priced on a per iteration basis. The throughput goal per iteration was estimated in story point based on projected load factor, planned work days, and staff plan. The development team was responsible for achieving the target throughput goal per

---

[2] Mike Cohen, "To Re-estimate or not; that is the question" Blog, 2007.

iteration[3]. This bidding approach was exclusively based on the total initial estimation of all stories. However, the original estimate was done during the exploration phase (the "Inception Phase"). Most of the stories needed to be re-estimated later because of the lack of knowledge of the domain, the underestimation of the system complexity, and unfamiliarity of back end code at the inception phase. But because of the way the project was bid, no new points could be introduced. We could only *re-distribute* rather than *re-estimate* stories. This caused significant confusion and risk.

The second project I worked on was a BI (Business Intelligence) reporting project for a giant online clothes retailer. The team did the estimation for about 200 stories in one week and after the development started, the team realized the estimation was considerably wide of the mark: almost every single story was misestimated. In addition, the relative story size was not right either. Unfortunately, since the release plan and date were already communicated, and also because this project was a time critical one, the estimation scope was not allowed to change.

Accuracy of estimation is a headache almost on every project. Though everybody admits the initial estimation is just an estimate, not the reflection of the actual effort, the release plan, iteration plan and the date are all built upon it. And once the date is out of door, it is hard to change. So, let's look at the problem from a different angle: Maybe we are not really bad at estimating. What we are really bad at is enumerating all the assumptions or uncertainties that lie behind our estimates[4]. Then the question becomes how to communicate the uncertainty along with the estimation, release plan and the date to stake holders and upper management at first hand?

3 Our Approach

As a spike on one of my projects, we tried a Monte Carlo (MC) simulation model and presented the estimation/probability diagram to our client. The client, a big retailer, wanted to build a robust online service center providing all types of products, services and guides to homeowners. The launch date was critical. The development team had only 3 months. Thus the client was very careful with the estimation of the stories, meaning they had to know how much and what exactly could be delivered within the 3 months. In order to provide the client a big picture showing the estimations with uncertainties, we applied Monte Carlo simulation approach to the estimation. The key to MC simulation is generating the set of random inputs.

First, we came up the complete story list with business users together. We had 61 stories covering the complete scope of the project. Then, we did the estimation together with business users who helped clarifying the stories, answering questions and validating some assumptions[5]. We had the team (4 developers, 2 of them are client developers) give the estimation for each of the story and we documented them

---

[3] See my paper "Project Bid on Iteration Basis", XP2007 conference proceedings, Springer Lecture Notes in Computer Science (Springer LNCS), 2007.

[4] Paul Rook, from his keynote on risk management, European Conference on Software Methods, London, October 1994.

[5] In some cases, business analyst or user proxy can represent business user to help the team with the estimation.

all. The estimation scale ranged from 1 to 5 with 5 the most complex. Next, we mapped the complexity to effort. In our case, we generated these by picking a random sample of stories and asking the developers who did the estimates to give us a guess

Table 1. Complexity and Effort Mapping

Complexity	Effort (Hours)
1	8
2	16
3	32
4	64
5	128

Table 2. Story list with initial estimation, MC value and MC effort

Story ID	Priority	Requirement	1st Estimation	2nd Estimation	3rd Estimation	4th Estimation	Random()	MC Value	MC Effort
6.3.1	1	Administrator can log in and navigate to the admin page	4	3	3	3	0.555921215	3	32
6.1.4	1	Administrator can search user by email or last name, then display the list of results	4	5	4	4	0.413699859	5	128
5.1.1	1	Administrator is able to edit user's preferences and profile information	5	2	2	3	0.630137989	2	16
6.1.3	1	Administrator is able to create users of different types	2	4	4	3	0.834879216	3	32
3.3.1	1	Administrator is able to delete user account	2	2	1	1	0.86269591	1	8
1.1.2	1	Using the Refine Search text box, a user can modify the existing question and resubmit a new search request, which will refresh the Answers results page	1	1	2	1	0.629504962	2	16
3.1.1	1	User will be able to rate and comment each Answer. The user must be registered.	4	3	3	3	0.47393431	3	32
1.1.1	1	A user will have the option when submitting a question to the Expert on whether they want to also submit their question to the community as well.	1	1	1	1	0.074078524	1	8
7.2.10	1	A third party will support AB testing to compare the effectiveness of the commercial messages based on the physical placements	2	2	1	1	0.951485484	1	8
3.4.2	1	A user may roll-over an underlined word and recive a pop-up ad with a click through to purchase	2	1	2	1	0.211061509	2	16
6.1.2	1	MMH will provide direction on how the thumbnail Image will be stored. There will be two work stream: one for uploading and checking format. second part will be to resize the image.	4	5	5	4	0.278954786	5	128
1.1.4	1	This tip should be deemed critical which will link to the specific tip detail page	3	4	3	3	0.899020875	3	32
2.2.2	1	Present a few key featured articles that the user can toggle through related three distinct dimensions: Improve, Repair, Maintain	2	3	2	2	0.349332009	3	32
2.2.1	1	Users will be able to remove the content that they saved previously in My Toolbox	2	2	2	2	0.873661367	2	16
7.2.2	1	General Search will include search into Community Answers as well as Articles and Ask the Expert.	2	2	2	2	0.018879821	2	16
2.3.1	1	Clicking on the video will bring up the article in a separate browser to play the movie.	2	2	2	2	0.929727827	2	16
3.2.2	1	Users can sort search results by type of content, date, created, alphabetic by titles	2	2	2	2	0.47580461	2	16
1.1.3	1	Expert Performance Report will include an average time of response to user questions and amount of workload per expert.	2	2	1	1	0.04172776	2	16

of effort required to complete the stories end-to-end. Then we averaged them to come up with the map.

Remark 1. The MC estimation value for each story is an uncertainty and should fall in the range of 1 and 5.

Remark 2. The formula to calculate the MC value for each story:

Estimation=IF(RAND()<(0.25),1^{st}estimation,IF(AND(RAN()>=(0.25),
(RAND()<0.5)),2^{nd}estimation,IF(AND(RAND()>=(0.5),(RAND()<0.75)),   (1)
3^{rd}estimation ,4th estimation))).

Remark 3. The four estimations represent the estimation given by each developer.

You can use the **Random Number Generation** tool in Excel's Analysis ToolPak Add-In to produce static random numbers for a few distributions. In our case, we made use of Excel's **RAND()** formula so that every time the worksheet recalculated, a new random number was generated.

Let's say we want to **run *max*=10000 evaluations** of our model and we can achieve this using the following Macro.

```
Sub MCmacro()
'
' MCmacro Macro
' Macro recorded 1/3/2008 by jzang
'

    Dim Counter As Integer
    Dim Max As Integer

    Max = 10000

    For Counter = 1 To Max
    Calculate
    Selection.Copy
    Sheets("Sheet4").Select
    Cells(Counter, 1).Select
    Selection.PasteSpecial Paste:=xlPasteValues, Operation:=xlNone, SkipBlanks _
        :=False, Transpose:=False
    Sheets("Sheet1").Select
    Application.CutCopyMode = False

    Next Counter
End Sub
```

In our case, we ran our model 10000 times. Here are the results:

Table 3. MC samples with estimation hours, frequency and accumulative probability

Effort(Hours)	Frequency	Probability	Cumulative Probability
1088	1	0.0001	0.01
1104	3	0.0003	0.04
1112	9	0.0009	0.13
1120	10	0.001	0.23
1128	18	0.0018	0.41
1136	24	0.0024	0.65
1144	31	0.0031	0.96
1152	46	0.0046	1.42
1160	52	0.0052	1.94
1168	65	0.0065	2.59
1176	84	0.0084	3.43
1184	93	0.0093	4.36
1192	114	0.0114	5.5
1200	124	0.0124	6.74
1208	171	0.0171	8.45
1216	198	0.0198	10.43
1224	227	0.0227	12.7
1232	242	0.0242	15.12
1240	270	0.027	17.82
1248	303	0.0303	20.85
1256	302	0.0302	23.87
1264	341	0.0341	27.28
1272	354	0.0354	30.82
1280	358	0.0358	34.4
1288	348	0.0348	37.88
1296	415	0.0415	42.03
1304	377	0.0377	45.8
1312	384	0.0384	49.64
1320	370	0.037	53.34
1328	356	0.0356	56.9
1336	339	0.0339	60.29
1344	351	0.0351	63.8
1352	359	0.0359	67.39
1360	347	0.0347	70.86
1368	307	0.0307	73.93
1376	269	0.0269	76.62
1384	265	0.0265	79.27
1392	217	0.0217	81.44
1400	210	0.021	83.54
1408	207	0.0207	85.61
1416	176	0.0176	87.37
1424	173	0.0173	89.1
1432	146	0.0146	90.56
1440	136	0.0136	91.92
1448	112	0.0112	93.04
1456	110	0.011	94.14
1464	95	0.0095	95.09
1472	88	0.0088	95.97
1480	70	0.007	96.67
1488	53	0.0053	97.2
1496	50	0.005	97.7
1504	53	0.0053	98.23
1512	41	0.0041	98.64
1520	27	0.0027	98.91
1528	19	0.0019	99.1
1536	25	0.0025	99.35
1544	15	0.0015	99.5
1552	13	0.0013	99.63
1560	12	0.0012	99.75
1568	9	0.0009	99.84
1576	2	0.0002	99.86
1584	7	0.0007	99.93
1600	6	0.0006	99.99
1608	1	0.0001	100

Remark 4. The hours represent the total effort in order to finish all the stories in the list.

4 Conclusion

Using the data in table 3, we came up with the Monte Carlo (MC) diagram which showed the frequency and the cumulative probability corresponding to each possible total effort to complete the project. As you can see from figure 1, the development estimation is associated with a probability.

Probability	Development Estimate (Hours)
50%	1312
65%	1345
75%	1370
90%	1432

Estimation is nothing that happens "to" business. Instead, it is always "with" the business. Without business requirements, there will be nothing for the team to estimate. Without business users' participation, there will be no validity of the estimation. Without new business information and changes flowing in, there will be no opportunity to re-estimate.

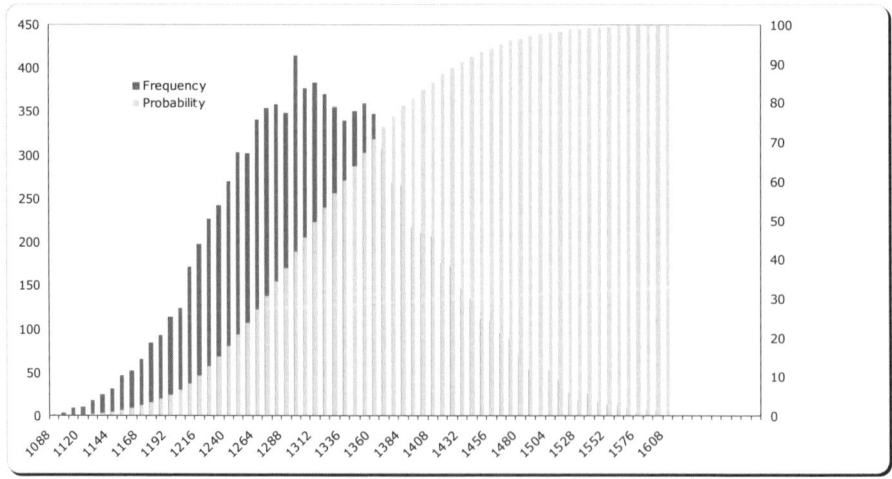

Fig. 1. MC estimation diagram

The presented approach doesn't serve as a solution to replace re-estimation. Re-estimation always happens. It is a very common phenomenon that business users feel quite hard to understand estimation is just an estimate instead of the actual work effort. When new information and knowledge come in, re-estimation needs to happen and this should happen iteratively with business. The communication with the business about the project progress and the impact on delivery caused by re-estimation should also happen iteratively. This approach doesn't replace all the iterative activities above. Instead, it gives awareness to business users and sets the appropriate expectation which prepares the business to understand and embrace the possibility of delivery date changes.

The development estimation along with the MC diagrams was well received by the business users, stakeholders and upper management. This set the right expectation. More importantly, stakeholders realized the uncertainty of the estimates, the probability of project completion date and the risk of over commitment.

References

1. Cohn, M.: User Stories Applied: For Agile Software Development. Addison-Wesley Professional, Reading (2004)
2. Cohn, M.: Agile Estimating and Planning. Prentice Hall PTR, Englewood Cliffs (2005)
3. Demarco, T., Lister, T.: Waltzing With Bears: Managing Risk on Software Projects. Dorset House Publishing Company (incorporated, 2003)
4. Highsmith, J.: Agile Project Management: Creating Innovative Products. Addison-Wesley Professional, Reading (2004)
5. Denne, M., Cleland-Huang, J.: Software by Numbers: Low-Risk, High-Return Development. Prentice Hall PTR, Englewood Cliffs (2004)

The Pomodoro Technique for Sustainable Pace in Extreme Programming Teams

Federico Gobbo[1] and Matteo Vaccari[2]

[1] Dipartimento di Informatica e Comunicazione,
University of Insubria, Via Mazzini 5, 21100 Varese, Italy
federico.gobbo@uninsubria.it
[2] Sourcesense Italy, Via Venezia 23,
20099 Sesto San Giovanni, Milan, Italy
m.vaccari@sourcesense.com

Abstract. One of the common challenges of an Extreme Programming (XP) team is to find strategies so to reinforce practices and increase velocity. Most practices have found at least one optimal strategy tested and approved practically by the community, while 'sustainable pace' is core tenet missing a clear strategy. The aim of the Pomodoro Technique (PT) is exactly to fill this gap. The PT is a timeboxing strategy originally meant for optimizing personal work and study and then applied to XP. The PT is widely applied by Italian Agile teams, but is still little known elsewhere. This paper examines how the PT is applied by them and how it integrates with XP.

1 Introduction

Starting an Extreme Programming (XP) team from scratch is always a challenge, just as it is to transform an "ordinary" software team in a genuinely XP one. One of the key point in enhancing an XP team is promoting team velocity, i.e. its productivity measured in story points completed in a given iteration. Team pressure in individual programmers' experience is well-known in XP literature and the use of Yesterday's Weather is the suggested practice so to manage the fear of censure and the risk of overwhelming [2]. Nevertheless, one of the known common errors in mentoring an XP team is to put too much attention to velocity too early, with unuseful stress. In other words, the risk in focusing on velocity is to reduce enthusiasm among team members: this risk should be addressed more clearly – after all, agile software developers' main mantra is 'coding as fun', and if this becomes untrue the whole process collapses. In our experience, achieving an equilibrium between team velocity and individual satisfaction is much more difficult for XP teams than "ordinary" ones, because of the very characteristics of this lightweight methodology. Usually the impact of (un)sustainable pace in a XP team's daily work so to achieve this equilibrium is underestimated. We found out that an unstressful – as well as efficient – way to help teams find their 'natural' rythm in daily work, in other words a sustainable pace, is the most direct way to achieve the necessary equilibrium between team and individual needs. The Pomodoro Technique (PT) can be used fruitfully in this sense.

P. Abrahamsson et al. (Eds.): XP 2008, LNBIP 9, pp. 180–184, 2008.

2   Pomodori for Time Boxing

The PT is a time boxing strategy people can apply in any situation, e.g., homework, study, cleaning house, and indeed software development, spread out from the psychological notions of time elaborated by Bergson and Minkowski [3]. It was invented initially for individual work, but it was then applied especially by XP teams. This paper covers only this last case. The goal of the technique is to perceive time as a value ("I'm doing my best at a right rythm"), instead of an enemy ("I have not enough time; I'm late"). When the PT is applied, we observe that wasted time and overwork are drastically reduced, while the distinction between free time and work time becomes clearer. The individual comes to respect the value of time more, both free time and work time. The heart of the PT is to start a 25-minutes timer and then focus completely on one task until it rings; no email, instant messaging or any other distraction is allowed. When the timer rings, people relax, push away the keyboard and rest for five minutes. This is a 'pomodoro': 25 minutes of focused, uninterrupted work on one task. The "pomodoro" name comes from the use of a common kitchen timer in the shape of a tomato (*pomodoro* in Italian). The 5 minutes break permits the performer to keep his or her own attention curve at its best, enhancing the rising points and at the same time minimizing the lowest ones. To improve this effect, every four subsequent successful pomodori a longer pause is recommended, usually 15 minutes long. This combination of breaks and pauses permit people not to work in overtime, being less efficient because of overtime work. This alternance of working time and breaks and pauses give the pace to the day, both to individuals and teams, and hopefully helps people adjust the rythm in order to reach a real sustainable pace.

There are two important rules in the PT: the Zero Pomodoro Rule and the Fundamental Rule. The Zero Pomodoro Rule states that if the pomodoro is interrupted, that pomodoro counts for nothing. This is a corollary of the Fundamental Rule: a pomodoro is indivisible. Practitioners become soon aware that there are two kinds of interruptions: the internal ones ("I should check email; I'll get me a coffee"), due to fear of being unsuccessful or to the difficulty of focusing on a single task for even as little as 25 minutes; and the external ones (a phone call, a request from a collegue), which are more difficult to manage. In fact, giving in to all sorts of unplanned and apparently urgent tasks can literally destroy all planning activity. This is made more visible in XP team, as the velocity is drastically reduced: "protecting the pomodoro" leads to fewer interruptions. The PT is also a valid tool for XP coaches, who want to protect the team members from external influences during their daily iterations. An Italian coach even introduces XP at the first glance by only retrospectives and the PT as the practices: the first practice tells which other practices are needed, while the PT get the team aware how much their daily work is really focused [7].

3   Applying the Pomodoro Technique in XP

During development, for every pair of developers there is a timer. The owner of the card is responsible for loading the timer, while recording is made on the card itself. During a meeting with people external to the team, the pomodoro may also be used to help people focus and reduce wasted time, and also to record precisely how much team effort was invested.

In XP teams, internal interruptions are easier to reduce, as no one is working really alone, so there is an implicit control so that everybody avoids at least explicit distractions. Different people deal with external interruptions differently, but some common patterns can be found. The most used pattern is called *inform, negotiate, callback* [3]. When someone interrupts, for instance a colleague, the developer *informs* that they are in working time, usually by saying "I'm in the middle of my pomodoro". Then they *negotiate* how urgent the request really is. In most cases the new task is delayed until the end of the pomodoro (e.g. "I'll finish my pomodoro in about 7 minutes, then I'll come"). In fact, there are few urgencies that can't be delayed for a few minutes, so people accept this *callback* strategy. Surprisingly, one of the most difficult aspects of the PT is the art of having a break. A break is *really* a break: people should relax during breaks, have a cup of tea or maybe just stand up and take a deep breath. One important thing is that you shouldn't actively think about the activity performed in the last pomodoro or what you expect to do in the next one. Thinking about something else relieves the mind, often leading to creative solutions, exactly because of the change of the attention focus. In spite of this it is not rare, while pair programming, to see the navigator calling the driver who is still juggling eggs in his mind, even after the ring of the timer.

It is worth to notice, that the ideal engineering days are different from the actual days: typically teams estimate eight pomodori for a project while half of them are actually spent in meeting, presales or support. In other words, there is no formula to convert pomodori to calendar time, because of interruptions on one side and of shorter successful pomodori on the other one (this is the No Formula Rule [3]). In our experience, teams learn to estimate every type of working activity, not only design and development.

There is a danger of viewing the pomodoro as a taylorist method for regulating the workers' day. It is not so, because the timer is used and regulated by the individual or pair. One might expect that, in a normal eight-hours work day, we should be able to do 15 or 16 pomodori. In practice, in a perfect day with no interruptions, it is rare to be able to do more than 12 pomodori. In a healthy, well-rested team it is reasonable to expect everyone to do about 10 pomodori per day. Where is the rest of the time going? For the most part in pauses or non-recorded activities, such as reading personal email. It might seem that this is quite unfortunate for the employer, as he's only getting 5 hours of concentrated work per day. But in fact, it is very advantageous to be able to see with this degree of precision how much *real* work he's getting and exactly *on what* it is spent.

How much does the technique cost? In the PT the first pomodoro is spent planning the rest of the day, and the last pomodoro is for recording of what was done. The overhead of two pomodori seems large; but there is much value in planning and in retrospecting. The first pomodoro can coincide with the daily stand-up meeting.

4   Case Study: XP User Groups and Teams

XP user groups collect people who are interested in exploring XP both in theory and practice. It is a good environment to share ideas, experience, and to experiment new techniques. In Milan the XP user group is highly business oriented, while in Varese it is more linked to the local University [5].

Pomodori came into user stories as an auxiliary tool for difficult estimation. In fact, as each pomodoro is dedicated to a single task, activites are planned along clearly defined subactivities estimated in pomodori: this is coverd by the More Than Five Pomodori and Less Than One Pomodoro rules. The first rule says that if you estimate an activity more than five pomodori, this should be split up. The complementary rule says that if several activities are estimated at less than one pomodoro, they should be joined together. The only exception is during the *last* pomodoro of a given activity: if the estimation of a given activity was of three pomodori and that activity is finished during the first 10-15 minutes of the third pomodoro, that pomodoro can be considered completed. Of course, if the activity is completed in the first 5-10 minutes, an overestimation occured, and that pomodoro shouldn't be counted.

Unlike XP user groups, XP teams should deal with the pressure of business needs and different work contexts. For instance, a team has chosen to deal with multiple simultaneous projects with pomodoro. The relative priority of the customers were given by management, and the available weekly pomodori were assigned according to proportions: if the most important customer is as important as all the others put together, then the team will dedicate 50% of the available pomodori to them [7].

There are different PT recording strategies among teams. For instance, in the Wallabiez team in Sinapsi (Milan) a big visible chart is used, where every day a different person is nominated the "Frodo of the Pomodoro", i.e. the bearer of the timer who is responsible for loading it and tracking: this allowed to the team to realize they were much less productive after lunch, so they started to colour the morning pomodori differently, so to make the problem visible [6]. In the Moonring team (Databtech, Milan), as well as in the Varese XP-UG, the pomodori are recorded in a wiki [5,8], while in other teams – e.g. in Sourcesense (Milan), Quinary (Milan) and XP Labs (Rome) custom applications were built for this purpose.

Sometimes people use the PT in open spaces where other people do not; in that case the ticking of the kitchen timer can cause problems. In those cases a software pomodoro can be used, but its use is highly controversial, as experience says that it is most difficult to have a break. In alternative, different hardwares seem to be more effective, e.g. hourglasses or countdowns on mobile phones, whose ringing is socially accepted. Furthermore, people invented strategies also for unnoticed breaks, i.e. to relax in front of their monitors, for example throughout unobtrusive qi gong exercises for the eyes [4].

5   Concluding Remarks

Sustainable pace is a practice of XP directly connected to the inner cycle of an XP team (e.g. where pair programming, simple design and refactoring are performed) and to retrospectives. Even if the PT doesn't improve velocity directly, so that it is difficult to find precise measures of its effect, in our experience it get people more aware on velocity so to improve it during the next iteration. Moreover, the PT is a lightweight measure of the effort easily understood: in our experience, retrospectives held after the introduction of the PT are more focused on work and on real working data, and creative solution about avoiding external interruptions are found. People learn to give priorities more explicitly, and, most importantly, they start feeling time as an ally.

References

1. Beck, K.: Extreme Programming Explained: Embrace Change, 1st edn. Addison-Wesley, Upper Saddle River (2000)
2. Beck, K., Fowler, M.: Planning Extreme Programming. Addison-Wesley, Upper Saddle River, NJ (2001)
3. Cirillo, F.: The Pomodoro Technique. XPLabs Technical Report version 1.3. English Version (Published June 15, 2007), http://www.tecnicadelpomodoro.it
4. Ferraro, D., Ma Xu, Z.: Qi-Gong Pour les Yeux. Guy Trédaniel Éditeur, Paris (1998)
5. Gobbo, F., Bozzolo, P., Girardi, J., Pepe, M.: Learning Agile Methods in Practice: Advanced Educational Aspects of the Varese XP-UG Experience. In: Concas, G., Damiani, E., Scotto, M., Succi, G. (eds.) XP 2007. LNCS, vol. 4536, pp. 173–174. Springer, Heidelberg (2007)
6. Wallabiez Team: La galleria dei Wallabiez [Wallabiez' gallery] (Cited January 5 2008), http://wiki.sinapsi.com/La_galleria_dei_wallabiez
7. Lana, G.: Personal communication (Cited January 5, 2008), http://www.gabrielelana.it
8. Mercanti, A.: Un'esperienza di Tracking [A tracking experience]. In: Italian Agile Day, Bologna, Italy (November 23, 2007), http://mythodology.com/iad07/IAD07-Mercanti.pdf

Adopting Iterative Development: The Perceived Business Value

Caryna Pinheiro, Frank Maurer, and Jonathan Sillito

University of Calgary
Calgary, Alberta, Canada
{capinhei,frank.maurer,sillito}@ucalgary.ca

Abstract. Iterative development is a common characteristic of agile methods. It is important to understand how the adoption of an iterative process provides business value, and how this value can be used to buy management support to implement other agile techniques. This paper exposes to the community an experience report of a large government agency's migration from a Waterfall process to an iterative methodology, the Rational Unified Process (RUP). Through field observations and semi-formal interviews with key business partners, we found five main areas of improvement: reestablishment of business involvement, better distribution of acceptance testing effort, introduction of a testing team, less pushback on necessary changes, improved communication and management of expectations.

Keywords: Iterative development, agile techniques, business value, Rational Unified Process, acceptance testing.

1 Background

This paper contributes to an understanding of the business advantages in adopting an iterative development practice in a bureaucratic industrial setting. Such an understanding is important as many business leaders prefer to adopt processes that have been successfully implemented by others, to reduce the risk of failure [1]. The company under study is a large Oil & Gas government agency that lacked the initial management support to adopt mainstream agile methods. This agency has a workforce of 900+ employees, with a large IT department comprised of over 10 different IT Programs. This study collected field observations and interviews from the key business representatives of the largest IT Program in the corporation, focusing on a set of three existing applications, and two newly developed systems. These multi-million dollar projects support business critical functions, such as the digital submission of information, internal processing of such information, and the publishing of the results to the public.

The original IT vision was to develop a simple solution to provide a central data management point to the business partners. The first release commenced in early 2001, with a group of 4-6 developers. The development team did not formally adopt a development methodology, but was following a Waterfall approach: gather all the system requirements, then develop the entire application, which is at last handed off to the business partners for testing and approval. After the first few releases, a new

P. Abrahamsson et al. (Eds.): XP 2008, LNBIP 9, pp. 185–189, 2008.

vision for a workflow system, that would allow digital submission of data for quicker turn-around times, was born. By 2004, the team increased to over 15 developers, with a total of 40+ team members (including business analysts, technical support, and managers). The former Waterfall process was not able to support the increasing pace of development, and many releases were delayed, resulting in poor software quality and cost overruns. Late in 2004, the corporation decided to adopt the IBM Rational Unified Process (RUP) [2], as it provided an iterative development approach as well as the degree of formality and traceability desired by the top-level management. Many Agilists consider the Rational Unified framework heavyweight, but since its inception in 1998, the RUP framework has been customized to fit more agile environments [4, 5] and the company adopted such a lighter version.

The adoption stages were identified as: pre-RUP, transition to RUP, and partial RUP adoption. IBM suggests an iterative approach to the RUP implementation, "adoption through execution" [2]. The company's current execution state includes: the iterative RUP lifecycle (inception, elaboration, construction, and transition), Rational Tools, role sets, and selected work products (Design and Use-Case Models, Software Architecture Document, Iteration Plan and Assessment, Risk List, Issues List, Test Case, amongst others). The partial RUP adoption refers to the pre-existing projects, as they did not benefit from the iterative approach since inception, missing the majority of the exercises that result in the above mentioned work products.

The Rational tools that were adopted during the transition stages included software for source code repository management, requirements gathering, and bug logging. The pre-existing systems moved to a spiral approach, where development was conducted in mini waterfall cycles of analysis, development, and testing, with release dates being booked according to business needs. The team later moved to scheduled releases, which are comprised of time boxed 6 week iterations. The two new projects followed the adopted RUP framework since inception.

2 Findings and Observations

Reestablishment of business involvement
During the first system release, the small team atmosphere allowed the business partners to have an active role in the requirements gathering stages of the system development. The project manager would set up business meetings with the involved stakeholders to gather requirements. Some requirements were documented in Word or Excel, others were only verbally communicated to the development team. Later, the development team would create screen mock-ups of the application, and present them to the business partners for feedback during meetings. Although acceptance testing did not occur until development was completed, business partners found the screen shoots extremely useful: *"even though we didn't get to test until the end, when we got the application, it was not about testing the screens and see how they looked like, it was testing to see if they worked, if they met the requirements."* They were very pleased with the first release of the system, which took approximately one year to be production ready. As the number of requirements increased, so did the IT team size. More rigorous management procedures were put into place. Developers needed to follow the project plan more closely, in some cases resulting in frustration, as the plan

was quickly outdated. Business partners were used to contacting developers with requests, who would in turn implement the requirements, causing a delay to the defined project plan, also found by Blotner [3]. As a result, managers prohibited business partners from contacting developers directly: *"we got cut off by management: 'that's it, no more talking to the developers!'"* It got to the point where management would complain about e-mails sent to developers by business: *"don't be seen talking to a developer, […] and really, that environment was not good. For us that doesn't work!"* Business partners felt that they lost the element of teamwork, causing friction and *"blaming games"* between IT management and Business, which was *"very disruptive to everyone involved."*

The introduction of the six week iterations has helped business partners become more involved in the iteration planning, by prioritizing which items need to be worked on first, and which ones require more analysis. They feel more ownership and accountability over the decisions made, which has helped rebuild the teamwork [1]. They are now allowed to contact developers: *"a developer came and sat with me [to discuss a task] and mocked it up in paper, and asked if it was ok with me, which was fantastic."* Still, involvement with developers is limited, as most of the communication goes through the project leaders and business analysts. Perhaps this can be attributed to the responsibilities defined in the RUP roles. Business feels that this *"middleman"* approach to communication has advantages, when dealing with developers that lack interpersonal skills, and drawbacks, as information gets *"lost in translation."* To mitigate this issue, key developers are invited to business meetings.

Business partners feel that the most visible gains come from the new systems that started development using the iterative RUP process, as they were involved in the process since inception. They were not given functional parts of the system to test until the construction stages, but they had iteration assessment meetings where demos were provided, allowing feedback on system functionality. As a result, the first full iteratively implemented system was the first project in more than six years to be delivered on-time and on-budget: *"which is significant for the organization, the first in years, [laughs] that says a lot. Our executive was very happy, from our perspective [it] is great."*

Better distribution of Acceptance Testing effort
The three business managers, corresponding section leads, and a few senior end-users conduct acceptance testing. The interviewed business partners felt that the original development process did not provide reasonable time for testing the system: *"you would get it [the application] for two days, and you need to approve it and its gotta go."* They felt rushed and uncomfortable by having to sign-off on a system that took over 10 months to develop, and only a few days to test. At the end of the development cycle, business had compounded testing to do, which caused an overwhelming workload: *"[testing] is not my full time job. I need to deal with core business. Testing work is supposed to be on the side, but [at that point] becomes fulltime work. I am basically doing two fulltime jobs, which makes things difficult."* Iterative development has time boxed the testing effort required by business to two weeks per iteration. Testing is not compounded, but it can still feel rushed based on the number of changes implemented during the iteration. The business partners see the organized and scheduled acceptance testing effort as a big improvement: *"it is better to plan*

that way, even from a personal life perspective. It is just way more organized than it used to be." Some interviewees actually stated that this organized schedule is the major improvement provided by the process changes made to the existing projects.

Introduction of testing team

A Quality Assurance (QA) team was not available in the pre-RUP stage, as management perceived formal testing as peripheral in comparison with other more pressing deliverables. The code would go from the developers who did not implement any automated tests, to the business partners for testing: *"we used to joke around saying what is the point? I open it [the application] and get the 'yellow screen of death[1]', so you are just wasting my time!"* As suggested by the six key RUP principles for business-driven development, management hired a full-time testing team at the end of the third transitional iteration. After the introduction of the testing team, all code goes through a round of formal testing before getting into the hands of the business users, and as a result the business partners find fewer fatal errors during acceptance testing. They can also focus on the areas that have been changed or included, as the testing team is responsible for the regression testing, which is considered a big time saver: *"it is night and day."* However, the testing required by the QA is complex and time consuming. The QA team is shared between all projects, and may not have enough resources to provide the appropriate levels of manual regression testing. That, in addition to the lack of unit tests, has been a sore spot for pre-existing systems, having problems reappear in production after being fixed. New systems are now implementing unit tests, which allow developers to regression test the application even before it is handed off to the formal testing team.

Less pushback on necessary changes

In the former Waterfall process, IT management would push back to implement changes: *"so you get stuck with it."* It is very difficult for business partners to define the project's scope to the degree of granularity needed at the initial requirements gathering stages: *"it is virtually impossible to foresee all the details and functionality of an application to define a hard scope document. To expect that when creating a scope document is unreasonable and shortsighted."* Business partners would have to make go-no-go decisions close to the production date, and many releases were delayed as much as a year due to poor testing results, and essential requirements being missed in the original scope document.

Iterative development has provided business with a set release schedule that are 6 weeks apart from each other, allowing critical items to be negotiated, prioritized and included in the next release. Also, for new development projects, the iteration assessments and demos allowed business partners to provide the feedback necessary to avoid major changes later on in the process. A visible result of that is the number of bugs[2] in production for the first system developed using RUP, which is less than a dozen compared to the hundreds found in the former ad-hoc projects.

---

[1] This refers to the fatal application errors in .Net, which display the error message in a yellow screen.

[2] Interviewees used the words "bug" and "defect" interchangeably, and both refer collectively to faults and failures. Enhancement requests were logged separately.

Improved communication and management of expectations
In the former process, issues were logged in Excel spreadsheets, discussed in business meetings, prioritized and put away in a place only accessible to managers. The RUP adoption involved the adoption of Rational Tools including a bug and enhancement logging software. Business partners have access to these tools, being able to view what is outstanding, which is very important to assist them in negotiations of shared resources, and to have more realistic expectations of what and when changes will be delivered. They also feel that overall the projects are much more organized, and due to the iterations, they are in constant communication with the team, which helps reduce *"surprises"* at the end of a release cycle.

3 Implications for Practice

The interviewed business partners see the adoption of the iterative RUP process as a definite benefit to the organization, with particular improvements in the areas of organization, communication, accountability, teamwork, and acceptance testing effort. In a bureaucratic governmental environment, bound to set regulations and continuous auditing, the patented IBM RUP framework provided the initial social change required to open the doors to other agile techniques. Management is now providing support for test and continuous integration automation, and new projects are holding daily stand-up meetings with the presence of involved business partners.

References

1. Hartman, F.: Don't Park Your Brain Outside. Project Management Institute (2000)
2. Barnes, J.: Implementing the IBM rational unified process and solutions: a guide to improving your software development capability and maturity. IBM Press (2007)
3. Blotner, J.A.: Agile techniques to avoid firefighting at a start-up. In: OOPSLA 2002 Practitioners Reports, Seattle, Washington, p. 1. ACM, New York (2002)
4. Hirsch, M.: Making RUP agile. In: OOPSLA 2002 Practitioners Reports, p. 1. ACM, New York (2002)
5. Ambler, S.: Agile Modeling: Effective Practices for eXtreme Programming and the Unified Process. John Wiley & Sons, Inc., New York (2002)

Explicit Risk Management in Agile Processes

Christopher R. Nelson, Gil Taran, and Lucia de Lascurain Hinojosa

Institute for Software Research
Carnegie Mellon University
Pittsburgh Pennsylvania 15213, United States
{crnelson,gil,ldelascu}@alumni.cmu.edu

Abstract. This paper explores the implicit nature of risk management in agile processes. It discusses why current techniques for managing risks in agile processes are not sufficient and how the processes can benefit from more explicit techniques. This is supported by the authors' experience with an industry project that was managed using Scrum. Initially, risks in the project were managed implicitly as is typical with agile processes, but more explicit techniques were adopted as the project progressed. The paper will discuss these techniques, mechanisms for incorporating them into agile processes, and lessons learned.

Keywords: Scrum, Risk Management, Software Risk Evaluations.

1 Introduction

Most agile processes [4, 6, 18] claim to be risk driven [15]. The processes themselves are an attempt to mitigate some risks, such as extremely volatile requirements. Agile processes manage risk, but in an implicit fashion. The techniques in these processes inherently deal with risks. However, by doing so, important steps in risk management are neglected. Missing steps include having defined processes or guidelines, mitigation strategies, risk repositories for tracking risks, and defining triggers to indicate the need for changes in the mitigation strategies.

There are commonalities between risk management and agile processes [15]. Risk management steps can be integrated into agile processes to explicitly address risk and this integration can be done in an efficient and lightweight manner to keep the processes honest to their agile spirit [6]. Traditional risk management approaches and tools, such as the Software Engineering Institute's (SEI) taxonomy based risk identification questionnaire and Software Risk Evaluation (SRE) [5,19], IEEE 1540 Standard for Lifecycle Processes – Risk Management [12] or the Project Management Body of Knowledge (PMBoK) [17], can be tailored to better suit smaller teams and agile environments. Risk identification, analysis, mitigation, and tracking can be incorporated into standard practices in agile processes such as prioritized task lists, iteration planning, and iteration reviews.

Section 2 gives a brief overview of the DaVinci Transform project sharing the authors' experience of using explicit risk management techniques with Scrum. Section 3 explores the implicit nature of risk management in agile processes and its

P. Abrahamsson et al. (Eds.): XP 2008, LNBIP 9, pp. 190–201, 2008.

limitations. Section 4 discusses the need for explicit rather than implicit risk management in agile processes. Section 5 describes the risk management framework applied by the DaVinci team. Section 6 details the DaVinci team's experience with explicit risk management in Scrum and the team's migration from an initial implicit risk management style. Section 7 draws out lessons learned from the project including effective and ineffective techniques. Section 8 concludes.

2   The DaVinci Transform Project

2.1   The Stakeholders

The DaVinci Transform project was completed as part of Carnegie Mellon University's (CMU) Master of Software Engineering (MSE) program [10]. The project consisted of five team members and two clients. The team members were students in the MSE program and the clients were senior members of the technical staff at the SEI. The MSE program uses a capstone element called the Studio project to allow students to try out tools techniques and methods learned in core courses and electives in a real project environment.

   While the project was conducted in an academic setting, the clients were still paying customers and the students were all experienced engineers with an average of 5 years of industry experience at companies including Siemens, Interdigital Communications, and IBM. The project lasted for four semesters (16 months) with varying time commitments (12 hours per week to 48 hours per week) depending on the semester. The project had a strict timeline, a budget of 5100 engineering hours, and was monitored and supervised by two senior faculty members of the MSE program. Three of the team members were located in Pittsburgh, Pennsylvania, with the client, and the remaining two were located in Long Island, New York.

2.2   Methodologies

The team used Scrum as their software process. One member on the team had prior experience with Scrum, agile processes in general, and distributed development. These concepts were new to the rest of the team members. Explicit risk management methods were new to all of the team members, but they were exposed to these methods in multiple classes as part of the MSE curriculum. In particular, continuous risk management was covered in a course on managing software development, and the students took a course on software architecture that covered architecture risks through the use of the SEI's Architecture Tradeoff and Analysis Method (ATAM) [2, 3]. Additionally, one of the team's faculty mentors was an expert in risk management.

2.3   The Product

The DaVinci Transform project involved developing a plug-in to the Eclipse [21] IDE that extended the functionality of the SEI's Open Source AADL Tool Environment (OSATE) [22]. OSATE is a tool that supports the modeling of embedded software architectures in the Architecture Analysis and Design Language (AADL)[1]. The AADL is a standard published by the Society of Automotive Engineers (SAE). The technical lead for the standard was one of the DaVinci team's customers. The second customer was the development lead for OSATE. The extensions to OSATE to be developed by the DaVinci team included a framework for developing transformations for AADL models and some example transformations. These transformations involved transforming AADL models to models in other target languages, transforming models in other target languages to models defined in the AADL, and transforming models defined in the AADL to new models defined in the AADL for the purpose of optimizing and re-factoring the input models.

3 Implicit Risk Management in Agile Processes

Agile processes that claim to be risk driven typically address risk management implicitly [15,16]. The processes themselves tend to be mitigation strategies for risks involving tight deadlines and volatile requirements, and the increased visibility by the customer aims at managing expectations while mitigating environmental and organizational risks [7]. In this way, risks are managed implicitly through the techniques commonly found in agile processes. Tasks (also called stories and features) are typically kept in a list (such as Scrum's backlog). These tasks are prioritized at the beginning of each iteration, which means that this implicit risk management is continuous. The prioritization sometimes explicitly calls for consideration of risks, but not always. When the prioritization does not explicitly call for the consideration of risks [15], it is likely that risks are still considered. When a business owner (also called a product owner, client, or customer) prioritizes tasks, it is likely that they are concerned with risks about what the market need is, what features competitors may be releasing, and how end users may react to feature sets. When developers prioritize tasks, they are also likely taking risks into account, subconsciously. Developers are concerned with tasks that seem technically difficult, may be hard to integrate, or may have technical unknowns.

Even when the prioritization does explicitly call for the consideration of risks - it is common in Scrum for developers to prioritize features in the product and sprint backlogs based on technical risk - risks are still being managed implicitly. The risks that make a task risky are not typically identified, that is, the task is not examined to determine what risks are involved in that task. The risks themselves are not analyzed, only the tasks are. No mitigation strategies, beyond simply working on the riskier tasks first, are created. Risks are not tracked to determine if they are mitigated, if they are on track to be mitigated, if they have been mitigated already, or if they have actually become problems (also known as issues). All of these missing pieces are left to the members of the development teams to address on their own with no direction.

4 The Need for Explicit Risk Management in Agile Processes

Simply placing a higher priority on riskier tasks is not managing risk. The risky tasks get addressed, and hopefully completed sooner, than less risky tasks. However, without analyzing a risk, and even more so without identifying the right risks, it is very difficult if not impossible to devise an appropriate plan for risk mitigation, tracking and control [13, 20].

Agile processes do not typically include risk management phases or policies on when and how to identify, analyze and mitigate risk [16]. The inherent belief is that agile methods use empirical process control to continuously monitor how the project is going and that doing so minimizes risks in itself. Furthermore, agile models do not provide a guideline on roles and responsibilities within a team for risk management activities leaving it up to the team to do it collectively. From a risk planning perspective, mitigation must be preceded by explicit risk identification and analysis, or it would be very difficult to track whether a risk is being mitigated, if a new mitigation strategy should be used, or if the risk has been mitigated [9].

To explicitly address risks, teams should spend some amount of time identifying them. Once risks are identified, they should be analyzed and prioritized [5,9,18,19]. Mitigation strategies and triggers can then be devised and built into action plans. The mitigation strategies are prioritized with other tasks for an iteration, and the action plans can be used to track the progress of risk mitigation.

At the end of each iteration, risks should be revisited and the action plans should be used to guide the team in next steps. Based on identification triggers, the team can decide if the current mitigation strategy is working, if a backup strategy should be put in place, if the risk has been mitigated, or if the risk has become a problem and the team needs to switch from prevention to damage control. Once these decisions are made, the results of the decisions can be fed into the planning phase of the next iteration. New risks are then identified, and tasks as parts of mitigation strategies can again be prioritized with other project-related tasks. This should be done continuously throughout the project.

While agile processes do address risk, doing so in an implicit way is dangerous. Implicit management of risks is a reasonable start, but it leaves much room for improvement. Managing risks explicitly, but with techniques that stay true to the spirit of agility, is a necessary next step to improve risk management in agile processes and increase the probability of successful projects.

5   Team DaVinci Risk Management Framework

Team DaVinci borrowed methodologies, tools, and techniques from the SEI to aid in risk management. They are presented here, along with how they were tailored to fit the needs of the project, to better understand the experiences that the team had with respect to managing the risks on their project. Since risk management was viewed as a continuous event, the team applied the SEI's Risk Management Paradigm [20] and, with it, the phases presented in figure 1.

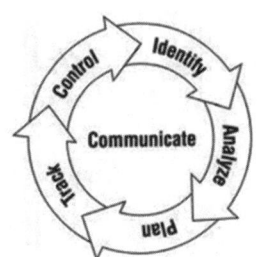

Fig. 1. The SEI Risk Management Paradigm

The steps of identification, analysis, mitigation, tracking and control occurred continuously and run concurrently - e.g., as new risks were identified and analyzed, other risks are being mitigated and tracked - and iteratively - e.g., one mitigation plan might yield new risks.

Communication is central to this risk management paradigm. Therefore, team members were encouraged to communicate the risk status to project (clients, faculty, and team members) during status and review meetings. The information that was shared included a current picture of the risks faced by the team, their status, and what was being done to help mitigate them.

6 Experiences with Explicit Risk Management and Agile Processes

The DaVinci team, as mentioned earlier, followed Scrum for their software development process and thus started out managing risks implicitly. The team felt early on that risk management should be addressed more explicitly than prescribed by Scrum, based on recommendations from CMU faculty, team mentors, and material covered in courses as part of the MSE curriculum. The team started managing risks more explicitly by creating a risk manager role. The person filling this role was responsible for helping the team identify and document risks. However, no tasks were defined for these activities at this point. Tasks for mitigation strategies were not defined either. Risks were identified through informal, and un-facilitated, brainstorming sessions. The captured risks were placed in an excel spreadsheet and the risk manager was responsible for prioritizing the risks based on their expected impacts and timeframes. A general risk mitigation task was included in iteration planning sessions for prioritization with other project tasks. This was not an effective approach. It was difficult for team members to understand what the mitigation task involved and how it supported the project. As a result, the task either did not receive a high enough priority rating to make it into an iteration plan, or it was the most likely task to be dropped if problems were encountered in other tasks. After a couple of

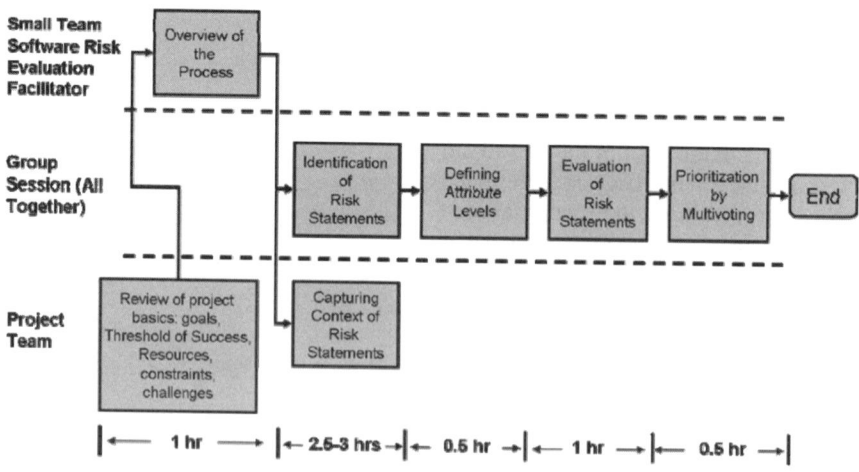

Fig. 2. Small-Team Software Risk Evaluation Process

iterations, the team realized a change in their risk management approach was required. This realization was fueled by several iterations that passed without mitigating a single risk. As a result, the team decided to elicit the help from risk management experts at Carnegie Mellon University and the SEI. Ray Williams from the SEI, and Gil Taran, from Carnegie Mellon University, were brought in to facilitate a small team software risk evaluation (see figure 2), a condensed version of the SEI's taxonomy based SRE method [19]. The goal of this evaluation was to identify and analyze those risks that might stop the team from reaching project success.

Using a technique called the Threshold of Success (ToS), the team was able to define a set of minimum objectives that needed to be met by projects' end for it to be called a success and against which those risks were identified. The result of this half-day evaluation involving all team members was a prioritized list of twenty risks formulated in a condition-consequence form as suggested by Gluch [11]. These risks were documented on the team's Wiki to allow for easy access for viewing and frequent updates. The final process the team followed and the way the risk management steps mapped to Scrum is depicted in figure 3.

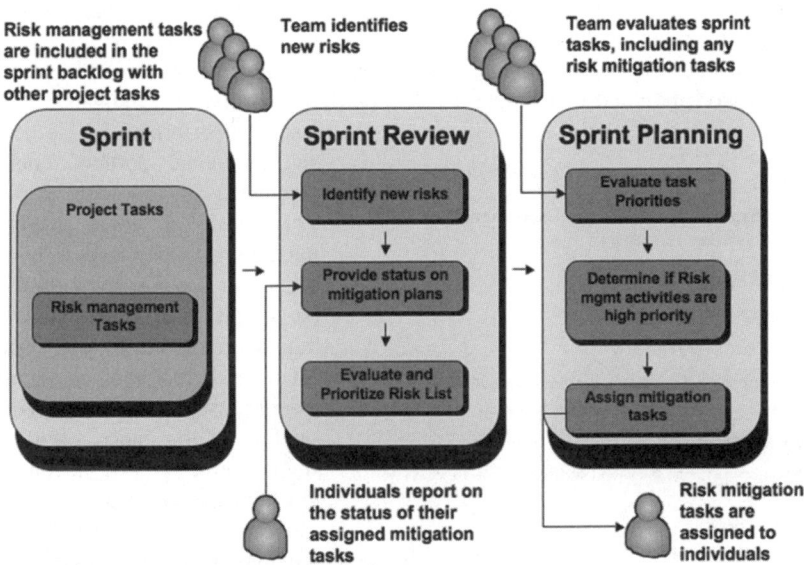

Fig. 3. Mapping Risk Management activities to Scrum Activities

The risk manager then documented the components of the risks - source(s), condition, consequence, impact, timeframe, and probability (see figure 4) - to facilitate the creation of action plans and mitigation strategies. The risk manager then worked with other team members to identify mitigation strategies that might lower the probability, reduce the impact, eliminate the source or consequences or, extend the time frame in which the risk needed to be addressed. Those team members involved (the risk manager, the team lead, and one distant team member) compiled a list of mitigation strategies for the top five risks.

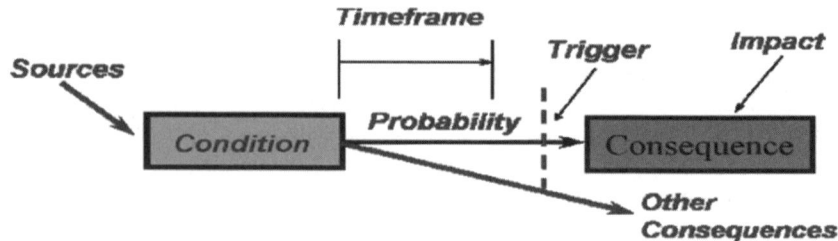

Fig. 4. Identifying the 6 considerations for risk mitigation

The mitigation strategies for each of the top 5 risks were then prioritized based on cost and the component of the risk that the strategy targeted (i.e., it is generally more beneficial to mitigate the source of a risk than the condition). The top two mitigation strategies for each of the top 5 risks were put into an action plan (figure 5 shows an example action plan) that also included triggers and timeframes for evaluating the mitigation strategies or re-evaluating the risk.

During iteration planning, the primary mitigation strategies (one for each of the top 5 risks) were included in the sprint backlog for prioritization. This sometimes required multiple tasks per mitigation strategy. The reason for multiple tasks was to break up the amount of work required to mitigate a risk such that a portion of a mitigation strategy could be performed in one iteration and additional portions could be completed in following iterations. This made it more likely for mitigation strategy tasks to be included in an iteration since they could be completed in small chunks. If a mitigation strategy was complicated and required a significant amount of time, it might be considered as too much effort for a single sprint because it could take too much time away from other aspects of the project that were required to show progress to the customers. At the end of each iteration, the team reviewed the triggers for risks that had timeframes associated with the end of the current sprint. If a trigger was triggered, then the team would take the appropriate next steps, such as moving to a backup strategy or closing the risk because the trigger indicated that the risk was mitigated.

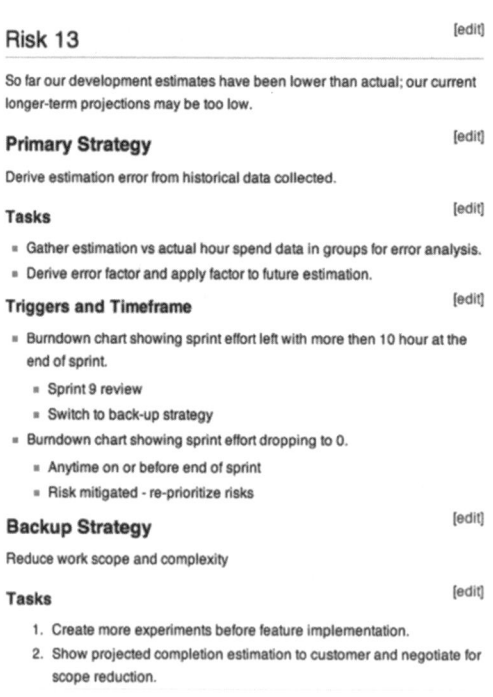

Fig. 5. An Example of an Action Plan

Once risks were mitigated, the top 5 risk list was updated. Also at the end of each iteration, the team would spend 10 to 15 minutes in the iteration review meeting discussing any changes in risks or any new risks that any team member had identified during the iteration. The risk list would be updated accordingly, and the risk manager would facilitate a quick re-prioritization of the list. If the top 5 risks changed resulting in risks in the top 5 that did not have defined action plans, then the team would allocate time in the coming iteration to devise the mitigation strategies for the new risks and define the action plans. This was a slight drawback. With this method it would be possible to identify a new risk that was critical and should be mitigated immediately, but the mitigation of the risk would have to wait until the following iteration. The current iteration would be used to define the mitigation tasks that could then be prioritized during the planning of the following iteration.

The adjustment to a more explicit risk management approach had significant benefits over the team's initial approach. The team was able to track their progress with risks. The triggers allowed the team to track the effectiveness of mitigation strategies. The updated top 5 risk list allowed the team to track which risks had been mitigated and where the team should be focusing their mitigation efforts at any given point in time. It was clear to the team that the new, more explicit, risk management approach was working because the team could see progress. On more than one occasion, the team switched from a primary mitigation strategy to a backup strategy. Additionally, prior to using the explicit approach, no risks were mitigated. After the change, the team effectively mitigated several risks.

7   Lessons Learned

Through the course of the DaVinci team's project, the team tried multiple techniques and constantly focused on process improvement through periodic reflections. These reflections and ongoing discussions with the MSE faculty supervising the project led to multiple insights with respect to the teams use of explicit risk management within the project. Following are some of these lessons in the form of both "Do" and "Don't" recommendations.

7.1   Risk Manager Role

The assignment of a risk manager role is important to ensure that risk management continues to get attention from the team. Someone needs to be a "risk champion," the person responsible for ensuring any necessary documentation is up to date, make sure that mitigation strategies are revisited at the end of each sprint, and ensure new time is spent identifying new risks. This role can easily be rotated between team members and these rotations should occur between iterations.

7.2   Wiki

To effectively manage risks, some documentation is required. It is necessary to document the current top risk item list, risk priorities, and their respective mitigation strategies. These documents need to be readily accessible to the whole team, and they need to be easy to modify. Risk documents can change frequently. A wiki works exceptionally well for risk management documentation. All members of a team can easily view and modify the documents, and most wikis also provide version control so that changes in the documents can be easily tracked.

7.3 Small Team Software Risk Evaluation

The SEI's SRE is a useful tool for identifying risks, but in its original form, is very time intensive and resource expensive. The use of the small team software risk evaluation (to a certain extent - a mini version of the longer SRE) is a great way to get risk management off the ground and establish an initial risk list for the project. However, multiple small team risk evaluations are likely to be too expensive to justify. All risk identification after the initial risk list is generated can be done less formally during iteration review meetings with the team going around and identifying new risks in a short brainstorming session.

7.4 Mitigation Tasks in Sprint Backlog

In order to integrate risk mitigation activities into an agile project, mitigation strategies need to be added to task lists. In Scrum, this is the product or sprint backlog. If mitigation strategies are not included as part of the tasks, they will not be prioritized with other tasks, will likely be looked at as simply overhead, and may be ignored or not given enough attention.

7.5 Multiple Tasks Per Mitigation Strategy

Mitigation strategies should be broken into a set of tasks that need to be completed. These tasks can be added to the list of tasks that need to be prioritized for an iteration. This allows for complicated mitigation strategies to be completed over the course of multiple iterations rather than depriving other aspects of the project while the risk is mitigated. This also allows for finer grained risk mitigation tracking through the tracking mechanisms already put in place for iteration tasks.

7.6 Mitigation Trigger

It is important to understand when a risk is mitigated so that efforts to mitigate the risk can be stopped. Many risks are clearly mitigated when certain tasks from the mitigation strategy are completed. Other risks require reoccurring tasks as part of the mitigation strategy. Risk triggers indicate to the team whether or not the existing efforts are effective. A trigger defines a specific event that may occur in the future. The trigger also defines what actions need to take place if the event occurs. Possible actions include closing the risk because it has been mitigated, or reexamine the risk and other possible mitigation strategies because the current strategy is not effective.

7.7 Mid-Iteration Triggers

Setting up triggers to be evaluated during the course of an iteration causes problems when a trigger is activated that requires action. Most agile processes talk about a frozen list of tasks during an iteration to protect the team from change during that short period of time. If triggers are evaluated in the middle of iterations, it may be the case that the team needs to switch to a back-up mitigation strategy in the middle of the iteration. Switching to a back-up strategy would require removing remaining tasks of the primary strategy from the task list and adding the tasks of the back-up to the task list. This goes against the flow of agile and can throw off the goals set during iteration planning. Amore appropriate way is to define all triggers such that they are reviewed at the end of an iteration, during the iteration review. This way, adjustments can be planned accordingly in the iteration planning that follows the iteration review.

7.8 Multi-voting

There are multiple ways to prioritize and reprioritize risk items. Team DaVinci found that the use of the multi-voting technique [9] was particularly effective in that the process was quick, easy to follow and included the opinions of all the team members within the prioritization effort. The swiftness allowed for the reprioritization of risks to be easily added as another activity into the regular Sprint planning meetings. The participation of all team members helped to ensure buy-in for the risk management activities and for the inclusion of mitigation strategy tasks in the teams sprint backlogs.

7.9 Mitigation Strategies for New Risks

When new risks are identified, mitigation strategies need to be formulated for the risks before anyone can start mitigating risks. Team DaVinci would identify new risks during sprint review meetings and plan for mitigation tasks during sprint planning meetings (see figure 1). If new risks were identified during a review meeting, a task to define the mitigation strategies was included in the planning of the following sprint. This is problematic if there is a critical risk that is identified. The next iteration would only include the task of identifying appropriate mitigations for this new risk but no tasks for implementing a strategy. The tasks to mitigate the risk would not occur until the following sprint. One recommendation would be to include a chunk of effort (roughly estimated) in the planning for the next sprint to be used for actual mitigation of the new critical risk in addition to determining appropriate mitigation strategies for that risk.

8 Conclusion

Agile processes inherently address risk in an implicit fashion. While addressing project risks implicitly is better than not addressing them at all, implicit risk management leaves much room for improvement. It lacks the ability to truly understand the risks a project is facing. Without this understanding, risks can not be effectively mitigated.

Explicitly engaging in risk management on agile projects involves extra time and structure seemingly defeating the 'agile' nature of the work. However, we have shown several options for integrating explicit risk management activities into tasks that already exist in most agile processes. This affords us the countless advantages to being formal when addressing risks, even in an agile setting. Specifically, explicit risk management allows for risks to be clearly identified and analyzed, and therefore directly targeted. Explicit risk management calls for mitigation strategies to be devised and mitigation tasks to be planned accordingly. Explicit risk management also provides mechanisms to track these strategies so as to determine if the they are effective and if the risks are being mitigated.

Explicit risk management can be incorporated into agile processes. Lightweight version of risk evaluation and identification techniques exist that are appropriate for small teams working with short iterations. The activities involved in continuous risk management (identification, analysis, planning, tracking, and control [5,8,9,15,19,20]) can be integrated into agile processes. The activities fit naturally in the iteration reviews, iteration planning, and iteration tasks.

Agile processes claim to be risk driven, but relying solely on their implicit style of risk management neglects important aspects of risk management. Any project using an agile process should seriously consider the value of adding explicit risk management techniques.

Acknowledgment

The authors would like to thank the other members of the DaVinci team (Carl, Chung-Hao, Harry, and Luis) for their help on the DaVinci project and insight into explicit risk management techniques used during the project. The authors would also like to thank Ray Williams for his guidance with the team's use of a condensed version of the SEI's taxonomy-based software risk evaluation.

References

1. Architecture Analysis and Design Language (Aadl), SAE Standard AS5506 (November 2004)
2. Barbacci, M., Ellison, R., Lattanze, A., Stafford, J., Weinstock, C., Wood, W.: Quality Attribute Workshops (QAWs), Third Edition, CMU SEI Technical Report CMU/SEI-2003-TR-016. Software Engineering Institute, Carnegie Mellon University (2003)
3. Bass, L., Clements, P., Kazman, R.: Software Architecture in Practice, 2nd edn. Addison-Wesley, Reading (2003)
4. Beck, K.: eXtreme Programming Explained: Embrace Change. Addison-Wesley, Reading (1999)
5. Carr, M.J., Konda, S.L.: Monarch, Ira, Ulrich, Carol F., and Walker, Clay F. Taxonomy-Based Risk Identification (CMU/SEI-93-TR-6, ESC-TR-93-183). Pittsburgh, PA: Software Engineering Institute, Carnegie Mellon University (1993)
6. Cockburn, A.: Agile Software Development. Addison-Wesley, Reading (2002)
7. Concha, M., Visconti, M., Astudillo, H.: Agile Commitments: Enhancing Business Risk Management in Agile Development Projects. In: Concas, G., et al. (eds.) XP 2007. LNCS, vol. 4536, pp. 149–152. Springer, Heidelberg (2007)
8. Conrow, E.H., Shishido, P.S.: Implementing Risk Management on Software Intensive Projects. IEEE Software 14(3), 83–89 (1997)
9. Dorofee, et al.: Continuous Risk Management Guidebook. Carnegie Mellon University (1996)

10. Garlan, D., Gluch, D., Tomayko, J.: Agents of Change: Educating Software Engineering Leaders. Computer 30(11), 59–65 (1997)
11. Gluch, D.P.: A Construct for Describing Software Development Risk (CMU/SEI-94-TR-14, ESC-TR-94-014). Pittsburgh, PA: Software Engineering Institute, Carnegie Mellon University (1994)
12. IEEE1540, IEEE 1540 Standard for Lifecycle - Processes-Risk Management. IEEE, New York (2001)
13. Lu, X.N., Ma, Q.G.: Risk Analysis in Software Development Project with Owners and Contractors. In: International Engineering Management Conference (October 2004)
14. McMahon Paul, E.: Bridging Agile and Traditional Development Methods: A Project Management Perspective, Crosstalk (May 2004)
15. Nyfjord, J., Kajko-Mattsson, M.: Commonalities in Risk Management and Agile Process Models. In: ICSEA 2007, Cap Esterel France (August 2007)
16. Paulk, M.: Agile Methodologies and Process Discipline. Crosstalk (October 2002)
17. Preston, G.: Smith and Roman Pichler, Agile Risks/Agile Rewards, Software Development, pp. 50–53 (April 2005) Project Management Institute, A Guide to the Project Management Body of Knowledge (PMBoK), 3rd Ed. ANSI/PMI 99-001-2004, Project Management Institute, Newton Square, PA (2004)
18. Schwaber, K.: Agile Project Management with Scrum. Microsoft Press (2004)
19. Williams, R.C., Pandelios, G.J., Behrens, S.G.S.: Method Description (Version 2.0) & SRE Team Members Notebook (Version 2.0) (CMU/SEI-99-TR-029). Pittsburgh, PA: Software Engineering Institute, Carnegie Mellon University (1999)
20. Williams Ray, C., Walker, J.A., Dorofee, A.J.: Putting Risk Management into Practice. IEEE Software 14(3), 75–82 (1997)
21. The Eclipse Development Platform, http://www.eclipse.org
22. The Society for Automotive Engineers Architecture Analysis & Design Language, http://www.aadl.info

APDT: An Agile Planning Tool for Digital Tabletops

Sebastian Weber, Yaser Ghanam, Xin Wang, and Frank Maurer

Department of Computer Science, University of Calgary
2500 University Dr. NW, Calgary, AB
Canada T2N 1N4
sebastian.weber@outlawtrail.de,
{yghanam,xin,maurer}@cpsc.ucalgary.ca

Abstract. This paper presents Agile Planner for Digital Tabletops (APDT) as a tool that facilitates agile planning meetings using large horizontal displays. Utilizing APDT on a reasonably sized digital tabletop allows collaborators to create, edit, move, rotate, toss and delete index cards just like they would do with paper artifacts. APDT provides a multimodal input system that supports gesture-, handwriting- and speech recognition as alternative input methodologies to conventional mouse and keyboard input.

Keywords: Agile planning, collaboration, digital tabletop, horizontal display, surface computing.

1 Introduction

In iterative software development models, planning meetings are a main venue where the customer conveys his needs and requirements to software developers. In agile planning meetings, index cards, so called story cards, are traditionally used to arrange tasks and feature requests into iterations. After filling in the required information, story cards are spread on a tabletop surface to allow for knowledge sharing among the attendees while they collaboratively discuss and organize the next iterations/release. Story cards may also be grouped into piles to indicate what tasks are to be accomplished in which iterations. Moving a story card from one position to another on the table surface for grouping or prioritizing purposes is a very common practice. Because of the setting of the meeting around the tabletop, reorienting story cards to make them easier to read for collaborators on the other side of the table is a common practice. Other story card related activities include modifying contents, passing the story card from one participant to another and trashing dispensable story cards. Most tools and commercial products focus on delivering the functionalities that are very likely to be needed in a planning meeting, but introduce a gap between what the traditional practice is and how the agile team needs to interact with such tools. For instance, the visualization of index cards as information holders is overlooked in many planning tools. The tool we present in this paper was specifically designed for use on digital tabletops to address usability and practicality issues found in other tools.

P. Abrahamsson et al. (Eds.): XP 2008, LNBIP 9, pp. 202–203, 2008.

2 Agile Planner for Digital Tabletops (APDT)

The digital surface we used in our project, shown in Fig. 1, is 210 cm X 120 cm with a resolution of approximately 10 mega-pixels. APDT was specifically developed for use on such a large horizontal display. APDT's ultimate goal is to make interaction with the planning objects feel as close to interacting with real paper cards as possible, and enhance this planning meeting by utilizing advantageous features of electronic devices. APDT allows for a multimodal interaction with the digital tabletop. That is, besides being able to use traditional input devices like mice and keyboards, users can use finger tips, electronic markers and even their voices to interact with the tabletop. The tool allows for unrestricted 360° rotation and movement of index cards. Using the RNT algorithm [1] implemented for APDT, users can manipulate the location and orientation of artifacts in the workspace in one fluid motion. Moreover, a tossing function allows for 'throwing' objects across the table to meet participants that are out of physical reach. The size of the table and the varying positions of the different users results in ordinary interfaces like menus or toolbars to be inconvenient. To create an orientation-independent environment, gesturing was implemented for creation, deletion and organization of planning objects. For instance, using a gesture for creation, story cards appear properly oriented towards their creator.

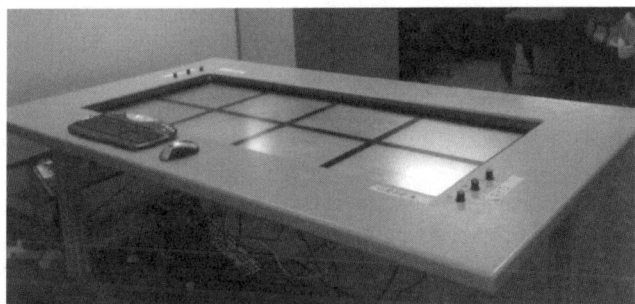

Fig. 1. The digital tabletop in our lab

Unlike some previously discussed tools that depend on external devices to feed recognized handwriting as input to the tabletop, APDT integrates handwriting recognition functionality directly into the table-interaction. The original handwriting and the recognized text are both displayed and can be edited afterwards. APDT also supports voice commands as an alternative channel for user input without the need to touch the tabletop surface.

Reference

1. Kruger, R., Carpendale, S., Scott, S., Greenberg, S.: Fluid Orientation on Tabletop Display. Computer Supported Cooperative Work, vol. 13, pp. 501–537. Kluwer Academic Publishers, Norwell (2004)

Investigating the Role of Trust in Agile Methods Using a Light Weight Systematic Literature Review

Eisha Hasnain and Tracy Hall

Brunel University, Uxbridge, Middlesex
UB8 3PH, United Kingdom
Eisha.Hasnain@brunel.ac.uk, Tracy.Hall@brunel.ac.uk

1 Introduction

In this paper we use a cut down systematic literature review to investigate the role of trust in agile methods. Our main motivation is to investigate the impact of the enhanced role of developers in agile methods. It is important to investigate the role of trust in agile methods because according to the agile manifesto the role of individual developers is central in an agile team: *"Individuals and Interactions over processes and tools"* and *"Build projects around motivated individuals. Give them the environment and support they need, and trust them to get the job done"* [1]. This suggests that managers must trust their staff to make decisions. The most direct forum for trust in agile projects is in the daily stand-up meeting. Project managers must trust that what developers say in the standup they are going to achieve during the day is what they actually achieve. In this paper we investigate the role trust plays in agile methods.

We report our systematic literature review to identify the role of trust in agile methods as reported in previously published studies. Full systematic literature reviews are very resource and time intensive. Consequently we have adapted Kitchenham's [2] guidelines to fit the time and resources we have available. This approach will allow us to generate the answers to our research questions based on a systematic analysis of previous published work in the area.

This paper is divided into five sections. The first section defines agile methods. The second section defines trust, explains the types of trust and describes how trust can be maintained. The third section describes how we carried out a systematic literature review. The fourth section presents results from our systematic literature review and the final section discusses our results and identifies future work.

2 Agile Methods

Agile software development challenges traditional software development methods. Rapidly changing environments characterized by evolving requirements and tight schedules require software developers to take an agile approach [3]. According to agile manifesto the key principles of agile methods are individuals and interactions over processes and tools, working software over comprehensive documentation, customer collaboration over contract negotiation, and responding to change over

P. Abrahamsson et al. (Eds.): XP 2008, LNBIP 9, pp. 204–207, 2008.
© Springer-Verlag Berlin Heidelberg 2008

following a plan. However one of the most important shifts in adopting an agile approach is the central focus given to people in the process. This is exemplified by the independence afforded to developers about the development work they do. Developer independence is usually structured within daily stand-up meetings. During stand-up meeting developers must say what they are going to achieve that day. We suggest that there must be an element of trust in 'believing' that developers will achieve what they say in the stand-up they will achieve. In this paper we investigate what role trust plays in agile teams by addressing the following research question: **RG: What role does trust play in agile teams?**

3 Trust

According to Jinwei and Fox [4]:

"Trust is the psychological state in which the trustor believes that the trustee behaves as expected in a specific context, based on evidence of the trustee's competence and goodwill; the trustor is willing to be vulnerable to that belief."

In this paper the trustor and trustee are the developers and project managers in a team and the competence is the capability of the developer to do the development work announced at the stand-up and goodwill is the good intention of the developer to do that development work. Trust is context-specific which means that if A trusts B to do C this doesn't means that A trusts B to do D. Our analysis of the trust literature suggests that the types of generic trust that can affect agile methods are interpersonal trust, relational trust, and system trust, trust in behaviour and trust in belief [4]. While the factors that maintain trust in agile methods are honesty, communication, cultural understanding, personal relationships, working together, performance and capability [5]. We will use these trust types and factors to analyse the importance of trust in agile methods.

4 Systematic Literature Reviews

Systematic literature reviews (SLR) are fairly new to software engineering but are long established in disciplines such as medical research. Systematic literature reviews are a method for analyzing all of the evidence addressing a particular research question. The outcome of a SLR is a landscape of evidence on a particular issues. Barbara Kitchenham recently introduced SLR's to software engineering [2].

In this cut down SLR we used only the IEEE Xplore search engine to identify papers. We searched for paper from 2000-2007. The searches were done in July and August 2007. We used the following search terms in our searches:

1. (Agile or XP) and (trust, developer, engineer, people, stand-up)
2. (Developer or Engineer) and Trust

These search terms retrieved 217 papers which we analyse in the next section.

5   Results

When we read the 217 papers only 11 papers are directly relevant to our research question. These papers discuss agile software development, the people factor and how successful teams can make an effect on eXtreme Programming. Further, 12 papers are indirectly relevant discusses different distributed projects, communication in these projects, and eXtreme Programming implementation in different university courses. The remaining 194 papers have been discarded as not relevant, as most papers are discussing trust related to network and security while other papers are discussing agile software development methods in software engineering field.

Overall our results shows that 188 of papers reported in the literature are experienced based while only 29 of papers is empirical as they contains all cases where data has been gathered either in qualitative or in quantitative forms. Division of results in these two forms will help us analyzing the material related to research question. Furthermore about 46 of articles are from the USA, while 171 are from rest of world. These demographics probably indicate cultural bias in the experiences and studies published.

6   Discussion

One of the key findings identified in this SLR is that rules are highly related to trust in development teams. If there is no trust between people then there are likely to be more rules. Empirical studies carried out by Sharp and Robinson [6] discusses the importance of trust in agile methods.

According to paper relative analysis between agile software development and war fighting written by Adolph [7]:

"... people who do not trust one another will end up cooperating only under a system of formal rules and regulations, which have to be negotiated, agreed to, litigated, and enforced, sometimes by coercive means. This legal apparatus, serving as a substitute for trust, entails what economists call "transaction costs"[7].

This finding raises issues such as: What type of rules will be agreed between people if there is no trust? How will these rules are implemented? And if these rules are not followed what will be the penalties? And who will enforce these penalties? All these questions make it clear that in the absence of trust, processes become complex.

It is clear that the importance of trust cannot be neglected. Without trust the development and implementation of rules is costly, complex and time consuming. All these factors increase the importance of trust in software development—especially in Agile Methods.

7   Conclusion

Our systematic literature review does not provide a comprehensive answer to the research question. This suggests that insufficient previous research has been published on the impact of trust in agile teams. Future research on this topic is important and could help increase the effectiveness of agile methods and also improve the quality of products developed using agile methods.

References

[1] Fowler, M., Highsmith, J.: The Agile Manifesto [November 10, 2007] (2001),
    `http://www.ddj.com/linux-open-source/184414755`
[2] Kitchenham, B.: Procedure for Performing Systematic Literature Reviews. Keele University Technical Report, 1353–7776 (2004)
[3] Cao, L.: Agile Software Development: Ad Hoc Practices or Sound Principles? IT Professional 9(2), 41–47 (2007)
[4] Huang, J.: Trust Judgement in Knowledge Provenance. In: Proceedings of Sixteenth International Workshop on Database and Expert Systems, pp. 524–528 (2005)
[5] Nguyen, T.P., Babar, A.M., Verner, J.: Critical Factors in Establishing and Maintaining Trust in Software Outsourcing Relationship. In: International Conference on Software Engineering, pp. 624–627 (2006)
[6] Sharp, H., Robinson, H.: Extreme Programming and Agile Processes in Software Engineering, pp. 139–147. Springer, Heidelberg (2004)
[7] Adolph, S.: Are we ready to be Unleashed? A Comparative Analysis between Agile Software Development and War Fighting. In: Proceedings of Agile Conference, pp. 20–28 (2005)

Agile Practices in a Product Development Organization

Frank Keenan[1], Tony McCarron[1], Shay Doherty[2], and Stuart McLean[2]

[1] Department of Computing and Mathematics, Dundalk Institute of Technology, Ireland
{frank.keenan,tony.mccarron}@dkit.ie
[2] Stiona Software, Ormeau House, 91 / 97 Ormeau Road, Belfast, BT7 1SH, UK

Abstract. Many reports highlight the advantages of using an agile approach to software development. However, as each case is different it is necessary to use practices that suit the particular situation under investigation. This paper reports on how agile practices, largely drawn from eXtreme Programming (XP), were used by Stiona Software for the development of their internet-based financial product *Fusion Accounts*.

Keywords: eXtreme Programming (XP), experience report, agile practices.

1 Introduction

The goal of Stiona's *Fusion Accounts* project was to develop a collaborative web-based accounting application to allow both accountants and their clients to work on the same accounts at the same time from anywhere. The Software As A Service (SaaS) model was used, allowing customers to *rent* part of the product rather than buying the whole. Development began in September 2006 with one dedicated developer. Others were expected to contribute as needed or as opportunities arose. A senior member took the role of *product owner* liaising with key potential customers while other members of the team included a marketing specialist and a tester.

A particular challenge, or perhaps opportunity, was the relationship with the customer base. It was hoped that in addition to existing customers changing from using traditional accounting packages, it would be possible to recruit new ones at an early stage of development. Frustrated by previous plan-driven experience, it was decided to follow an agile approach influenced by XP [1].

2 Introduction of Agile Practices

The agile practices that were adopted are now described.

Work Area: the development office was organized so that the team was located in the same area with workstations organized around three whiteboards. At various stages the information displayed changed to reflect development focus. For example, relevant screenshots would be displayed on one board with another used to perform use case analysis. Off-site members were kept up-to-date with a shared spreadsheet and communicated through a wiki and by skype, sharing emerging requirements.

P. Abrahamsson et al. (Eds.): XP 2008, LNBIP 9, pp. 208–209, 2008.

Real Customer Involvement: The product owner was in continuous contact with an accountant with a large client base. Other potential customers were also engaged. From an early stage, although in a separate office, an accounts clerk was contactable. However, this contribution was enhanced significantly when the clerk relocated to join the team, using a live version of the product.

Incremental Development and Deployment: Weekly meetings allowed progress updates, identification of impediments, requirements brainstorming and integration of emerging concerns. Through feedback, *invoicing* was chosen as the highest priority. In short cycles, (one or two weeks) fully functioning and tested software was produced and made available for demonstration.

Common Ownership: All members had access to the requirements list and source code allowing requirements to be added at weekly meetings or as they emerged.

Negotiable Scope: The sales approach taken here was to recruit major clients with their customers in turn becoming Stiona customers. In both cases contracts were agreed on a short-term basis with an emphasis on the customer *renting* software rather than purchasing it. Later, customers can select from a larger package. This allowed the implementation of the highest priority needs first.

Testing: A dedicated tester participated two days per week. There was also *customer testing* by major clients while on-site clerks provided daily feedback. The first official release was available for pilot testing with a doctor's surgery in May.

Two significant factors enabled the introduction of these practices were the technology used and the ability of the team. Development was mainly in .NET 2.0 and AJAX, with specialist software used to create the interface. Tests were documented in NUnit. SQL Compare was used to compare development and test databases. Northern Ireland government standards for financial software were followed. *Issue Tracker* was used for sharing and tracking requirements and errors.

3 Conclusion

These practices helped "satisfy the customer through early and continuous delivery of valuable software". A suitable work environment, supported by various customer input, helped to realize the SaaS model. Reflecting their initial progress, "Fusion Accounts" was short listed for the national British Telecom *Inspired IT* Awards 2007. A particular challenge that now arises is to support a live product while developing new software. Ways of supporting this are being investigated including the provision of customer support through wikis. The work described in this experience report was supported by the Fusion programme funded by Inter*Trade*Ireland.

Reference

1. Beck, K., Andres, C.: Extreme Programming Explained, 2nd edn. Addison Wesley, Reading (2005)

Building and Linking a Metaphor: Finding Value!

Frank Keenan[1], David Bustard[2], Namgyal Damdul[1], and David Connolly[1]

[1] Department of Computing and Mathematics, Dundalk Institute of Technology, Ireland
{frank.keenan,namgyal.damdul,david.connolly}@dkit.ie
[2] School of Information and Software Engineering, University of Ulster,
Coleraine, BT52 1SA, UK
dw.bustard@ulster.ac.uk

Abstract. Initially System Metaphor was included as one of twelve practices of Extreme Programming (XP) to facilitate participants' common understanding and description of the problem under consideration. However, the practice was removed in the second version of XP as practitioners found it difficult to understand, devise and link it to implementation activities. This poster describes how a metaphor can be constructed and linked to development by using practices associated with Soft Systems Methodology (SSM). Initial, positive, feedback from an educational exercise is presented.

Keywords: Metaphor, Soft Systems Methodology (SSM).

1 Introduction

XP evolved from a fixed set of twelve practices now described as a "process of experimentation and improvement" [1]. Despite its removal as an explicit XP practice this poster describes how describing a *metaphor* and linking it to development provides benefit. Here, parts of SSM [2], a well-proven method for analyzing problems including the development of software is combined with XP. Traditionally, SSM has been described as a seven-stage process. Problem situations are usually captured diagrammatically as *rich pictures*. Although subjective, with no rules defined for drawing them, they help achieve a shared understanding of a situation among interested parties. Models of 'relevant systems' are then developed, based on that knowledge and are expressed as *root definitions* and *conceptual models*. A root definition is a short textual statement that defines the important elements of the 'relevant system' providing a particular perspective on the system under investigation. A conceptual model is derived from the root definition by identifying the activities present or implied and their inter-relationship. These models provide a basis for further debate on the activities involved. Next, change recommendations are derived from the results and action to improve the situation undertaken is recommended.

This approach used *rich picture analysis* to build a metaphor and then detailed examination to develop a conceptual model. The activities of this model were then used to create user stories.

P. Abrahamsson et al. (Eds.): XP 2008, LNBIP 9, pp. 210–211, 2008.

2 Evaluation

An evaluation study was conducted with two final year groups of Degree students. All had previous knowledge of agile methods, particularly XP, and were introduced to SSM and the combined approach. One team used only XP and the other SSM-XP. Both had access to a customer throughout development. In the first SSM-XP session the customer outlined the problem. After a discussion, drawing of a rich picture was facilitated and the various issues raised were easily and quickly clarified by the customer. This session was interactive with members offering suggestions, raising questions and amending the diagram. Finally, the rich picture was photographed and transcribed. Thus, the metaphor was created. The main challenge appeared to be reaching agreement on the problem rather than drawing the diagram. As the conceptual model developed more focused discussion took place. Essentially, one or two related activities formed an XP release. User stories were agreed and estimated facilitating the link between metaphor and development. Project scope was not a difficulty at this stage—a problem that did arise for the XP team. In subsequent sessions the team used the recorded pictures to recall objectives and stay focused.

The SSM-XP team implemented more user stories which seemed to be of higher quality. Also, despite extra initial effort, after five sessions they reached the same stage as the XP team. Feedback indicated that the Rich Picture was "very helpful" and "effective" in understanding the problem. The conceptual model helped "prioritize the requirements" from the Rich Picture and helped "clarify stories" for implementation.

3 Conclusion

This poster has proposed that there is still benefit in developing a metaphor for XP as originally indicated. The new version of XP allows inclusion of other practices so there is no reason why metaphor should not be implemented. The key is to provide guidance on how one can be constructed and linked to development. This has been achieved through the combination of parts of SSM with XP. Student exercises, although limited, have provided positive feedback indicating that this combination is beneficial without detracting from the overall development time. Our future work includes the examination and development of tools to build a metaphor while enabling communication within a distributed team.

References

1. Beck, K., Andres, C.: Extreme Programming Explained, 2nd edn. Addison Wesley, Reading (2005)
2. Checkland, P.: Systems Thinking, Systems Practice (with 30-year retrospective). John Wiley & Sons, Chichester (1999)

The Story of Transition to Agile Software Development

Gadi Lifshitz[1], Ayelet Kroskin[1], and Yael Dubinsky[2]

[1] Cisco Systems, 32 Hamelacha St., Netanya 42504, Israel
{glifshit,akroskin}@cisco.com
[2] IBM, Haifa Research Lab, 31905 Haifa, Israel
dubinsky@il.ibm.com

Cisco Systems, Inc. (Nasdaq:CSCO) is the worldwide leader in networking for the Internet. Inside Cisco's Development Organization, the Network Management Technology Group (NTMG) is the group responsible for developing and delivering Network Management software for Cisco devices. The Converged Management Platform (CMP) Development Group within NMTG is building the Next Generation Network Management software called Active Network Abstraction (ANA), a platform which is aimed at converging numerous network management applications into a single platform, leveraging the capabilities of scale and distribution, and allowing the benefits of advanced technologies and a uniform interface. In this report we tell the story of a transition to agile software development in the Active Network Abstraction (ANA) project, including lessons learned.

The process of transition to agile software development [2,4] was composed of two main phases: The *first-team phase* in which one team (consisting of eight developers and two testers) developed two releases working according to the agile approach, and the *scale phase*, in which two additional teams working on the same project made the transition to agile. In what follows we focus on the first-team phase.

The agile room. The team moved into a large meeting room with a large meeting table. Working in a single room with developers, testers, a manager and a customer (the project architect as a *proxy* customer) enabled communication and collaboration they had never dreamed of. The main challenge of working in the agile room was controlling the noise level. The team focused on small improvements that could be made to ease the noise e.g., all cellular phones were put on vibrate; personal conversations, arguments and phone calls were taken outside the room; soft background music was played; a role to enforce noise rules was instated. The walls in the agile room symbolized the evolvement of the agile team as they were slowly filled up with a variety of measurements, post it notes displaying the iteration story status, quotes of the day and work procedures, for example: the Test Driven Development (TDD) [1] cycle, the continuous integration process and design diagrams. The team worked in mixed pairs during agile hours between 10:00-16:00.

Agile roles. The team members were encouraged from the beginning of the release to take on individual roles [3]. These roles included for example: the methodologist who was the process protector; the tracker who was responsible for all measurements; the integrator who was responsible for the continuous integration process which included

P. Abrahamsson et al. (Eds.): XP 2008, LNBIP 9, pp. 212–214, 2008.

a continuous integration machine and a traffic light which signaled the build status; the tester who was responsible for forming an acceptance test framework, and defining the methodology of acceptance and unit testing. Acceptance tests were written for each story and were defined by the customer. TDD was initially practiced by the team members, but was a disappointment as it was abandoned early on.

The Agile Business Day. The team held a Business Day at the end of each 2-week iteration. The schedule of this day included a demo to the customer of the stories completed during the iteration, customer feedback, measurement analysis, reflection, and planning for the next iteration.

The Demos: The team focused on showing visible, time-boxed demos to the customer. The demos were initially long but gradually became more efficient.

The measurements: The team initially began with tracking a single measurement which was a variation of the well known burndown chart. As the team and process evolved, additional measurements came up as needed by the team, for example, a team satisfaction measurement, average team overtime (hours worked on stories outside agile hours) and manager/customer presence time in the agile rooms. Most measurements were brought up by teammates and were measured in order to deal with problematic situations the team was facing: not working at a sustainable pace and the customer not being present to answer questions during the iteration.

The reflections: Reflections [2] were held frequently and were a very significant part of the transition to agile as they were a tool for continuous improvement. Reflections were held either on topics that were determined ahead of time, for example, how do the testers and developers work together as one team, or on spontaneous topics brought up during the reflection.

The planning process: During the planning process the customer would present the stories for the next iteration, the team would break down the stories into tasks and estimate the tasks. The team tried several methods of estimations including estimating tasks in hours, in buckets (small, medium or large) which team members complained was not accurate, estimating in relative units and using planning poker. Currently, the team is estimating in days but still using the planning poker technique.

Outcomes: The first agile team phase was found to be a success at Cisco. Not only did team members feel the quality of the product was higher, but the team was consistently delivering at the end of each iteration. The great support of the management played a big factor in the success of the agile experiment. There were some topics that the team struggled with throughout the release e.g., the issue of 'agile hours' was questioned and some motivation issues were found among more experienced engineers.

The experience and lessons learned described during the transition to agile are used today for the in-progress scale phase in the project. Emphasis is put on the mechanisms to control the process of multiple teams e.g., working procedures, common measurements and derived policies.

References

1. Beck, K.: Test-Driven Development By Example. Addison Wesley, Reading (2003)
2. Beck, K., Andres, C.: Extreme Programming Explained. Addison-Wesley, Reading (2004)
3. Dubinsky, Y., Hazzan, O.: Using a role scheme to derive software project quality. Journal of System Architecture 52(11), 693–699 (2006)
4. Highsmith, J.: Agile Software development Ecosystems. Addison-Wesley, Reading (2002)

Predicting Software Fault Proneness Model Using Neural Network

Yogesh Singh, Arvinder Kaur, and Ruchika Malhotra

University School of Information Technology, GGS Indraprastha University,
Kashmere Gate, Delhi-110403, India
ys66@rediffmail.com, arvinderkaurtakkar@yahoo.com,
ruchikamalhotra2004@yahoo.com

Importance of quality software is increasing leading to development of sophisticated techniques for exploring data sets, which can be used in constructing models for predicting quality attributes. There have been few empirical studies evaluating the impact of object-oriented metrics on software quality and constructing models that utilize them in predicting quality attributes of the system. Most of these predicted models are built using statistical techniques. Most of these prediction models are built using statistical techniques. ANN have seen an explosion of interest over the years, and are being successfully applied across a range of problem domains, in areas as diverse as finance, medicine, engineering, geology and physics. Indeed, anywhere that there are problems of prediction, classification or control, neural networks are being introduced. ANN can be used as a predictive model because it is very sophisticated modeling techniques capable of modeling complex functions.

Khoshgoftaar et al. presented a case study of real time avionics software to predict the testability of each module from static measurements of source code. They found that ANN is a promising technique for building predictive models, because they are able to model nonlinear relationships. The LR and ANN approaches are inherently different, raising the question whether one approach has better performance than the other. To investigate this question, the performance of LR and ANN methods was compared in the study for predicting software fault proneness. The goal of this paper is to empirically compare regression and machine learning technique to assess software quality. The binary dependent variable in our study is fault proneness. Fault proneness is defined as the probability of fault detection in a class. The study used data collected from public domain NASA data set. We find the effect of software metric on fault proneness. The fault proneness models were predicted using logistic regression and decision tree methods. The performance of the two methods was compared by Receiver Operating Characteristic (ROC) analysis. Most of these prediction models are built using statistical techniques.

The study is divided into following parts:

(i)   Software fault proneness model is constructed using multivariate analysis to predict fault proneness of classes using LR and ANN technique.

(ii)   The performance of the models is evaluated using ROC analysis.

P. Abrahamsson et al. (Eds.): XP 2008, LNBIP 9, pp. 215–217, 2008.

The predicted model shows that metrics are related to fault proneness. The network used in this work belongs to Multilayer Feed Forward networks and is referred to as M-H-Q network with M source nodes, H nodes in hidden layer and Q nodes in the output layer. The input nodes are connected to every node of the hidden layer but are not directly connected to the output node. Thus the network does not have any lateral or shortcut connection. Figure 1 presents structure of ANN used in this study.

ANN repetitively adjusts different weights so that the difference between desired output from the network and actual output from ANN is minimized. The network learns by finding a vector of connection weights that minimizes the sum of squared errors on the training data set. The summary of ANN used in this study is shown in Table 3. The ANN was trained by standard error back propagation algorithm at a learning rate of 0.005, having the minimum square error as the training stopping criterion.

The input layer has one unit for each input variable. Each input value in the data set is normalized within the interval [0, 1] using min-max normalization. Given an n by m matrix of multivariate data, Principal component analysis [] can reduce the number of columns. We performed Principal component analysis on the input metrics to produce domain metrics []. In our study n represents the number of classes for which OO metrics have been collected. Using Principal component analysis, the n by m matrix is reduced to n by p matrix (where p<m).

We use one hidden layer as what can be achieved in function approximation with more than one hidden layer can also be achieved by one hidden layer. There is one unit in the output layer. The output unit with value greater than a threshold (cutoff point) indicates the class selected by the network is fault prone otherwise it is not.

The accuracy of models predicted is somewhat optimistic since the models are applied on same data set from which they are derived from. To predict accuracy of model it should be applied on different data sets thus we performed 10-cross validation of LR and ANN models. For the 10-cross validation, the classes were randomly divided into 10 equal parts of approximately. The models predict faulty classes with more than 70 percent accuracy. The areas under the ROC curves 0.78 and 0.76 for the LR and ANN model, respectively.

Based on these results, it is reasonable to claim that such a model could help for planning and executing testing by focusing resources on fault-prone parts of the design and code. This study confirms that construction of ANN is feasible, adaptable to systems, and useful in predicting fault prone classes. While research continues, practitioners and researchers may apply ANN method for constructing model to predict faulty classes.

As in all empirical studies the relationship we established is valid only for certain population of systems. In this case, we can roughly characterize this population as "medium-sized systems."

From the design phase, one can make software measurements and then predict which classes will need extra attention during the remainder of development. This can help management focus resources on those classes that cause most of the problems. Also, if required, developers can reconsider design and thus take corrective actions. In order to draw strong conclusions, however, more replicated studies are needed.

These design measurements can be used as quality benchmarks to assess and compare products, once one knows the metrics to be measured. More such studies can provide quality benchmarks across organizations, whereas within an organization, quality benchmarks can be set comparing metric values with the existing operational good quality software. If deviation is found in the metric values further investigation to know the cause of deviation could be done. Thus, corrective actions could be taken before final delivery or future releases of the software. This is particularly important when systems are maintained over a long period and new versions are released regularly.

More similar type of studies must be carried out with large data sets to get an accurate measure of performance outside the development population. In future we plan to replicate our study on large data sets and to validate OO design metrics across different fault severities. We plan to replicate our study to predict models based on machine learning algorithms such as genetic algorithms. We will also focus on cost benefit analysis of models that will help to determine whether a given fault proneness model would be economically viable.

Multi-modal Functional Test Execution

Shelly Park and Frank Maurer

University of Calgary
Department of Computer Science
2500 University Drive NW, Calgary, Alberta, Canada
{parksh,maurer}@cpsc.ucalgary.ca

Abstract. Multi-modal test execution allows execution of the same test against various layers of a software system, e.g. the GUI layer, the web service layer and the business logic layer. Multi-modal test execution helps with identifying the location of software bugs during debugging and maintenance as well as in tracking the progress of the development effort. This paper presents a method that effectively encodes multi-modal functional tests without creating large test maintenance overhead. Our approach extends the Fit table specification structure by multi-modal fixtures and presents the results of test execution in a way to help with debugging and progress reporting.

Keywords: Executable Acceptance Testing, Test Driven Development, Functional Specifications, Functional Testing, Validation Testing, Architectural Design Decisions, Multi-modal Test Execution.

1 Introduction

In Executable Acceptance Test Driven Development (EATDD) – also called story-test driven development – software requirements are specified in form of executable acceptance tests or executable specifications. The purpose of acceptance testing is to give confidence to the customer that the functional specifications defined in the requirements are correctly implemented in the software product and to ensure high customer satisfaction through critical examination of the quality of the software through continuous regression testing.

In an agile environment, acceptance tests are developed by a customer in collaboration with BAs, QAs and/or developers. The tests can be seen as a contract between the developers and the customer and it defines criteria for a finished product. In an EATDD environment, the acceptance tests play an important role throughout the software development cycle due to the ubiquity of their presence in all aspects of the development cycle. Everyone in the development team and all stakeholders are at least partially involved in either specifying, testing, implementing or communicating through acceptance tests at some point in their work. Acceptance tests are not just for customers, but an important communication tool for all stakeholders – users, customers, analysts, developers and testers – in the development project.

Following the discussions at the Agile Alliance Functional Testing Tools Visioning Workshop as well as Andrea's paper on envisioning the next functional testing tools [1],

P. Abrahamsson et al. (Eds.): XP 2008, LNBIP 9, pp. 218–219, 2008.
© Springer-Verlag Berlin Heidelberg 2008

this paper argues that the next generation of functional testing tools needs to be multi-modal: tests need to be expressible in multiple formats to satisfy the requirements from different stakeholder groups and need to be executable against different layers of the software system. We call the first *multi-modal test definition* and the second *multi-modal test execution*.

2 Multi-modal Functional Test Execution

There are two problems in regards to multi-modal functional testing. The purpose of *multi-modal test execution* (MMTE) is to provide one-to-many mapping between the test definition and the test executions: a single test is executed against different layers and/or components of the software system.

A functional feature can appear in different layers of the software architecture or different components of the software. Rather than duplicating the acceptance test definition per appearance of the functionality or completely ignoring the multi-layer aspect of the software in the acceptance testing, the next generation of acceptance testing tools should acknowledge the need for MMTE and actively practice MMTE in all testing processes.

It is important that non-developers are also aware of the MMTE result based. One of the benefits of having architectural information embedded in the acceptance tests through MMTE is quick feedback about the impact of system-wide architectural or business requirement changes that may occur during the development project. Resource allocation or feature negotiation is easier when all stakeholders are informed with more concrete evidence to base their decisions.

MMTE can also play an important role in deriving requirements. Often customers may not be aware of exactly what they need, thus the requirements may be too vague. Having MMTE capability in the testing tool can help business analysts or testers to work with the customer to derive more detailed requirements in terms of multi-layered system components or platforms.

Based on the requirements and motivations provided above, we have implemented multi-modal test execution based on a popular executable acceptance testing tool called Fit.

References

1. Agile Alliance Functional Testing Tools Visioning Workshop (October 2007),
   http://www.agilealliance.org/show/1938
2. Gamma, E., Helm, R., Johnson, R., Vlissides, J.: Design Patterns: Elements of Reusable Object-Oriented Software. Addison-Wesley, Reading (1994)

Social Network Analysis of Communication in Open Source Projects

Guido Porruvecchio, Selene Uras, and Roberta Quaresima

Department of Electric and Electronic Engineering, University of Cagliari,
Piazza d'Armi, 09123 Cagliari, Italy
{guido.porruvecchio,s.uras,roberta.quaresima}@diee.unica.it

Abstract. In agile methodologies communication is a fundamental value because understanding communicational practices keeps together all the different aspects that improve team performance. In Open Source (OS) teams communication is also important because of the nature of the communities. We present a study of Mailing Lists (MLs) of some of the most successful OS projects to analyse their communicational flow. We adopted Social Network Analysis (SNA) approach to quantitatively describe these communities and to evaluate the communicational practices.

1 The Value of Communication in Open Source Teams

In this work, we focus on one of the key values behind agile methodologies - communication, and on the quantitative study of communication in OS communities. We analyse these communities - and namely the interactions between developers and users - under the perspective of communicational patterns, as determined by social network analysis. Our analysis focuses on considering the interaction between developers and users as a network, and uses the quantitative indicators proposed by Freeman [2]. We previously found that the virtual place where developers meet users is the developers Mailing List [3] [1]. It is used to share information, to gather all users' needs and proposals, and to create a link between users and developers.

2 Social Network Analysis

SNA has been defined as a way to describe relationships among social entities, as well as the patterns and implications of these connections [4]. Adopting the SNA approach, the people are actors in contact with one another; to depict the network for each team, actors become nodes and each relationship between two of them is represented by a link. One of the most important aspects of SNA is the identification of the most central actors, that is, those who are particularly visible to other actors in the network, and who are able to maintain several relationships with them [2]. The chosen centrality indexes (degree, betweenness, closeness), by identifying the most central members in the networks, can help us to find a possible relationship between prominent members and OS projects' success, quality and maturity.

P. Abrahamsson et al. (Eds.): XP 2008, LNBIP 9, pp. 220–221, 2008.

3 The Social Network of Open Source Communities

We chose the 70 most active projects as of December 2006 in Sourceforge, observing that not all the developers mailing lists were available. In fact, with respect to these projects, 30 did not even have a mailing list, and only 9 had a sufficiently active list. These projects, which we used for our research, are: Arianne, Gaim, Gallery, Geotools, Gimp-Print, Licq, MinGW, Miranda, Netatalk. We built a framework to extract key data from mailing list archives (for each mail: sender, subject, date and thread starter). The network representing the OS community was defined as follows:

- **nodes** are the mail senders, in other words each community member who posted a message in a discussion thread
- **links** are established between two members participating in the same thread.

So two nodes are connected if both participated to the same thread. If a thread involved several members, the sub-network composed by them is fully connected. This network was analyzed extracting the three centrality measures previously mentioned, making possible to better describe interactions and communication flow among members of the MLs. We found the SNA indexes we used to describe the networks suited to individuate the most prominent actors in the communities. They display leadership behaviors and play a major role in team coordination, information management and sharing. The synthetic indicators of network features (the centralization indexes) can be used to characterize with a few parameters a network, easing to discriminate among various possible structures and flows of control.

References

1. Concas, G., Lisci, M., Pinna, S., Porruvecchio, G., Uras, S.: Learning communities in open source projects. In: Proceedings of CELDA 2007, IADIS, Portugal, pp. 73–78 (2007)
2. Freeman, L.C.: Centrality in social networks: Conceptual clarification. Social Networks 1, 215–239 (1979)
3. Uras, S., Concas, G., Lisci, M., Marchesi, M., Pinna, S.: Communication flow in open source projects. In: Concas, G., Damiani, E., Scotto, M., Succi, G. (eds.) XP 2007. LNCS, vol. 4536, pp. 261–265. Springer, Heidelberg (2007)
4. Wasserman, S., Faust, K.: Social network analysis: methods and applications. Cambridge University Press, Cambridge (1994)

Toward Empowering Extreme Programming from an Architectural Viewpoint

Amir Saffarian, Amir Azim Sharifloo, and Fereidoun Shams

Department of Computer Engineering, Faculty of Electrical and Computer Engineering,
Shahid Beheshti University, Tehran, Iran
a_saffarian@std.sbu.ac.ir, a.sharifloo@mail.sbu.ac.ir,
f_shams@sbu.ac.ir

The XP method is one of the noticeable approaches among agile software development methodologies. Besides its valuable features and capabilities there is a lack and that is about how to control the quality of the system and the effects of quality attributes on each other. In the last decade, software quality requirements have been especially addressed by software architecture. Since software architecture knowledge has grown and matured in recent years, many of agile methods, like XP, have not considered the importance of architecture in their development process. This paper introduces two practices (*Continuous Architectural Refactoring* and *Real Architecture Qualification*) in order to empower XP's development process toward improving system's architecture. The main characteristic of proposed solution is that it is derived from values and practices of XP so as to keep its agility intact.

Although there is no explicit support for the concept of architecture in XP methodology, it leads to a software system that should have some specific structures which we call it implicit architecture. One is not fare if he says that XP is free of any architectural activities because there are three of them by which the mentioned implicit architecture will be influenced. Spike Solutions, Metaphors and Refactoring are the main XP elements that could affect the architecture of the system but they are inadequate. Generally, quality attributes could be divided into two categories considering the perspective to be used. The first category is related to the quality attributes that are evaluated based on developers' concerns like modifiability, testability, reusability, understandability, scalability, and maintainability. Ordinarily, this evaluation is done by the architect, who has the knowledge about architectural design, through system models and diagrams in the CAR process. The other category contains quality attributes which should be evaluated using the real working system like performance, usability, availability. These quality attributes are observable externally considering users view. Therefore, customer is the person to evaluate these qualities through RAQ [1].

Architectural smells represent inefficiencies that could gradually mislead the system`s architecture toward an unmanageable and unsuitable shape unless resolved as soon as possible. In *Continuous Architectural Refactoring* (CAR) smells are discovered and solutions to revise them would be identified by using architectural refactoring techniques [2]. Furthermore, CAR initially designed to be used in parallel with the development process of XP so as to not affect the performance of a pure XP and keep agility intact. To make CAR possible, we need a role called Architect who is responsible to decide on candidate solutions to remove architectural smells. The

P. Abrahamsson et al. (Eds.): XP 2008, LNBIP 9, pp. 222–223, 2008.

architect will continuously receive partial models by development teams. Class diagram seems to be a suitable model for the architect because the dependencies between classes and their interfaces are clearly defined in it. The architect could use formal (fully detailed) class diagrams to depict other informal (shortly detailed) models like package and layer diagrams to identify smells. As many smells could be attached to certain patterns, the idea of doing automatic smell checking (e.g. using JDepend [3]) is not infeasible.

On the other hand, *Real Architecture Qualification* (RAQ) is almost a kind of brainstorming session based on a working system and architectural models. RAQ focuses on achieving customer observable quality requirements. In order to enable programmers to have an insight about this category of quality attributes each pair programming team needs to have clear information about each quality attribute. Therefore the criteria of customer satisfaction have to be attached to e all user stories. This task is achievable by using general scenarios` checklist [4] to prepare suitable concrete scenarios. After that, besides functional test cases, developers should design quality test cases so as to check their code considering the non-functional requirements provided through quality scenarios. In fact RAQ has two parts. The first part (discussed above) is mainly performed by developers through pair programming and the second part is the one mentioned in [1] which becomes active in the end of all iterations. Steps of the second part of RAQ could be summarized as 1) Preparing the structure of the session and identifying representatives of stakeholders to join the session, 2) Describing, in brief, final architectural model of the iteration that is integrated using partial models, 3) Describing, in brief, refactoring decisions that have be made by architect and ask members to express their opinions about them, 4) Identifying architectural aspects (quality attributes) that should be analyzed in the session, 5) For each quality attribute specified in step 4: a) Start a brainstorming sub-session, taking stakeholder`s opinions into account about their experience when working with current working system, b) Decide about solutions for new needs and requests that current working system cannot provide or handle, c) Defining new solutions as concrete new tasks and taking them as unfinished tasks.

References

1. Azim Sharifloo, A., Saffarian, A.S., Shams, F.: Embedding Architectural Practices into Extreme Programming. In: Proceedings of the 19th Australian Software Engineering Conference, Australia (to appear, 2008)
2. Lippert, M., Roock, S.: Refactoring in Large Software Projects: Performing Complex Restructurings Successfully, 1st edn. John Wiley & Sons, Chichester (2006)
3. JDepend, http://clarkware.com/software/JDepend.html
4. Bass, L., Klein, M., Moreno, G.: Applicability of General Scenarios to the Architecture Tradeoff Analysis Method. Technical Report, CMU/SEI-2001-TR-014, Software Engineering Institute, Carnegie Mellon University (2001)

A Metric-Based Approach to Assess Class Testability

Yogesh Singh and Anju Saha

GGSIP University, India
ys66@rediffmail.com, anju_kochhar@yahoo.com

Abstract. In today's world people have become highly dependent on software systems for almost everything. Hence it necessitates the need for reliable and quality software. Software quality and reliability can only be achieved if the testing is made effective. One way of making testing effective is to improve software testability. Software testability is an external attribute of the software which provides a guideline for testing. Software testability has been defined by numerous researchers from different points of view. An extensive survey of the literature on software testability was done. During the survey, it was found that there were very few researchers who had analyzed the relationship between source code metrics and test metrics. Hence this study aims at performing an empirical study to evaluate some of the source code metrics that have a bearing on the testing effort for object oriented development. Testing effort in turn provides an insight of software testability. This study is performed at the unit level of testing .i.e class level using JUnit testing framework. JUnit framework allows users to create a test class for every java class. Two open source Java projects have been used for this empirical study. In these systems, JUnit test classes have been written for java classes. This study aims to judge the capability of the object oriented metrics to assess class testability. A correlation is found between object oriented metrics and test metrics. To find the correlation the Spearman's rank-order correlation coefficient is calculated for each object oriented metric of the java classes and three test metrics of the corresponding test classes. The definition used in this study is by ISO[2] which defines testability as: "attributes of software that bear on the effort needed to validate the software product. The attributes of software that we consider are the source code metrics of object oriented software. Object oriented languages have different features like class, method, inheritance, polymorphism, dynamic binding etc. Hence these features also have a bearing on the testing effort and hence on testability. This study focuses on source code factors only and investigates the effect of source code factors on the testing effort. Through testing effort we can quantify testability using two factors given by Brutink[1]. These two factors are *test case generation* and *test case construction* factors. Test case generation factor is defined as the factor which influences the number of required test cases. Test case construction factor is defined as the factor which influences the effort needed to construct a test case. For each of the source code metrics we identify which of them is a test case generation and test case construction factor. This in turn, provides an insight into the required testing effort and testability. Hence through source code metrics we can assess software testability. After finding the results, first of all, we observe that some of the source code metrics are highly correlated amongst themselves. Second

P. Abrahamsson et al. (Eds.): XP 2008, LNBIP 9, pp. 224–225, 2008.

observation is that, the test metrics are also correlated. There are four size related metrics: LOC, NOA, NOM and WMC. All the four metrics are correlated to all the three test metrics (Except NOA in one of the case study). We find that high LOC, high NOM and high WMC lead to low testability. We can not categorize NOA as leading to high or low testability because of the inconsistency among results of two case studies. High LCOM leads to low testability. So, more cohesive classes have high testability. There is an inverse but weak correlation between DIT and test metrics because in these java projects as the DIT increases the testing decreases in the sense that the core functionality is tested in the parent class and child classes only test their own specific features. Although this correlation will vary depending upon the testing technique used whether the child class tests the features of its parent class or not which is not the norm. In case of NOC we are not able to draw any conclusion because there is no consistent correlation between NOC and test metrics. Although there can be found a correlation among NOC and test metrics if the testing strategy used makes a thorough testing of parent class with the increase in number of children, with an intention that if parent class is having a fault it does not creep into the child class. We foresee the following future work. First, this experiment should be extended to a large number of systems, using different development methodologies like Test driven development, extreme programming and agile software development. Second, this experiment has been conducted at the class level; it should be extended to package level testing. Third, the number of metrics we have considered are very few. This experiment should be extended to a number of other source code metrics which deal with polymorphism, exception handling etc. Fourth, other strong statistical methods should be used to find the correlation between source code metrics and test metrics.

References

1. Bruntink, M., Deursen, A.V.: Predicting class testability using object oriented metrics. In: Proceedings of the IEEE International Workshop on Source Code Analysis and Manipulation, pp. 136–145 (2004)
2. ISO, International standard ISO/IEC 9126. Information technology: Software Product Evaluation: Quality Characteristics and Guidelines for their Use (1991)

Inside View of an Extreme Process

Sara Shahzad, Zahid Hussain, Martin Lechner, and Wolfgang Slany

Institute for Software Technology, Graz University of Technology, Graz, Austria
{sshahzad,zhussain,mlechner,wsi}@ist.tugraz.at

1 Introduction

Agile processes encourage embracing change in an efficient and flexible manner. Extreme Programming (XP), being a popular agile methodology, has been widely experimented with by software development teams and many case studies have been presented by the research community. Our team has employed the XP methodology to develop a mobile multimedia application. The aim of this paper is to define our project and team setup and the prevailing XP environment in order to highlight various aspects of our process.

1.1 XP Motivation

The goal of the project is to develop a multimedia streaming application for mobile devices with an emphasis to utilize huge archives of TV and radio programs and other documentary and entertainment content. Having the option for selecting the development methodology, the team selected XP with an intention to use it in a progressive manner: conscious of applying each practice, that can be applied, and looking for the improvement and optimization of the whole XP process to make the basis for a profound academic research. In recent years, many development teams have adopted XP to evaluate the methodology and to get hands-on experience of an agile development methodology [4]. Among the less satisfied in the developer community some conclude that it is not the process which lacks in providing a proper base for software development, but it is a short coming on the side of the developers who fail in applying the necessary practices to their full extent and ignore some practices altogether [3]. The XP process is so agile that each practice can be optimized as suited. As in our case we have to consider that we are not a usual XP team but rather a team of researchers who aim to participate in the software development as a test-bed for their PhD research. In a sense it is the agility of the process which has provided us this opportunity to go deep into research, by experimenting it in different ways, along with application development.

2 The Project

The project team consists of six PhD students, five developers (a mix professional programmers and members from academia) and one business person. Also, the team differs in social and cultural backgrounds, as two of the team members are from Asia and the rest of the team is European. The business person, having a degree in business science,

P. Abrahamsson et al. (Eds.): XP 2008, LNBIP 9, pp. 226–227, 2008.

deals with project partners and also acts as a replacement for the on-site customer. He acts as a mediator in team discussions as he has a professional experience in team mediation. The XP-room provides enough space for having individual places as well as pairing stations for the team. The room setting also facilitates team discussions as it is surrounded by six white boards, to place the story cards as well as for drawing graphs and diagrams.

2.1 Evaluating the Process

Each developer, also being a researcher, takes part in the analysis, development and improvement of XP. The data required for analyzing the process performance is collected by actually implementing each practice. The developers do their best to fulfill completeness requirements of the data collected for analysis. Different tools for planning (e.g., Xplanner [1]) and for empirical data collection (e.g., Shodan 2.0 Input Metric Survey [2]) are in use since the start of the project to analyze the performance of XP practices under the project umbrella. Iteration and release velocities are recorded to visualize the throughput performance of the team over a period of time. The team is continuously working to tailor the planning and velocity calculation processes for incorporating application, business and research related stories that it has to schedule. Pair programming, collective code ownership, simple design, and working in small releases are some of the main practices which constitute the core XP process for the team and the project. In order to develop the base for research and development side-by-side the team takes a routine weekly retrospective view of the process in "reflection meeting". In this meeting the team presents application, process and team related problems, discusses possible solutions, and decides on changes in the overall process. Test-first programming, regular refactoring of code and system metaphor are some of the current discussion points in reflection meetings.

3 Conclusion

Being agile, it is inviting to mold and reshape the methodology according to the requirements of the project. Our experience shows that even though the XP methodology is simple, a serious effort should be made to apply its practices and in maintaining a balance between agility and discipline in order to get the maximum benefits from it.

Acknowledgement. The research herein is partially conducted within the competence network Softnet Austria (www.soft-net.at) and funded by the Austrian Federal Ministry of Economics (bm:wa), the province of Styria, the Steirische Wirtschaftsförderungsgesellschaft mbH. (SFG), and the city of Vienna in terms of the center for innovation and technology (ZIT).

References

1. http://www.xplanner.org/ (visited on 04.01.2008)
2. http://agile.csc.ncsu.edu/survey/shodansurvey.html (visited on 04.01.2008)
3. Rainsberger, J.B.: My greatest misses: Xp 2000-2007, agile 2007(August 18, 2007)
4. Tessem, P.: Experiences in learning xp practices: A qualitative study, xp2003. In: Marchesi, M., Succi, G. (eds.) XP 2003. LNCS, vol. 2675, pp. 131–137. Springer, Heidelberg (2003)

To Track QA Work or Not; That Is the Question

Juanjuan Zang

Jzang@thoughtworks.com

Abstract. In the past few years, I have been coaching several clients and numerous projects on Agile management methodology. Unanimously, I was asked the same question many times: Can we track QA (Quality Assurance) work as we do with development? In another word, can we capture all the QA activities and work in a backlog list and do the iteration and release planning based on the QA staff plan, and assumed QA velocity? Can we also generate QA status report such as the burn up or burn down chart? Before answering these questions, my first response would be why. No doubt, QA is a core part for an Agile project. Suppose developers achieve the throughput per iteration as scheduled, does it mean the project will be released as planned? Not necessarily, what if QA could not complete testing all stories from previous dev iterations? What if QA has to support interim release testing? What if QA is pulled into other activities than iteration testing? What if QA team is mixed of on shore and offshore members, and has to support multiple dev teams at the same time? All these questions become the reasons behind the very first one – "Can we track QA as we do with our Dev?" The first project I worked on was for an investment banking client who had a QA team of 6 people with 4 on shore and 2 off shore, supporting testing for 5 development teams of almost 30 developers. The team faced several issues: There was no QA estimation for story; QA spent lots of time on non-story activities without tracking; the ratio QA to developers was 1:5. The second team I worked with was a QA team of an e-commerce retailer IT department. The team had 3 people supporting 6 developers. The team mixed the dev velocity with QA's. By their definition, velocity was the amount of work that passed UAT[1] in an iteration, measured in dev estimation points, while at the same time, Iteration planning only took dev velocity into consideration. The QA estimation for each story was well off mark. And as same as the first team, QA team members were pulled regularly to support release testing and other non project related activities. We helped both teams by adopting similar tracking mechanism we used for the dev team. We first created a complete QA backlog list including all the stories, plus the non-story QA tasks. In the backlog list, we indicated which dev iteration and QA iteration each story was schedule in. We then did QA estimation for each story using the "triangulation" rule[2]. We separated QA velocity from Dev's. We

---

[1] User Acceptance Testing. In our case, UAT is more like a formality. Most of times, UAT is passed if QA signs off the story.

[2] Triangulating an estimate refers to estimating a story based on its relationship to one or more other stories. In this case, QA should have its own baseline QA story and triangulate the baseline story and other QA stories when estimating.

P. Abrahamsson et al. (Eds.): XP 2008, LNBIP 9, pp. 228–229, 2008.
© Springer-Verlag Berlin Heidelberg 2008

planned QA iteration as we did for Dev, and provided QA status report and burn up chart per iteration. Both projects achieved good results:

1. We better managed QA work load – By having a complete QA backlog list and giving QA estimation for each story, the team had a clear idea about QA scope.
2. We better managed QA non story activities – By having QA non-story activities in the QA backlog list, and having them prioritized along with the stories, QA team could schedule these activities along with stories in each iteration. Thus QA team could work on these technical debts without being unnoticed.
3. We better tracked QA velocity and load factor – Tracking QA team velocity and load factor separately helped the team with QA iteration planning, velocity measuring and monitoring and team status reporting.
4. We better managed QA team staffing – Since now the QA team had the complete scope measured in points, the team velocity, the project release plan and date, it served better for QA to figure out how many people the team needed in order to finish all the testing to make sure the project could be released on time.
5. We clarified the definition of team velocity – "Never mix the QA velocity with team velocity". This is the lesson we learnt. Using QA velocity as team velocity could mislead the business users and mis-communicate the team status to the upper management. For example, the burn up chart shows the total amount of work in dev estimation points, the dev velocity per iteration, expressed in story points and the trend line which predicts the possible completion date based on the team velocity so far. If the team velocity is defined as the total points of stories only signed off by QA, it means even the stories are completed, but they are not credited if QA hasn't signed off yet. In another word, the team velocity is more QA velocity rather than Dev's, while the scope line still represents the total dev estimation points. Obviously, you will immediately realize these two are not incommensurable. This can also sets wrong expectation for business users who would expect the dev team velocity instead of the QA's.

Keywords: QA, Agile, Iteration, Release, Story, Story Point, Estimation, Load Factor, Velocity.

References

1. Cohn, M.: User Stories Applied: For Agile Software Development. Addison-Wesley Professional, Reading (2004)
2. Cohn, M.: Agile Estimating and Planning. Prentice Hall PTR, Englewood Cliffs (2005)

Build Notifications in Agile Environments

Ruth Ablett, Frank Maurer, Ehud Sharlin, Jorg Denzinger, and Craig Schock

University of Calgary, Canada
{ablettr,maurer,ehud,denzinge,schock}@cpsc.ucalgary.ca

1 Introduction

Agile methods [1] are becoming popular in the software industry. In agile software development projects, it is imperative that all software written by each developer integrates properly into the entire project. To this end, most agile teams adopt *Continuous Integration* (CI). CI is the practice of automatically compiling, deploying and testing the entire codebase against a suite of prewritten tests. This occurs after any change to the codebase, usually multiple times per day.

When integration is finished, it is important for the developers to become aware of the result so that any problems can be immediately fixed. Undetected bugs can cause further problems as other developers may synchronize with a broken version of the codebase, and this may result in increased effort required to fix the problem and delays in integrating their changes to the latest build. Thus, awareness of the build status is essential, especially immediately after submitting new code to the codebase.

2 Previous Work

A study by Saff and Ernst [2] evaluated continuous integration when used by a single developer to ensure new code passed regression and unit tests. They found that continuous integration had a positive effect on the completion of programming tasks. Our research focuses on how agile teams can be notified when build breakages occur.

Alberto Savoia [3] created a build notification system using peripheral awareness [4] to inform developers of the build state. The system uses two lava lamps, one red and one green. The continuous integration tool turns on the green lamp when the build was successful, and the red when it was broken.

3 Experimental Setup

The goal of the experiment described herein is to evaluate three notification mechanisms - e-mail (virtual), lava lamps (ambient), and BuildBot (active) - within the context of a shared project. Notifications were sent out when code is committed. The goal was to determine which of the three modes would be most effective.

Java Lava Lamps were used as an ambient device in this study. An ambient display is a way of keeping people informed about the build state without disrupting them.

The BuildBot [5] robotic notification device was designed as an active, ambient build notification tool to study the effect of such a device on an agile team in the context of a shared project. If the build fails, BuildBot follows a network of lines to reach the responsible developer's workstation and kindly barks until the build is fixed.

P. Abrahamsson et al. (Eds.): XP 2008, LNBIP 9, pp. 230–231, 2008.

The three-week experiment was set up as follows: During the first week, email was sent only to the developer responsible for a build breakage. During the second week, a pair of *Java Lava Lamps* were installed and showed the build status. BuildBot was used as the physical notification device instead of the lava lamps for the third week.

4 Results and Discussion

Email was preferred by some developers because each message is nearly instantaneous, simple, not location dependent, not obtrusive to others, and shows the entire build break message such as tests failed. However, too many can become spam.

Some participants liked the lava lamps because they were simple, unobtrusive, and fun. However, most participants did not notice the lamps because of the cubicle walls, and thought the information was too limited on its own (only red or green). And finally, a developer must be present in the same room to see the lava lamps.

BuildBot's popularity among some developers and observers may be due to the fun and the novelty factor. Others, however, did not like the fact that the robot notifies everyone. Also, some expressed concern of the robot's singling out of one developer.

5 Conclusion and Future Work

The results of this evaluation show that the social nature of the group must be considered when introducing any continuous integration notification device.

The Java Lava Lamps used in this study were well-received in that they were fun and unobtrusive, but we believe they would be better in a more open environment.

Introducing something as potentially disruptive as BuildBot can cause friction. Since we found that to the developers, email was the most popular, followed by the lava lamps, we conclude that the most effective for an agile development team would be a combination of an openly visible but unobtrusive ambient and a virtual one.

The results presented here are those of a small-scale, short-term study. A longer-term evaluation (months or years) is needed involving many more developers. Also, there are also many kinds of alert mechanisms that have yet to be evaluated, such as ceiling-mounted rope lighting, system tray alerts, or a visit from a project manager.

References

1. Manifesto for Agile Software Development (2005). Accessed 5 June 2007, http://agilemanifesto.org
2. Saff, D., Ernst, M.D.: An Experimental Evaluation of Continuous Testing During Development. In: International Symposium on Software Testing and Analysis, ISSTA (2004)
3. Savoia, A.: On Java Lava Lamps and other eXtreme Feedback Devices (August 26, 2004), http://www.artima.com/weblogs/viewpost.jsp?thread=67492
4. Cadiz, J.J., Venolia, G.D., Jancke, G., Gupta, A.: Sideshow: Providing peripheral awareness of important information. Microsoft Research Technical Report MSR-TR-200181 (2001)
5. Ablett, R., Sharlin, E., Maurer, F., Denzinger, J., Schock, C.: BuildBot: A Robotic Self-Supervision Mechanism for Agile Software Engineering Teams. In: IEEE RO-MAN 2007 (2007)

Supporting Distributed Pair Programming with the COLLECE Groupware System: An Empirical Study

Rafael Duque and Crescencio Bravo

Department of Information Systems and Technologies
University of Castilla – La Mancha (Spain)
Paseo de la Universidad 4, 13071 Ciudad Real (Spain)
{Rafael.Duque,Crescencio.Bravo}@uclm.es

Abstract. This article presents a comparative study between distributed pair programming and solo programming practices.

1 Supporting Distributed Pair Programming: An Empirical Study

The COLLECE (COLLaborative Edition, Compilation and Execution) system [1] is a groupware tool that enables users who are located in different workstations to collaborate in the same time (real time) in the building of a computer program. COLLECE was used in a study to compare the activity of distributed pair programmers (DPPs) [2] and solo programmers. In this study particular attention was given to work productivity and program quality. The dependent variables considered to evaluate both productivity and quality are described below:

- **Productivity:** This quantifies the time that programmers spent completing the programming task. Moreover, in order to get a more detailed analysis of how the users' efforts are distributed during the working process, the following variables are analyzed:
  - **NI_edic:** Number of interactions of edition (e.g., to insert a character).
  - **NI_exec:** Number of interactions aimed at executing the program coded.
  - **NI_com:** Number of communication interactions (chat messages).
  - **NI_coor:** Number of coordination interactions. (e.g., the interactions refer to the synchronization of the compilation and execution processes).
- **Quality:** The programs built by the users were subjected to a process where a number of experts evaluated their quality. The *quality* variable is quantified with a natural number belonging to the set $\{1, 2, 3, 4, 5\}$ (1: very low quality- 5: very high quality). In addition, the number of compilation errors of the programs built was analyzed beforehand.

Three different tasks were proposed to the participants in the experiments. The participants were 51 programmers that had at least one year's experience in the implementation of software projects using the Java programming language. The first task asked the participants to create a program that test if a string is palindrome. The second task was aimed at creating a program to calculate the greatest common divisor

P. Abrahamsson et al. (Eds.): XP 2008, LNBIP 9, pp. 232–233, 2008.

of two numbers my means of the Euclidean algorithm. The third task required to build a program that calculated the first n numbers in the Fibonacci series.

Table 1 shows a global analysis of the results obtained in the study. When the DPPs have enough experience in the use of the groupware tool and work collaboratively with their partner, the quality of programs is better than of those built by solo programmers. In all tasks, the number of compilation errors (CE) made by DPPs is always lower than those made by the solo programmers.

Table 1. Quality (average values; in brackets the standard deviation)

	Solo programmers			Distributed pair programmers		
	$Task_0$	$Task_1$	$Task_2$	$Task_0$	$Task_1$	$Task_2$
Quality	2.6 (1.2)	3.3 (1.1)	3.2 (0.8)	2.4 (0.8)	3.5 (0.75)	3.7 (0.7)
CE	2.2 (2.1)	0.8 (1.2)	0.4 (0.7)	1.6 (1.5)	0.5 (0.8)	0.1 (0.5)

The data collected in Table 2 show that DPPs spent more time completing their tasks. They had to carry out additional interactions in order to coordinate and communicate in a distributed collaborative synchronous environment.

Table 2. Productivity (average values; in brackets the standard deviation)

	Solo programmers			Distributed pair programmers		
	$Task_0$	$Task_1$	$Task_2$	$Task_0$	$Task_1$	$Task_2$
Time	2560.5 (581.6)	2300.7 (395.1)	1745.5 (495.7)	2901.2 (469.8)	2495.6 (355.1)	2050.7 (833.9)
NI_edic	1052.2 (293.8)	843.0 (257.5)	878.2 (236.4)	446.8 (134.7)	475.3 (118.8)	448.3 (170.0)
NI_exec	5.2 (5.8)	8.8 (10.3)	6.8 (5.4)	1.73 (2.0)	2.1 (1.9)	3.7 (2.0)
NI_coor	0 (0.0)	0 (0.0)	0 (0.0)	18.40 (12.9)	21.4 (10.5)	23.3 (10.3)
NI_com	0 (0.0)	0 (0.0)	0 (0.0)	26.03 (15.5)	22.9 (9.4)	20.7 (8.3)

We can conclude that DPPs make programs of higher quality. The additional effort they make to coordinate and to communicate is offset by fewer edition interactions.

Acknowledgments

This research is partially supported by the Comunidad Autónoma de Castilla - La Mancha (Spain) in the PAC07-0020-5702 and PCI08-0069-7887 projects.

References

1. Bravo, C., Duque, R., Gallardo, J., García, J., García, P.: A Groupware System for Distributed Collaborative Programming: Usability Issues and Lessons Learned. In: International Workshop on Tools Support and Requirements Management for Globally Distributed Software Development, Centre for Telematics and Information Technology, pp. 50–56 (2007)
2. Williams, L., Kessler, R.: Pair Programming Illuminated. Addison-Wesley, Reading (2002)

Experience on the Human Side of Agile

Angela Martin[1], James Noble[1], and Robert Biddle[2]

[1] Victoria University of Wellington, Wellington, New Zealand
angela.m.martin@gmail.com
[2] Carleton University, Ottawa, Canada
robert_biddle@carleton.ca

Abstract. This brief paper describes an XP2008 conference workshop on the subject of experience on the human side of agile development. By this, we include such topics as the customer role, user interaction design, and the social nature of teams. The workshop will allow practitioners and researchers interested in these topics to develop a common map of resources, and a model to assist collaboration on further exposition and study.

Keywords: Agile Software Development, Human Factors, Development Experience.

1 Overview

This brief paper describes a half-day workshop at XP2008 on "Experience on the Human Side of Agile Development". By the "human side", we mean to address all those aspects of agile development that relate primarily to people working together, rather than technical practices. The workshop will involve both practitioners and researchers, and the emphasis will be on experience in the agile teams, projects, and workplaces. We will especially invite practitioners interested in human aspects, especially including customers, coaches, managers, user interaction designers, as well as developers. No workshops have previously been held on this topic, but tutorials and panels on related topics at both XP200X and Agile200X conferences have received strong attendance and acclaim.

An emphasis on human factors has been evident in Agile Development from the beginning. For example, the first comparison in the Agile Manifesto is "Individuals and interactions over processes and tools". However, some tension arises even in the next line: "Working software over comprehensive documentation". And although all agile processes acknowledge the importance of the human factor, the truth is that most writing on agile development, most sessions at conferences, and indeed most participants at conferences, address technical aspects. Even ideas with a human focus, such as "whole team", too often involve only the team involved in technical development, and leave outside the customers, interaction designers, end users, and others. We believe that the core of agile development involves human aspects; but we believe we need better understanding of those human aspects to allow agile development to grow and flourish.

There are a number of available resources related to the topic of the workshop. Some of the Agile Alliance programs have involved work with an emphasis on the

P. Abrahamsson et al. (Eds.): XP 2008, LNBIP 9, pp. 234–235, 2008.

human side. In particular, the "Agile Narratives" program has captured many stories from individual practitioners on their experience working in agile development. Also, there are experience reports from all the major conferences, XP200X, Agile 200X, and the earlier XP Agile Universe and Agile Development Conferences. These typically focus on a development story in a business context, but in doing so frequently highlight key human experience. As well, the same venues have featured research papers, and some of these focus on the human aspects. We ourselves have contributed some of this work, including research on the customer role [4, 3], user interaction design [2, 1], and motivation and social issues [5, 6]. Several other groups also focus on issues on the human side, and we propose this workshop to facilitate collaboration between us, and others who are interested in this area.

The major agenda items are as follows. First, we will pool our knowledge of all the writing and resources that address the human side of agile development. Second, we will collaborate in the design of a structure of the broad subject, identifying areas that have been well covered, and areas in need of further study. Finally, we will plan collaboration on new projects in this area.

References

1. Ferreira, J., Noble, J., Biddle, R.: Agile development iterations and UI design. In: Proceedings of the Agile Software Development Conference, IEEE, Washington D.C (2007)
2. Ferreira, J., Noble, J., Biddle, R.: Up-front interaction design in agile development. In: Proceedings of the 8th International Conference on eXtreme Programming and Agile Processes in Software Engineering. LNCS, Springer-Verlag, Como, Italy (2007)
3. Martin, A., Biddle, R., Noble, J.: The XP customer role in practice: Three studies. In: Alpert, S. (ed.) Proceedings of the Second Agile Development Conference, pp. 42–54. ACM SIGSOFT, Salt Lake City, USA (2004)
4. Martin, A., Noble, J., Biddle, R.: Being Jane Malkovich: a Look into the World of an XP Customer. In: Marchesi, M., Succi, G. (eds.) XP 2003. LNCS, vol. 2675, pp. 234–243. Springer, Heidelberg (2003)
5. Whitworth, E., Biddle, R.: Motivation and cohesion in agile teams. In: Concas, G., Damiani, E., Scotto, M., Succi, G. (eds.) XP 2007. LNCS, vol. 4536, pp. 62–69. Springer, Heidelberg (2007)
6. Whitworth, E., Biddle, R.: The social nature of agile teams. In: Proceedings of the Agile Software Development Conference, IEEE, Washington D.C (2007)

Retrospective Exploration Workshop

David Hussman[1] and Lasse Koskela[2]

[1] DevJam Inc., USA
David.Hussman@devjam.biz
[2] Reaktor Innovations, Finland
Lasse.Koskela@ri.fi

Abstract. Inspecting and adapting is pitched as being an essential ingredient for continuous learning and improvement. In Scrum, for example, there's an explicit opportunity for doing this - it's called the sprint retrospective meeting. Now, it's one thing to say, "we're going to inspect and adapt", and to actually do it. Furthermore, facilitating such a meeting is not exactly a skill we inherit in our genes. It's something we need to learn. Without mastering the skill, we're effectively losing on a lot of important interaction and learning. This workshop is an opportunity to improve that skill through a combination of a brief tutorial and a series of hands-on exercises, letting participants experiment with a number of retrospective techniques in small groups.

1 Overview

Inspecting and adapting is pitched as being an essential ingredient for continuous learning and improvement. In Scrum, for example, there's an explicit opportunity for doing this—it's called the sprint retrospective meeting. Now, it's one thing to say, "we're going to inspect and adapt", and to actually do it. Furthermore, facilitating such a meeting is not exactly a skill we inherit in our genes. It's something we need to learn. Without mastering the skill, we're effectively losing on a lot of important interaction and learning. This workshop is an opportunity to improve that skill through a combination of a brief tutorial and a series of hands-on exercises, letting participants experiment with a number of retrospective techniques in small groups.

The exercises follow the five-phase structure [1] of a retrospective: setting the stage, gathering data, generating insights, deciding what to do, and closing. These phases are described in more detail below. Select exercises will be carried out in small groups, each group receiving a scenario to simulate, and each member of the team taking turns in being the facilitator. After each phase, the whole workshop will share their observations about the experience—both from a facilitator's and a participant's perspective. Retrospectives often follow a five-phase structure: setting the stage, gathering data, generating insights, deciding what to do, and closing.

A fundamental principle underlying a retrospective is the Prime Directive: "Regardless what we discover, we understand and truly believe that everyone did the best job they could, given what they knew at the time, their skills, and abilities, the resource available and the situation at hand." Establishing ground rules such as the Prime Directive is a primary goal for the "set the stage" phase, along with facilitating an environment where the participants can safely express their feelings and concerns.

P. Abrahamsson et al. (Eds.): XP 2008, LNBIP 9, pp. 236–237, 2008.

The purpose of the "gathering data" phase is to create a common understanding among the participants about what happened during the iteration. Having data on the events, highlights and low points helps the participants not just to remember what had happened but also to recognize and appreciate patterns. Furthermore, the hard data contributes to constructive discussions.

Once everyone is on the same page, it's time to generate insights. In this phase, the participants look for the big picture and try to get to the root causes of the observed patterns and behaviors, mining the data gathered in the previous phase.

Once the participants have identified a number of potential improvements, root causes for dysfunction, conflict, or inefficiency, it's time to decide what the participants are going to commit to doing - the fourth phase in the retrospective.

Finally, the fifth and last phase of a retrospective is the closing. This is where the focus shifts from retrospecting on the past iteration and the group's working agreements to retrospecting on the retrospective itself. After all, we wouldn't want to not improve our retrospectives, would we?

2 About the Session Organizers

David Hussman has been creating software for more than 15 years in a variety of domains. For the past 7 years, David has mentored and coached agile teams in the U.S., Canada, Europe, Russia, and Ukraine. Along with presenting and leading workshops / tutorials at conferences in the U.S. and Europe, David has contributed to several books (Managing Agile Projects and Agile in the Large), and worked on agile curriculum for The University of Minnesota and Capella University. David is currently writing a book for the Pragmatic Programmer series. David leads DevJam, a Minneapolis based company composed of agile collaborators.

Lasse Koskela works as a coach, trainer and consultant, spending his days helping clients and colleagues at Reaktor Innovations create successful software products. He has trenched in a variety of software projects ranging from enterprise applications to middleware products developed for an equally wide range of domains. In the recent years, Lasse has spent an increasing amount of time giving training courses and mentoring teams on-site, helping them improve their performance and establish a culture of continuous learning. When not working with clients, Lasse hacks on open source projects, moderates discussions at JavaRanch, or writes about software development—most recently a book on Test Driven Development [2].

References

1. Derby, E., Larsen, D.: Agile Retrospectives: Making Good Teams Great. The Pragmatic Programmers (2006)
2. Koskela, L.: Test Driven: TDD and Acceptance TDD for Java Developers. Manning Publications (2007)

Exposing the "Devils" within: Agile Taboos in a Large Organization

Lars Arne Skår[1] and Jan-Erik Sandberg[2]

[1] Miles, Norway
lars@miles.no
[2] Det Norske Veritas, Norway
Jan-Erik.Sandberg@dnv.com

1 Workshop Overview

In the last couple of years, some agile practitioners are moving away from the core values and principles. We are now seeing that many of the practices we love in Agile is reduced to academic ramblings. This fuzziness has lead parts of the community back to vague and undisciplined processes. In large organizations this is becoming particularly prevalent since many people that really never understood the core values, now adopt simplified ways of Agile, ignoring the hard and still most important parts of it.

Thus, we propose this workshop for agile2008 to challenge participants to discuss how to get back to the core agile values; Delivering high quality software at a racing pace, with a happy team. Even in large globally distributed organizations. We want the participants of this workshop to be able to reveal who and what is blocking their efforts and how to get through them to make a real difference.

Below are some examples on concerns we have had based on our own experiences in the environments we have been working in:

- Project managers who takes an interest in Scrum, but due to lack of experience in agile practices neglect the importance of self-directing team and tries to impose direction and delegation and tasks. Unfortunately this happens often. Project managers may be uncomfortable leaving the normal command-and-control style. We would like to discuss such experiences and how those could be dealt with.
- Similarly projects that just introduces daily stand-up meetings but no other practices to support agile development. I have heard projects claiming they are agile just because they run what they call scrum-meetings. What happens then, and how can we get it right from there.
- Test-driven development is catching on, and project managers have started an interest in the coverage reports and want to follow up ridigly on the coverage numbers. In some cases we have seen that the members have created tests just to increase the coverage, not really adding useful tests. In such cases you can create a good environment to discuss the quality and attitude towards the tests itself, and the purpose of those.

The point of the session is to dare to challenge and assess all the experiences the participants have had and use those experiences to move forward in an even more positive direction.

P. Abrahamsson et al. (Eds.): XP 2008, LNBIP 9, pp. 238–239, 2008.
© Springer-Verlag Berlin Heidelberg 2008

The format of the workshop will be in a modernized way of structured "open space".

1. The presenters give a small introduction based on their experience with large distributed organizations to set the tone for the workshop.
2. In the good nature of standup meetings, all participants are asked to name and quickly explain issues and taboos they have encountered. We will make sure to follow a very strict approach, so that this does not take more time than it needs to.
3. Together with the attendants, we select the two most pressing matters and split into groups. The groups will discuss one subject each. Participants are free to choose which group they want to attend.
4. After the first discussion, we have another very quick standup where the participants are asked to name new subjects they want to discuss.
5. Since new issues and subjects should have emerged from the first discussion, the participants vote for two new items to discuss and we divide into two new groups.
6. We repeat the process once more, so that we have in total three discussions.
7. The presenters sum up the output of the discussions.

We are two presenters and we will be active in one discussion group each. Our responsibility will be to make sure that the discussions are relevant to the subject and that all participants get to state their experience and opinions. We will take notes and sum up the workshop at the end.

2 Organizers' Experience

We would like to point out these experiences for the purpose of this workshop:

1. We started early; Jan-Erik started 8 years ago, Lars started 6 years ago in introducing agile practices in our own work
2. Through the years we have seen the evolution of the practices, new fads come and go, and the real usefulness of them as well as the current risk of not achieving what we expect due to missing important pieces of the puzzle
3. The "taboo" in question could very well be Scrum—we all enjoy the positive interest in agile practices that Scrum have created; however has the popularity come at the expense of other important practices?
4. We have now worked for larger organizations for a couple of years (Lars in a 18.000 people European based IT company; Jan-Erik in a 5.000 people global naval certification company); and have first hand experience in scaling agile practices, and the value of scaling agile to larger organizations as well as the added challenges such organizations impose on making agile practices deliver on the promise
5. Still—this is a workshop format, and our intention is to bring people together who have started to experience these challenges, and encourage discussions and sharing of these experiences. We will be happy to share our own, and focus on bringing out the groups experiences on the table in order to facilitate how we can improve.

BIOHAZARD – Engineering the Change Virus

Patrick Kua

Thoughtworks
168-173 High Holborn, London
WC1V 7AA, United Kingdom
pkua@thoughtworks.com

Abstract. Introducing change into organisations and influencing the way people work is a slow and potentially rewarding task. Adapting to changing circumstances is a key aspect to agile methods and helping others develop healthy habits in this area is often difficult to accomplish. We will investigate why it is so difficult as well as principles and practices for introducing change in effective ways that will help you to spread the change virus.

Keywords: Change, influence, organisational change, agile patterns.

1 Synopsis

We think that agile software development is currently the best way of developing software, yet it hasn't been adopted by all software companies in the world. Why? The answer – it's really hard for people to fully embrace change.

Teams and organisations get stuck in their ways, and even cultures of continuous improvement and openness to change slowly build up a resistance until change no longer occurs.

This ninety-minute workshop aims to raise your awareness of agents against change, and equip you with practical skills and techniques that will help you bolster the strength of the change virus. We'll look at ways of taking it to a point where it's so contagious that it has a life of its own.

Specifically we will:

- Investigate sources of resistance to agile practices
- Look at a number of patterns for helping others to embrace change
- Examine influence and different styles of influencing
- Share a number of case studies where these were applied to improve agile adoption and inspire a culture of continuous change.
- Recognise where change patterns can fail and common pitfalls

2 Who Should Attend?

This session will interest anyone who wants to improve their working environment. It's especially for people working with teams or organisations where agile adoption is not yet widespread, and continuous improvement is not built into the practices.

P. Abrahamsson et al. (Eds.): XP 2008, LNBIP 9, pp. 240–241, 2008.

Everyone who attends this will benefit from an improved awareness of why process change fails, and come away equipped with some skills they can leverage to improve their situation for the better.

Participants do not need any experience in agile software development to participate in this workshop.

3 Presenter's Background

Patrick Kua is an agile coach, facilitator and developer for ThoughtWorks. He has been working with individuals on teams in agile environments for the last four years, and understands how powerful and responsive people can be when working together in a common manner. He is always interested in aspects of continuous improvement, and how light weight processes can boost team effectiveness.

He brings a blend of deep technical skills and deep understanding of processes that help his teams succeed in their goals. He's presented at the last few XP conferences about Test Driven Development and Information Radiators.

4 Workshop History

This workshop is based on a set of training classes we run inside of Thoughtworks. Patrick ran these training classes for the last three months, refining the material based on feedback from the class participants. This has not been presented at any other conferences so far.

The material in this workshop has been very useful for consultants who work with organisations who are about to, or are continuing to adopt agile software development.

Patrick presented "Reface Your Team Space", a workshop on Information Radiators at last year's XP2007 and "Test Driving Your Swing" at XP2006.

Architecture-Centric Methods and Agile Approaches

Muhammad Ali Babar[1] and Pekka Abrahamsson[2]

[1] Lero, Univeristy of Limerick, Ireland
malibaba@lero.ie
[2] VTT, Finland
pekka.abrahamsson@sintef.no

1 Overview

Agile practices have recently gained popularity among large number of companies as a mechanism for reducing cost and increasing ability to handle change in dynamic market conditions. Based on the principles of the Agile manifesto [1, 2], researchers and practitioners have proposed several software development approaches such as Extreme Programming, Scrum and Feature-Driven Development. These and other agile approaches have had significant impact on industrial software development practices. However, there is also a significant concern and perplexity about the role and importance of the issues related to a system's software architecture, which is considered one of the most important initial design artefacts. It is argued that software architecture is an effective tool to cut development cost and time and to increase the quality of a system. Many practitioners of Agile approaches appear to view software architecture in the context of the plan-driven development paradigm [3]. For them, upfront design and evaluation of software architecture requires too much work, which may have very little value to the customers of a system. Hence, they perceive architectural work as part of high ceremony processes, which usually require large amount of documentation. We maintain that these two seemingly opposing views to software engineering can be integrated but it requires that experts from both fields work together to overcome evident challenges in bridging these two paradigms together. Indeed, software architecture researchers and practitioners appear to believe that sound architectural practices cannot be followed using Agile approaches. However, these two extreme views of Agile and architecture appear to neglect that many agile experts emphasises the importance of paying attention to good design and architecture early in the development process [4, 5]. Recently, there is growing recognition of the importance of paying more attention to architectural aspects in agile approaches [3, 6, 7]. We argue that there is a vital need for devising a research agenda for identifying and dealing with architecture-centric challenges in agile software development. Such research agenda should make it possible to guide the future research on integrating architecture-centric methods in agile approaches and give advice to the software industry on dealing with architecture related challenges. Some of the questions to stimulate discussion in the workshop are:

- What is the role of software architecture in Agile software development?
- What are the key architecture-centric challenges and potential solutions in Agile software development projects?

P. Abrahamsson et al. (Eds.): XP 2008, LNBIP 9, pp. 242–243, 2008.

- What is the strength of the evidence that attention to architectural issues can be counterproductive in Agile development or vice versa?
- What are the prerequisites for integrating Architecture-Centric methods in agile development and potential implications of such integration?

2 Objectives

The workshop aims at bringing together both researchers and practitioners from agile approaches and software architecture backgrounds to discuss the importance and challenges of integrating architecture-centric methods in agile approaches in the context of developing large (or ultra large) scale software intensive systems. The overall goal of the workshop is to develop a common research agenda for studying agile software development and software architecture-centric issues in tandem. This event will also provide a platform to identify the mechanics of bridging the gap between agile approaches and architecture-centric methods.

3 Workshop Format

The workshop is planned to provide the attendees with an opportunity to develop a common research agenda through brainstorming, discussion and building consensus on important directions. To foster discussions at the workshop, the prospective attendees will be asked to post questions and/or views about the workshop theme and main research questions on a Wiki to be setup for the workshop. The workshop organizers will identify a few main topics to be debated during the workshop in order to develop a proposed common research agenda. The material produced in the workshop will be collected and refined to produce a workshop report by the organizers. All the discussions and workshop report will be placed on the workshop Wiki and open contributions will be sought from all the interested researchers and practitioners to build a community around the workshop topic.

References

[1] Abrahamsson, P., Warsta, J., Siponen, M.T., Ronkainen, J.: New Directions on Agile Methods: A Comparative Analysis. In: ICSE 2003 (2003)
[2] Manifesto for Agile Software Development
[3] Nord, R.L., Tomayko, J.E.: Software Architecture-Centric Methods and Agile Development. IEEE Software 23(2), 47–53 (2006)
[4] Beck, K.: Extreme Programming Explained: Embrace Change. Addison Wesley Longman, Inc., Reading (2000)
[5] Martin, R.: Agile Software Development, Principles, Patterns, and Practices. Prentice Hall, Upper Saddle River (2002)
[6] Parsons, R.: Architecture and Agile Methodologies - How to Get Along. In: WICSA (2008)
[7] Ihme, T., Abrahamsson, P.: Agile Architecting: The Use of Architectural Patterns in Mobile Java Applications. International Journal of Agile Manufacturing 8(2), 1–16 (2005)

Exploring Agile Coaching

Rachel Davies[1] and Liz Sedley[2]

[1] Agile Experience Limited, United Kingdom
Rachel@agilexp.com
[2] Agile Coaching Limited, United Kingdom
liz@agilecoach.co.uk

Abstract. The surge in Agile adoption has created a demand for project managers rather than direct their teams. A sign of this trend is the ever-increasing number of people getting certified as scrum masters and agile leaders. Training courses that introduce agile practices are easy to find. But making the transition to coach is not as simple as understanding what agile practices are. Your challenge as an Agile Coach is to support your team in learning how to wield their new Agile tools in creating great software.

1 Workshop Summary

The goal of this workshop is to produce a set of guidelines that agile coaches can use to help their teams in applying agile techniques.

1.1 Participation

This workshop is aimed at the growing number of scrum masters, agile project managers and agile coaches. It assumes participants are already familiar with at least one agile methodology and the most common agile practices. And provides the opportunity to meet other practicing Agile Coaches and hearing how they work with their teams. Come along to share coaching experiences of what worked (or did not work) for you.

To find out more about participation, please see our webpage at:

http://www.agilexp.com/XP2008-AgileCoachingWorkshop.php

1.2 Deliverables

The workshop is to develop a set of coaching guidelines which we will make available on our website. The presenters will arrange to take digital photographs of all workshop outputs and arrange for these to be uploaded to the workshop web page or conference wiki website.

2 Content and Process

The workshop will start with introductions followed by a short presentation on coaching agile teams. The purpose of the presentation is to introduce the topic and share some examples from real projects.

P. Abrahamsson et al. (Eds.): XP 2008, LNBIP 9, pp. 244–245, 2008.

Next participants will share their experience with the group by presenting their position papers. The workshop will then move into working in small groups to try an exercise in coaching agile practices. Following a break for coffee, we will debrief the exercise and discuss aspects of coaching revealed.

Now the groups start working to distill their ideas into guidelines for coaching agile teams. Each work group will take a turn to present their set that they develop to the session group.

2.1 Timetable

12:30 - 12:35	Introductions
12:35 - 13:00	Presentation/Position papers
13:00 - 13:30	Exercise
	Lunch
15:00 - 15:15	Debrief and discussion
15:15 - 15:45	Groups explore coaching guidelines
15:45 - 16:00	Each group presents what they learned to the session group.

3 Workshop Organizers

Rachel Davies is a highly respected Agile Coach whose expertise is recognized internationally across the XP, Scrum and DSDM communities. She has 20 years experience in software development and started her own agile journey in 2000 as a programmer in an XP team. Rachel has served on the board of directors of Agile Alliance for 5 years and is conference chair for Agile2008. Rachel has presented at numerous conferences on topics related to agile coaching and has participated in the XP 200x conference program every year since 2001.

Liz Sedley has been working as an Agile Coach for the last 4 years, in 3 companies. Previously to that she was a software engineer working in C++ and C# since graduating with a Computer Science Degree in 1992.

Liz presented an 'Introduction to Lean Value Stream Mapping' at the XPDay 2007 conference in London.

The Agile Technique Hour

David Parsons

Institute of Information and Mathematical Sciences
Massey University, Auckland, New Zealand
d.p.parsons@massey.ac.nz

Abstract. This workshop addresses issues around how various techniques may be integrated within an agile methodology, how these techniques interact with each other, and how certain techniques may be regarded as more or less critical to the success of an agile software development project.

Keywords: Agile technique, workshop, process miniature, simulation.

1 Introduction

In recent years, a large number of agile software development methods have been promoted by various practitioners, with many overlapping techniques. These methods tend to vary in the prescriptiveness of their approach, in the particular combinations of techniques they recommended, and in the balance between technological and managerial emphasis. Some research into agile methods in practice suggests that the combination and usage of particular techniques varies tremendously even within the umbrella of a particular agile method [1]. Therefore agile method adoption is not as significant as agile technique adoption. The main objective of this workshop is to focus on the influence of particular techniques, using an approach based on *process miniatures* [2], a method for simulating agile project processes in a short time scale.

2 The Aims of the Workshop

This workshop aims to explore some of the techniques used within agile methods and to try to assess their relative usefulness within a simulated agile process. This workshop is in the spirit of a number of previous approaches to exploring agile methods by using game-like simulations. These include Process Miniatures [2], the eXtreme Hour [3], the XP Game [4] and the Planning Game [5]. However the focus of most of these other efforts has been to concentrate on the managerial aspects of agile methods. In contrast, the 'Agile Hour' enables us to explore the 'technique' subset of agile practices, which focuses not so much on planning and estimating (though this is necessary too to provide us with a framework for the other activities) but on how agile techniques are used within an iteration. We are particularly interested in what techniques are used within agile methods, how they may synergise with one another, and which practices might be regarded as 'core'.

The approach of the workshop is to do a process miniature that gradually introduces subsets of the available techniques, and by doing so, helps us to assess which techniques

P. Abrahamsson et al. (Eds.): XP 2008, LNBIP 9, pp. 246–247, 2008.
© Springer-Verlag Berlin Heidelberg 2008

may be the most helpful. Of course we cannot test all the techniques in this way because not all techniques can reasonably be simulated in a workshop. Therefore the techniques that we address are the following; active stakeholder participation, pair programming, co-location, refactoring, regression testing, common coding guidelines, continuous integration and test driven development.

3   Overview of the Process

The task is to design a human powered vehicle. Teams are allocated a set of user stories describing required features of a human powered vehicle. The vehicle is created by overlaying features drawn on A4 transparencies, and each transparency can depict exactly one feature. Teams develop these features concurrently, and new user stories are introduced with each iteration. Each feature has a score representing its business value, which is useful for the teams when choosing development priorities. The teams consist of; stakeholders (who specify requirements on story cards), developers (who estimate and design solutions) QA (who acts as judge and acceptance tester), and Tracker (who records and times everything).

The schedule is broken down into three twenty minute stages. In each stage the first five minutes consist of planning tasks, such as selecting user stories, making estimates, and prioritizing stories. The following ten minutes is a development phase, during which QA writes acceptance tests and developers build using a subset of techniques. This phase includes a mid-term review. The final five minutes is a review stage, including acceptance testing. We have eight techniques in total. The first three techniques are controlled and must be used as advised. Developers may request one additional technique during the first and second post-iteration review.

At the end of the workshop we discuss the design outcomes, discuss our experiences with the different techniques and vote on the perceived usefulness of the techniques. We then reflect on the experience and share our responses.

References

1. Parsons, D., Ryu, H., Lal, R.: The Impact of Methods and Techniques on Outcomes from Agile Software Development Projects. In: McMaster, T., Wastell, D., Ferneley, E., DeGross, J. (eds.) Organisational Dynamics of Technology-Based Innovation: Diversifying the Research Agenda, pp. 235–252. Springer, New York (2007)
2. Cockburn, A.: Agile Software Development. Addison-Wesley, Reading (2002)
3. Extreme Hour Wiki (2005), http://c2.com/xp/ExtremeHour.html
4. Peeters, V., Van Cauwenberghe, P.: The XP Game (2006),
   http://www.xp.be/xpgame.html
5. Planning Game Wiki (2007), http://c2.com/cgi/wiki?PlanningGame

AOSTA: Agile Open Source Tools Academy

Werner Wild[1], Barbara Weber[2], and Hubert Baumeister[3]

[1] Evolution Consulting, University of Innsbruck, Management Center Innsbruck
[2] University of Innsbruck, Austria
[3] Technical University of Denmark, Lyngby

1 Workshop Description

Our workshop provides a platform to share experiences, exchange success stories and discuss potential pitfalls when using Open Source Tools (OST) for Agile Development. The goal of this workshop is to create awareness of useful OST and help to improve one's portfolio of tools for Agile Development. This ninety-minute workshop is a follow up on the highly successful AOSTA workshops at XP'2006 in Oulu Finland – there were more than 25 participants and a mid-night (!) sun BOF on the same topic attracted more than 10 additional attendees and XP'2007, Como, Italy. We will continue our discussions and share new up-to-date experiences among all new and repeat participants.

Everyone who already uses or plans to use OST for developing software the Agile Way can participate. All, from hard-core developers via project managers to CIOs are welcome to share their experiences and expectations. In addition, OST developers should attend to gain additional insights in their "customer's" agile needs to better steer their ongoing open source projects. Finally, whoever wants to get a quick overview on the state of the art in OST for Agile Development can participate in the discussions and/or demos; however, we kindly ask participants to get ready to demo, or at least share some stories about their favourite tool(s). Bring your Laptop!

To get started a comprehensive overview on OST is given by the organizers when presenting the results of two Master Theses (e.g. Value Benefit Analysis) at the MCI (Management Center Innsbruck). After this brief introduction workshop participants should present a short summary of their agile open source toolbox, including the pros and cons they find noteworthy. Then, like in an Open Space, "workshoppers" should demo their agile toolkit, or, at least, their favourite OST at given timeslots. Short "hands on" sessions would be great, if there are the "right" number of participants at each spot in the Open Space. Finally, a wrap up session with all participants will give a chance to discuss open questions, share "war stories" and get feedback.

This workshop provides participants with the unique opportunity to profit from the experience of real practitioners using OST in their current projects and, equally important, to leave with the gratifying feeling of having been able to help others with your expertise. Participants will gain a quick perspective whether a specific tool can ease their daily work and learn how to avoid well know and not-so-well-known pitfalls.

A comprehensive list of OST for Agile Warriors will be created as one of the publicly available outputs from this workshop. It will be made available on the web. However, physically present, active participants will learn the most, e.g., through the

P. Abrahamsson et al. (Eds.): XP 2008, LNBIP 9, pp. 248–249, 2008.

shared stories and networking opportunities. And, last but not least, you will be able to spend a fun and nice morning with great people like you!

2 About the Facilitators

Werner Wild has been in IT for almost 30 years and currently is a consultant with Evolution, Innsbruck. He also lectures at the University of Innsbruck, the University of Bolzano and the Management Center Innsbruck (MCI). He has long-term experience with many practices of XP as a developer, project manager and consultant and tries hard to convince his students to become more agile! He also is an elected board member of the steering committee for the Austrian IT Industry at the Federal Chamber of Commerce.

Barbara Weber is a full-time researcher at the Computer Science Department, University of Innsbruck, Austria and specializes in Business Process Management/ Business Agility. She has given lectures in Agile Methods for several years and managed numerous XP projects with graduate students. Her development projects are almost exclusively done with Open Source tools.

Hubert Baumeister is associate professor at the Technical University of Denmark, Lyngby, and is one of the few people who has been attending all (!) XP 2000-2007 conferences! In addition, he served as Program Chair of XP 2005 and as Academic Chair of XP 2004.

There's No Such Thing as Best Practice

Moderator: Steve Freeman

Abstract. The Agile movement presents itself as a carrier of "Best Practice", tools and techniques that any self-respecting development organisation should follow. Most of these practices were first written up from a few iconic projects and other groups' attempts to imitate them -- without the original organisation, technologies, or personalities. Now we have a lot of useful ideas and can even be certified to prove we know what we're doing. But is this right?

Do we really believe in reproducible methodologies? Surely organizational context trumps everything -- which is why some Agile adoptions don't last. Or are there fundamental concepts that we can apply everywhere? And how can we figure out what's fundamental and what's circumstantial?

P. Abrahamsson et al. (Eds.): XP 2008, LNBIP 9, p. 250, 2008.

Culture and Agile: Challenges and Synergies

Steven Fraser[1], Pekka Abrahamsson[2], Robert Biddle[3],
Jutta Eckstein[4], Philippe Kruchten[5], Dennis Mancl[6], and Werner Wild[7]

[1] Director – Engineering, Cisco Research, USA
sdfraser@acm.org
[2] Professor, VTT Technical Research Centre, Finland
pekka.abrahamsson@vtt.fi
[3] Professor, Human-Oriented Technology (HOT) Lab, Canada
robert_biddle@carleton.ca
[4] Partner, IT Communications, Germany
jutta@jeckstein.com
[5] Professor, UBC, Canada
philippe@kruchten.com
[6] Member of Technical Staff, Lucent-Alcatel, USA
mancl@alcatel-lucent.com
[7] Consultant, Evolution, Austria
werner.wild@evolution.at

Abstract. Culture offers both local and global challenges to software teams as they collaborate to understand requirements, build systems, and deliver product. Agile software practices through iteration, incremental delivery, and customer proximity can ameliorate cultural challenges to create synergies. Alternatively, some cultural barriers may prove insurmountable. This panel brings together community experts to share and discuss research and field experience.

1 Steven Fraser *(panel impresario)*

STEVEN FRASER recently joined Cisco Research in San Jose California as a Director (Engineering) with responsibilities for developing and managing university research collaborations. Previously, Steven was a member of Qualcomm's Learning Center in San Diego, California with responsibilities for technical learning and development and creating the corporation's internal technical conference - the QTech Forum. Steven held a variety of technology management roles at Bell-Northern Research, NT, and Nortel including Process Architect, Senior Manager (Disruptive Technology and Global External Research), and Advisor (Design Process Engineering). In 1994, he was a Visiting Scientist at the Software Engineering Institute (SEI) at Carnegie Mellon University (CMU) collaborating with the Application of Software Models project on the development of team-based domain analysis (software reuse) techniques. Fraser was the General Chair for XP2006, the Corporate Support Chair for OOPSLA'07 and OOPSLA'08, and Tutorial Chair for both XP2008 and ICSE 2009. Fraser holds a doctorate in EE from McGill University in Montréal - and is a member of the ACM and a senior member of the IEEE.

P. Abrahamsson et al. (Eds.): XP 2008, LNBIP 9, pp. 251–255, 2008.

2 Pekka Abrahamsson

PEKKA ABRAHAMSSON is research professor at VTT Technical Research Centre of Finland. He holds also an adjunct chief scientist's position in SINTEF, Norway. He is currently a visiting professor at Free University of Bozen-Bolzano in Italy. His current responsibilities include managing a FLEXI-ITEA2 project, which involves 35 organizations from 7 European countries. The project aims at developing agile innovations in the domain of global, large and complex embedded systems development. His previous project was awarded an ITEA Achievement for outstanding industrial impact. His research interests are centred on business agility, agile software development, empirical software engineering and innovation theories. He has coached several agile software development projects in industry and authored more than sixty scientific publications focusing on software process and quality improvement, agile software development and mobile software. He was recently awarded a Nokia Foundation Award for his achievements in software research.

In the field of organizational behaviour there are two opposing thoughts of schools representing fundamentally different views on organizational culture. One argues that the culture, *per se*, cannot be changed. Rather, it merely develops or evolves over time to a certain direction. This direction is difficult or even impossible to control or manage. The other school holds a belief that cultures can indeed be changed, if certain determinants are in place and concrete actions are taken. In this view, cultures can somehow be managed. Agile software development represents, in my view, a culturally sensitive view on software development. It is a unique approach to software engineering since it explicitly states the values and principles it holds valuable over others. It goes further and provides a set of concrete practices that are likely to influence on behaviour of the developers, managers and customers. These elements can be viewed as a vehicle for the development of an organizational culture. I find that the direction of this change vehicle is towards professionalism in the field of software development. Maybe this is the reason explaining why agile implementations differ from one company to another so widely. Being a culturally sensitive approach places several challenges as well. As an example, the third parties are experiencing great difficulties in viewing from the outset how deeply the professionalism promoted by agile methods has penetrated into the behaviour of the software teams. As agile approaches are being adopted globally, it will be interesting to see how national cultures, habits and customs conflict or support the type of openness and transparency supported by agile methods.

3 Robert Biddle

ROBERT BIDDLE is Professor of Human Computer Interaction at Carleton University in Ottawa, Canada, where he is a member of the graduate faculties of both Computer Science and Psychology. His active research is in human aspects of agile development, computer games, and computer security.

Agile methods emphasize the importance of people working together. This emphasis is a timely and refreshing change from the emphasis on production-line automation that has been the dominant, if seldom acknowledged, ideal of software development since its inception. Despite this new emphasis, we lack much theoretical and operational understanding of how to work together well. Too often, this results in us inappropriately applying to people the techniques we know from computer systems. To work well as people, we must acknowledge and embrace our human character: our behavior and our culture. In turn, this means that we as software developers need to understand human behavior and human culture much better than we do now. In our recent research work, we are conducting studies from the viewpoints of human activity, teams as social organizations, and involving varying cultural dimensions. We are finding some good explanations for situations where agile methods work well, and some surprises about where there are challenges. We increasingly believe that being good software developers means recognizing our nature as humans. Although we work with machines, and we build machines, we must recognize that we ourselves are not machines.

4 Jutta Eckstein

JUTTA ECKSTEIN is a partner of IT Communication and an independent consultant-trainer from Braunschweig, Germany. Jutta has over ten years experience with agile processes in developing object-oriented applications. She has helped many teams and organizations all over the world to make the transition to an agile approach. She has a unique experience in applying agile processes within medium-sized to large mission-critical projects. This is also the topic of her book *Agile Software Development in the Large*. Besides engineering software, Jutta has designed and taught Object Technology courses for industry. Jutta has completed a course on teacher training and led many train-the-trainer programs. Another focus area includes techniques, which help teach OT, and she is the lead for a pedagogical patterns project. Jutta has presented work at conferences including ACCU, JAOO, OOPSLA, XP, and Agile.

Often, when people discuss culture they have different geographic areas or diverse religions in mind. However, on second thought you will find that as well a company shapes a culture (e.g. the difference between the culture in a small company compared to a large organization is significant) and so do branches and roles (e.g. analysts seem to be of a different tribe than programmers), etc. Now let's take a look at the origin of Agility: definitely the breeding ground was the Smalltalk community - and the ones who are around long enough know that the Smalltalk-guys had their own culture, especially if you compared them with the C++ crowd. After the first successes of Agile many doubted that this will work in a culture that C++ provides. In the mean time this question isn't asked anymore and I am aware of projects which followed an agile approach in a mainframe environment.

So yes, a different culture (no matter if it is geographic area or a programming language) makes a difference in the implementation of agile. However, I came to the conclusion that the more difficult any kind of culture seems to be for applying agility at first glance, the more essential it is to recollect and understand the agile value system and the principles and take those as a guidance for establishing an agile culture. So in a sense a more difficult culture asks for a deeper understanding of agile, whereas a more "natural" agile culture might allow people to get away with only a vague idea of it.

5 Philippe Kruchten

PHILIPPE KRUCHTEN is a Professor of Software Engineering in the Department of Electrical and Computer Engineering of the University of British Columbia, in Vancouver, Canada. He joined UBC in 2004 after a 30+ year career in industry, where he worked mostly in with large software-intensive systems design, in the domains of telecommunication, defense, aerospace, and transportation. Some of his experience is embodied in the Rational Unified Process (RUP) whose development he directed from 1995 until 2003, when IBM acquired Rational Software. RUP includes an architectural design method, known as "RUP 4+1 views". Philippe's current research interests still reside mostly with software architecture, and in particular architectural decisions and the decision process, as well as software engineering processes, in particular the application of agile processes in large and globally distributed teams. He is a senior member of IEEE Computer Society, the cofounder of Agile Vancouver, a BC Professional Engineer, and a member of the APEGBC council.

In recent research, we have taken a systematic look at how intercultural factors affect the outcomes of software development practices. We have identified patterns and anti-patterns of organizational behavior that affect the outcome of off-shoring or outsourcing software projects. In the past decade, the North American and Western European IT industry has observed a rapid increase in the number of companies outsourcing software projects for development abroad or starting their own development centers in remote locations. In spite of great promises and anticipation, not all global software development projects succeed. When they fail, people are quick to blame it on "them", their lack of diligence or commitment, or to blame it on technology, but we observed that they often fail because of subtle intercultural issues. To explore this matter, we have studied the concept of culture and the potential impact of intercultural dynamics on global software development projects. There has been little analytical research done in this area and impact is assessed based on anecdotal accounts by project managers. Our research takes a grounded theory approach, starting with a collection of critical incidents in a range of global projects, obtained through semi-structured interviews. Our recent work has presented a descriptive conceptual framework for coordination between individuals and teams, which we have used to analyze and explain some of our findings. Our ultimate objective is to provide project managers with tools to help identify and mitigate the risks associated with a given mix of cultures in a software project.

6 Dennis Mancl

DENNIS MANCL is a member of Technical Staff at Alcatel-Lucent Bell Labs. He has been a researcher and internal consultant on the use of object-oriented technologies for telecommunications software, with a special emphasis on leveraging legacy software.

We have witnessed many successful and unsuccessful attempts to introduce agile practices in teams of software professionals. Three reasons for resistance to the adoption of more agile practices include: "we have always done things this way," "we are afraid that quality will suffer," and "we don't have time to change." These teams have all had one thing in common: they are trying to use the most efficient techniques to build what they believe to be a well-defined system. On the other hand, the teams that have successfully employed agility also have one thing in common: everyone admits that they have a lot to learn, both about the system under development and about the process of building and delivering systems. Agile methods are seen by many team members as a way to attack the "discovery costs" that are inherent in any large project. Iteration, prototyping, unit testing, refactoring, and other related practices -- these are viewed as the most effective ways of learning what they need to know. For green field system, we all need to fill in the gaps that are inevitable in the initial problem specification. In extending or reengineering legacy systems, we all need to understand things that might be missing in the design documentation. In short, the culture in an agile environment is a "lifelong learning" culture, and the biggest challenge in introducing agility to a new organization is to convince them that their current understanding is incomplete.

7 Werner Wild

WERNER WILD is a long-term agile consultant and university lecturer and has introduced several hundred students to agile and lean ideas. He introduced small and medium-sized enterprises to eXtreme Programming and has run several Agile Software Development projects in Central Europe. Together with Barbara Weber he researches and publishes on the agile management of business processes. As an elected official of the Austrian Chamber of Commerce he spreads Agile Software Development through local events, workshops and the media.

My experience with cultural synergies and challenges stems from introducing more than a hundred students and several Central European small/medium-sized enterprises to agile development practices. While we did not conduct a full scientific study, several observations were repeated. There appears to be a significant difference between Austrian (Germanic culture) and Italian (Romanic culture) students - the ones south of the Alps are more used to "non-plan driven" environments and learn agile development (specifically Lean and XP) within 2-4 weeks, while their Austrian colleagues take 4-8 weeks to be productive. This is not gender-specific, although my observations indicate that female students on both sides of the Alps pick up the concepts significantly faster than their male counterparts. Most students don't want to go back to "traditional" methods, once they experienced Agile, except possibly for those who seem to live in a "culture of blame." Similar observations were made within enterprise organizations. Is there a pattern emerging?

Architecture and Agility Are Not Mutually Exclusive

Moderator: Lasse Koskela

Abstract. Over the recent years, we've seen a constant stream of tutorials and workshops on "agile architecture" in conferences and there seems to remain a variety of suggested answers to this question - how should agile methods and architecture relate to each other and whether evolutionary design should include architecture or stick to what's inside the boxes?

The idea of emergent design through Test Driven Development and Refactoring has been a popular concept in discussions ever since Extreme Programming Explained was published but many consultants suggest that we shouldn't let it all emerge from code and rather carry out some up-front design in the form of iteration design workshops, for example. Some even suggest that TDD tends to lead to downright bad architectures.

What is the answer? Can we reach agreement? Can we agree on a good approach for a given scenario? Or is architecture the software community's wild west where whoever holds the gun is right?

P. Abrahamsson et al. (Eds.): XP 2008, LNBIP 9, p. 256, 2008.

Author Index